D0284066

# Party On!

Alexander Hamilton and Thomas Jefferson laid the foundations for today's political debates between Democrats and Republicans. Hamilton believed that freedom must be married with a strong central government and especially an energetic president, while Jefferson believed freedom derived from local civic virtues. Throughout history, Democrats and Republicans have chosen sides in this eternal debate—and sometimes even changed sides. Today, those debates have become sharper and more polarized, as the two parties square off on major issues such as healthcare, taxes, regulation, the role of the federal government, and what discretion should be given to local authorities. The debate can be loud and shrill, even as the public yearns for some accommodation between these two schools of thought. People may generally desire an active government to deal with acute problems, but localism still has widespread appeal, and political dysfunction often results when these outcomes are presented as polar opposites and elections are reduced to zero-sum contests. Social media adds to the polarization, as Americans gravitate to websites that often ratify their preexisting points of view. The parties struggle to function in this environment as they try to adapt to the political realities of the social media age and the Trump era.

**John Kenneth White** is Professor of Politics at the Catholic University of America. His most recent book is *What Happened to the Republican Party?: And What It Means for American Presidential Politics*.

**Matthew R. Kerbel** is Professor and Chair of Political Science at Villanova University. His most recent book is *Next Generation Netroots: Realignment and the Rise of the Internet Left*.

# Party On!

*Political Parties from Hamilton and Jefferson to Trump*

Second Edition

*John Kenneth White*
*Matthew R. Kerbel*

Routledge
Taylor & Francis Group

NEW YORK AND LONDON

Second edition published 2018
by Routledge
711 Third Avenue, New York, NY 10017

and by Routledge
2 Park Square, Milton Park, Abingdon, Oxon, OX14 4RN

*Routledge is an imprint of the Taylor & Francis Group, an informa business*

© 2018 Taylor & Francis

First edition published by Paradigm Publishers 2012

*Library of Congress Cataloging-in-Publication Data*
Names: White, John Kenneth, 1952– author. | Kerbel, Matthew Robert, 1958– author.
Title: Party on! : political parties from hamilton and jefferson to trump / John Kenneth White, Catholic University of America, Matthew R. Kerbel, Villanova University.
Description: Second edition. | New York, NY : Routledge, 2018. | Includes index.
Identifiers: LCCN 2017015600 | ISBN 9781138103047 (hardback) |
    ISBN 9781138103054 (pbk.) | ISBN 9781315103051 (ebook)
Subjects: LCSH: Political parties—United States—History.
Classification: LCC JK2261 .W55 2018 | DDC 324.273009—dc23
LC record available at https://lccn.loc.gov/2017015600

ISBN: 978-1-138-10304-7 (hbk)
ISBN: 978-1-138-10305-4 (pbk)
ISBN: 978-1-315-10305-1 (ebk)

Typeset in Bembo
by Apex CoVantage, LLC

*For our daughters, Jeannette White and Gabrielle Kerbel*

# Contents

# Preface

## Political Parties in a Time of Transition

With the election of Donald Trump, the Republican and Democratic parties face an existential crisis.

For Democrats, the quandary is clear: they control neither the presidency nor Congress, and will have difficulty preventing Republicans from maintaining their hold on the Supreme Court. Their situation at the state level is even worse. Barack Obama departed the White House with Democrats in control of both the governorship and legislature in a mere six states.[1] In 2017, you can travel the 2,500 miles between Hartford, Connecticut, and Sacramento, California, without passing through a single state with a dominant Democratic majority. As president, Obama did little to invest in the Democratic Party—preferring to maintain his own campaign organization called "Obama for America," later renamed "Organizing for America." But Organizing for America could not duplicate the functions of a political party, and Democrats paid a steep price. They lost 958 state legislative seats during Obama's presidency, depleting the talent pool that parties rely on for future national candidates. One need only recall that Obama himself was an obscure Illinois state senator just four years before ascending to the presidency.

As Democrats shift to a defensive position after relinquishing the White House, they find themselves with limited resources for blocking or derailing the Trump agenda. Trump's 2016 victory gave the Republican Party an opportunity to enact legislation that had been previously subject to Obama's veto pen. Trump also won the chance to fulfill GOP wishes by signing executive orders contrary to those put in place by Obama on matters ranging from immigration to energy policy, as he did in the first days of his presidency. Democrats will have some parliamentary options like the Senate filibuster and can use the courts to slow or derail some Republican initiatives, and they can rally public opinion when the president's actions are unpopular. But they hold few formal levers of power, an enormous problem when you consider that political parties exist to contest and win elections.

If the short-term prospects for the Democratic Party look bleak, the long-term prospects for the Republican Party may be even worse—despite their temporarily dominant political position. Donald Trump's nomination and subsequent election was, in many ways, a repudiation of the leadership of the Republican Party. During the 2016 primary campaign, most Republican leaders shunned Trump, preferring mainstream alternatives like Ohio governor John Kasich, Florida senator Marco Rubio, and, when all other options were exhausted, Texas senator Ted Cruz as viable alternatives. The Republican establishment feared and loathed Trump. They feared that if his primary campaign failed, he would run as a third-party candidate and split the conservative vote, going so far as to require him to sign a pledge supporting the party's nominee should he suspend his campaign. They loathed him for his egotism and personal failings, and for positions that ran counter to long-standing Republican beliefs dating back to Ronald Reagan. Trump returned the favor, running against Republican orthodoxy and casting bipartisan aspersions on what he described as the political swamp of Washington, DC.

Republican voters ate it up. Frustrated by the party's inability to roll back the Obama agenda and angered by what they perceived to be the ineptitude of the party's establishment, they backed Trump in one contest after another. Republican elites proved helpless to stop this revolt by their rank-and-file despite efforts to deny Trump the nomination that continued until the Republican convention in the summer of 2016. Many assumed his nomination would lead the GOP to its third straight presidential defeat, while others feared that his populist message would drive conservatism from the party.

Few thought about what they would do if he won, because few thought that possible. When he did, establishment Republicans scrambled to accommodate themselves to a president who had savaged them in his campaign. The GOP establishment prostrated itself before Trump, and the new president let them. He dangled (and eventually withdrew) a potential secretary of state nomination in front of 2012 Republican nominee Mitt Romney, who had been a vocal Trump critic during the campaign. There was no doubt that Trump was calling the shots. With his election, he had staged a hostile takeover of the Republican Party.

Trump inherited a party with significant long-term worries. The party whose label he now wears is, in many respects, out of touch with the driving demographic and social forces of the early twenty-first century. Minority voters, Millennials, and single women continue to grow as a share of the overall population, strongly favoring the Democratic Party, while the Republican base of older, white, and rural voters decreases with every election. Despite his Electoral College victory, Trump lost the national popular vote to Hillary Clinton by nearly 2.9 million, the sixth time in the last seven elections that Republicans have fallen short in the national tally. A paltry 77,744 ballots made the difference in Pennsylvania,

Wisconsin, and Michigan, the three states that cemented Trump's 304 to 227 win in the Electoral College.

His failure to resonate in more diverse corners of the American electorate was on display as Trump began his presidency with historically low job approval ratings.[2] Large protests after the election and following Trump's inauguration showed the depth of hostility directed toward the new president by significant numbers of Americans who consider his policies anathema to their vision of the country. Conservative radio host Hugh Hewitt warned that a general lack of "goodwill" meant that Trump could face impeachment should Democrats return to power in the House, noting that Trump's many conflicts of interest put him on "constitutional thin ice."[3] At the very least, dramatic changes are often undermined without broad popular support, and Republican leaders who opposed candidate Trump, then ingratiated themselves to President Trump, will be wedded politically to the actions of the Trump administration regardless of its record. The future of the Republican Party is now in his hands.

If this makes it sound like the political party system as it stands today is chaotic and uncertain, that's probably because it is. We are living through a moment when both major parties are struggling to hold together their coalitions in the wake of dramatic economic and cultural upheaval. Such moments are rare but hardly unprecedented, and, in many respects, we have been here before. During the 1970s, both parties were historically weak. Republicans reeled from Watergate and the resignation of Richard M. Nixon in the face of impeachment by the House and certain conviction by the Senate. Meanwhile, Democrats nominated an outsider with little interest in party affairs, Jimmy Carter—whom voters later judged to be ineffective largely because many of Carter's fellow Democrats refused to cooperate with him.[4]

In 1972, journalist David Broder encapsulated the views of many political scientists in his aptly titled book, *The Party's Over*.[5] Political scientists everywhere lamented the lassitude of the major parties and warned of danger ahead. The Committee for Party Renewal, a bipartisan organization consisting of academics and party activists, declared: "Without parties there can be no organized and coherent politics. When politics lacks coherence, there can be no accountable democracy."[6] Committee co-chair Gerald M. Pomper concurred: "We must either acknowledge the mutual reliance of our parties and democracy—or lose both."[7]

Yet less than two decades later, political scientist Larry Sabato authored a book titled *The Party's Just Begun*. In it, Sabato noted that the parties had staged a comeback, as Ronald Reagan cared deeply about rebuilding the Republican Party, and both parties acquired more campaign dollars to hire more staff and became increasingly technologically proficient. In the process, voters were attuned to ever-wider partisan differences and began to cast their ballots accordingly.[8]

Throughout the centuries, parties have had to adapt to new and challenging circumstances. When they could not, they went the way of the Federalists and the Whigs, bowing out while new, more robust parties took their place. By the mid-nineteenth century, competition between Democrats and Republicans had taken hold, and although it has endured for more than a century and a half, the coalitions constituting the parties have changed and changed again in response to political conditions. Party coalitions are fluid entities.

In 1888, Englishman James Bryce wrote in *The American Commonwealth*: "Parties are inevitable. No free large country has been without them. No-one has shown how representative government could be worked without them. They bring order out of chaos."[9] While Bryce believed parties were in need of reform, he thought they mattered even more in the United States than in Europe. Today, the Democratic and Republican parties are buffeted by a myriad of challenges, including the seizure by voters of the nominating process away from the party establishments; a cacophony of opinions expressed on social media that compete with the muted voices of party leaders; wealthy individuals who create Super PACs that fund their preferred candidates, independent of the preferences of party leaders; and growing partisanship in government that has made compromise difficult to achieve. Voter dissatisfaction with both parties is high, and with viable third-party opportunities lacking, it is easy to picture both parties reimagining themselves in response to these external pressures.

This volume will explore the challenges facing both parties, placing them in historical context to make sense of where the party system stands at the dawn of the Trump administration. Seeing the past as prologue, we remain confident that the party system will once again adjust to changing times. We believe Democrats will find their way during the Trump era, even as they confront the hurdles of being out of power. We believe Republicans will either reconcile with Donald Trump and allow him to remake their party in his image, or reject him and work through a potential divorce between Trump voters and traditional conservatives. Both parties will continue to adapt to new forms of social media, and we expect them to vigorously engage at the state and local levels, where party organizations are likely to revive in an altered form. While large campaign dollars continue to flow unfettered, small contributions will also proliferate and will be an important element of future campaign funding, as voters become increasingly engaged in the issues of the day.

Americans are rediscovering the meaning of citizenship as they take to the streets, contribute money to political causes, write emails to elected officials, make telephone calls, or canvass for favored candidates. Political parties are at the center of this activity, in the eye of the storm, as party leaders attempt to adjust to the political conditions swirling around them. As in the past, the parties will have to adapt or die. We believe they will find a way to rise to the occasion and renew themselves once more. In the pages ahead, we will explore how, despite what at times appears to be evidence to the contrary, Democrats and Republicans will manage to address the critical problems facing a twenty-first century electorate and, as they have so often done in the past, find a way to *Party On!*

# NOTES

1.   Those are Connecticut, Rhode Island, Oregon, California, and Hawaii.

2.   A Quinnipiac poll taken days after Trump's inauguration found his job approval at 36 percent, an all-time low for a newly sworn-in President. See Quinnipiac poll, January 20–25, 2017. Text of question: "Do you approve or disapprove of the way Donald Trump is handling his job as President?" Approve, 36 percent; disapprove, 44 percent; not sure, 19 percent.

3.   Quoted in Paulina Firozi, "Hewitt: Trump on 'Constitutional Thin Ice,' Could Face Impeachment," *The Hill*, January 25, 2017.

4.   A 1988 poll found that of the previous nine presidents, 46 percent judged Carter the "least able to get things done." See Harris poll, November 11–14, 1988. Text of question: "I'd like to ask you about the last nine presidents of the United States. Please keep in mind Roosevelt, Truman, Eisenhower, Kennedy, Johnson, Nixon, Ford, Carter, and Reagan. If you had to choose one, which president do you think was least able to get things done?" Roosevelt, 1 percent; Truman, 2 percent; Eisenhower, 3 percent; Kennedy, 2 percent; Johnson, 6 percent; Nixon, 13 percent; Ford, 15 percent; Carter, 46 percent; Reagan, 6 percent; not sure, 10 percent.

5.   David S. Broder, *The Party's Over: The Failure of Politics in America* (New York: Harper and Row, 1972).

6.   "Strengthening the Political Parties," a position paper adopted by the Committee for Party Renewal in 1980 and presented to both national party committees.

7.   Gerald M. Pomper, "The Contribution of Political Parties," in Gerald M. Pomper, ed., *Party Renewal in America: Theory and Practice* (New Brunswick, New Jersey: Praeger, 1980), p. 5.

8.   Larry J. Sabato, *The Party's Just Begun: Shaping Political Parties for America's Future* (Glenview, Illinois: Little Brown, 1988).

9.   Quoted in Leon D. Epstein, *Political Parties in the American Mold* (Madison: University of Wisconsin Press, 1986), p. 18.

# Introduction

# Of Elephants and Donkeys, Candidates and Institutions, Patriots and Progressives

I t wasn't supposed to end this way. The 2016 presidential election upended the predictions of nearly every poll, pundit, and political scientist, almost all of whom believed Hillary Clinton would defeat Donald Trump to become the nation's first female U.S. president. Many indicators pointed to a Clinton victory: the Democratic Party had an on-message nominating convention; polls showed Clinton convincingly winning all three presidential debates; the Democratic all-stars (Barack Obama, Michelle Obama, and Bill Clinton) vigorously campaigned on her behalf, while the two George Bushes, John McCain, and Mitt Romney shunned Donald Trump; the political demography of the country favored Clinton as racial minorities grew in importance; and Barack Obama's job approval stood at 53 percent on Election Day, the highest number in years.[1] A majority of voters viewed Clinton's opponent as temperamentally unfit to hold the nation's highest office, and the final pre-election polls showed her with a small, but seemingly durable and insurmountable, lead. The latter proved correct, as Clinton won the popular vote by nearly three million over Trump, the largest vote lead for a losing candidate in modern times, but narrow losses in Pennsylvania, Michigan, and Wisconsin kept her out of the White House.

Trump's triumph in the Electoral College (304 votes for Trump to 227 for Clinton[2]) happened because after eight years of the Obama presidency, voters wanted change. Of those who cast ballots in 2016, 39 percent cited "can bring change" as the most important quality they were looking for in the next president and, of these, *83 percent* supported Donald Trump.[3] In addition to his surprising win, Republicans retained their majority in the U.S. Senate, with only a two-seat Democratic gain (another surprise), and they held onto their majority in the U.S. House of Representatives, with Democrats adding just six seats—far less of a surprise, given Republican control of the statehouses and the party's ability to draw congressional district lines favorable to their candidates. Republican control of the federal "trifecta"—i.e., the presidency, House, and Senate—following the 2016 election was akin in many ways to the GOP's triumphant win under Ronald Reagan in 1980. Back then, Reagan's Republican Party also controlled the presidency and the U.S. Senate, and the addition of more Republican representatives gave the new president de facto control of the U.S. House of Representatives.

But there are several key differences between the 1980 and 2016 outcomes. Ronald Reagan replaced an unpopular president, Jimmy Carter, while Donald Trump succeeded a popular two-term incumbent, Barack Obama. Especially important were Reagan's dual commitments to the Republican Party and a conservative philosophy of governance he helped shape. As Reagan once said: "A political party isn't a fraternity. It isn't something like the old school tie you wear. You band together in a political party because of certain beliefs of what government should be."[4] Reagan had decades of experience in the Republican ranks, serving as a two-term governor of California, and before his 1980 win was a two-time candidate for the Republican Party's presidential nomination. Donald Trump, on the other hand, conveniently changed parties five times since 1987, having been initially registered as a Republican, then a member of New York State's Independence Party, subsequently changing his registration to Democrat, again switching to an unaffiliated status, and finally reverting back to the Republican Party.[5]

Ronald Reagan's political history gave him cachet within the Republican establishment, as key Republicans endorsed his 1980 candidacy, and later unanimously put their support fully behind him once he captured the GOP nomination. Donald Trump, however, was held in near-universal contempt by the Republican establishment during the entire 2016 campaign. Steve Schmidt, campaign manager for John McCain in 2008, expressed the anti-Trump sentiments of most Republican leaders:

> You see someone who is manifestly unprepared for the duties of the office of President of the United States, who has no idea what he's talking about from a policy perspective, who lacks the requisite dignity required of someone who wishes to be the Head of State of the government of the United States, and someone who lacks the capacity to be the Commander-in-Chief of the most powerful military and the world's most potent nuclear arsenal.[6]

Schmidt was hardly alone. Ohio governor and former Republican presidential candidate, John Kasich, refused to endorse Trump, even boycotting the party's convention held in his home state. George H. W. Bush let it slip that he would vote for Hillary Clinton, while both George W. and Laura Bush left their presidential ballots blank on Election Day. Mitt Romney was especially contemptuous of Trump, describing the New York billionaire and former reality television host as "a phony [and] a fraud," adding:

> [T]his is an individual who mocked a disabled reporter, who attributed a reporter's questions to her menstrual cycle, who mocked a brilliant rival who happened to be a woman due to her appearance, who bragged about his marital affairs, and who laces his public speeches with vulgarity. . . . The president and, yes, even the nominees of the country's great parties helped define America to billions of people around the world. All of them bear the responsibility of being an example for our children and grandchildren. . . . Now, imagine your children and your grandchildren acting the way [Donald Trump] does. Would you welcome that? Haven't we seen before what happens when people in prominent positions fail the basic responsibility of honorable conduct? We have. And it always injures our families and our country.[7]

The contempt the Republican establishment had for Donald Trump was returned in kind. In an unprecedented attack on his adopted party, Trump trashed the presidencies of his Republican predecessors. In 1987, Trump took out advertisements in the *New York Times*, *Boston Globe*, and *Washington Post* lambasting Ronald Reagan.[8] He later called George W. Bush's Iraq War a "big fat mistake."[9] As for his immediate Republican standard-bearers, Trump labeled John McCain's heroism as a tortured prisoner of the Vietnam War as a badge of dishonor ("I like people who weren't captured"[10]); and he described Mitt Romney as someone who "choked like a dog" for having lost to Obama.[11] Instead of welcoming the endorsements of Republican officials, Trump relished their contempt:

> There are people who look at a problem . . . and shake their heads, thinking it can't be done. There is a name for people like that: Governor. Then there are people who talk about the issue, throw around other people's money, and maybe even show you drawings. There's a name for those people, too: Senator.[12]

Former Republican National Committee chair Haley Barbour described the source of Trump's popular appeal: "Trump is the manifestation of people's anger. People all around the country want to send Washington [, DC] the bird, and they see him as the gigantic middle finger."[13]

Trump's surprising win has important ramifications for both political parties—consequences that are described throughout this book. Foremost is the fact that the role party elites once exercised as mediators between leaders and the mass public has been relegated to the ash heap of history. Replacing once-powerful party titans are candidates who ask, "Why not me?" and are driven by a personal "politics of ambition."[14] Of course, presidential candidates have always been ambitious—after all, it was once said of Abraham Lincoln that "his ambition was a little engine that never quit."[15] But the peer review that party leaders once exercised to ensure a basic level of fitness in their candidates has faded away as voters in both parties have taken the reins to determine who should lead their party—often without regard to what their choices would do to the institutional presidency they would inhabit. In 2016, Democratic and Republican voters wanted to send their party establishments a message, not necessarily a president. As one Trump Republican put it, "The more he riles up the establishment, the better I like it."[16] Democratic voters sent a similar message. Many supported Bernie Sanders, an independent social democrat who only joined the Democratic Party to seeks its presidential nomination. Sanders nearly beat the establishment favorite, Hillary Clinton, in the 2016 primaries and contested the former secretary of state right into the summertime Democratic Convention.

The result has been an inability of both Republican and Democratic Party leaders to have much of a say in awarding the highest prize any party can give: its nomination for the presidency of the United States. Historically, party leaders sought and found candidates they believed were worthy of inhabiting that sacred office. Hence, Republicans nominated Abraham Lincoln, Dwight D. Eisenhower, and Ronald Reagan to fulfill the role. Democratic leaders also elevated candidates who would best serve the national interest: Franklin D. Roosevelt, Harry S. Truman, John F. Kennedy, and Lyndon B. Johnson are but a few examples. More than merely finding nominees who would advocate mutually agreeable policies, party leaders searched for candidates who could inhabit the presidency and serve as the nation's chief of state. As Franklin D. Roosevelt once said, the presidency must be "a place of moral leadership."[17] This theme was later eloquently echoed by George W. Bush:

> After power vanishes and pride passes, this is what remains: The promises we
> kept. The oath we fulfilled. The example we set. The honor we earned. We are
> united in a common task: to give our children a spirit of moral courage.[18]

Today, the ability of party leaders to act as a buffer between candidates and the public has all but disappeared following decades of reform—in the nominating process described in Chapter 4; how political monies are raised and spent described in Chapter 7; and the rise of new forms of social media that bypass parties altogether, which is discussed in Chapter 6. In an *Atlantic Monthly* article, author Jonathan Rauch deplored the passing of the political establishments whose presence once managed conflicts behind closed doors, and whose collapse became a victim of populist-inspired reforms:

> Our intricate, informal system of political intermediation, which took many
> decades to build, did not commit suicide or die of old age; we reformed
> it to death. For decades, well-meaning political reformers have attacked
> intermediaries as corrupt, undemocratic, unnecessary, or (usually) all of the
> above. Americans have been subtly demonizing and disempowering political

professionals and parties, which is like spending decades abusing and attacking your own immune system. Eventually, you will get sick.[19]

The weakening of the party establishments has been decades in the making. In 1972, journalist David S. Broder published a book titled *The Party's Over*. In it, he set forth an unsparing diagnosis of the many ailments afflicting what remained of the once-grand old parties:

> My view is that American politics is at an impasse, that we have been spinning our wheels for a long, long time; and that we are going to dig ourselves ever deeper into trouble, unless we find a way to develop some political traction and move again.[20]

As party establishments weaken, political personalities (and their self-created organizations) loom large. After eight years of the Obama presidency, the Democratic Party emerged in a perilous condition. More than 1,100 Democratic officials were ousted by voters—including a loss of 11 U.S. Senate seats, 60 House seats, 14 governorships, and *900* state legislative seats.[21] Following the 2016 election, Republicans won control of the governorship and state legislatures in 24 states, while Democrats have complete control in just six states. Simply put, the Democratic Party is so enfeebled that its position has been compared to the 1920s, when it remained out of power until Franklin D. Roosevelt's 1932 landslide win in the midst of the Great Depression. In the two crucial midterm elections during his eight-year presidency (2010 and 2014), Barack Obama sat on the sidelines, even as his personal creation, Organizing for America, an outgrowth of his 2008 campaign organization, Obama for America, continued to compete for funds with other Democratic Party entities. In a similar way, Donald Trump has transcended the Republican Party establishment to create a personalized following. Trump's unprecedented use of Twitter has given him a platform to bypass the media and speak directly (and candidly) to his loyal followers. During the Republican primary campaign, Trump used Twitter to brand his rivals—e.g., Jeb "low energy" Bush, "Little Marco" Rubio, and "Lyin' Ted" Cruz. In the general election, Trump always referred to Hillary Clinton as "#Crooked Hillary," and continuously exploited her misuse of classified emails while serving as secretary of state, goading audiences into a chant of "Lock Her Up!" In a candid moment, Trump admitted, "The show is Trump, and it is sold-out performances everywhere."[22]

The creation of a more personalized presidency poses a unique threat to the American party system. In 1950, the American Political Science Association issued a stern warning should the parties ever find themselves in such a weakened position that a president could easily overpower them:

> When the President's program actually is the sole program . . ., either his party becomes a flock of sheep or the party falls apart. In effect, this concept of the presidency disperses the party system by making the President reach

directly for the support of a majority of the voters. It favors a President who exploits skillfully the arts of demagoguery, who sees the whole country as his political backyard, and who does not mind turning into the embodiment of personal government.[23]

Following publication of the report, President Harry S. Truman wrote to Bertram M. Gross, executive secretary to his Council of Economic Advisers, inviting members of the just-published report, *Toward a More Responsible Two-Party System*, to visit him at the White House. In his letter, Truman expressed his interest in "maintaining our two-party system," and warned that "unless we are very careful it can become obsolete and that we don't want."[24]

Donald Trump's disagreements with traditional Republican Party positions are well known. Dating back to Ronald Reagan, the GOP has been the party of free trade, limited government, and anti-communist, pro-defense. Donald Trump would negate trade agreements negotiated by presidents since Reagan; would institute tariffs on goods coming into the U.S. from overseas; wants to spend $1 billion (or more) on rebuilding the nation's highways, airports, and railroads; and questioned the intelligence community's assessments that Russia interfered in the 2016 election while aligning himself closely with Russian President Vladimir Putin in the days leading up to his taking the oath of office. Noting the newly won Republican control of the presidency and Congress, one of the authors of this book, Matthew R. Kerbel, writes that the Republican Party of 2017 will be "at the peak of its formal power at the same time it is self-destructing."[25] Like many analysts, Kerbel sees a rising American electorate—including single women, minorities, and young people—that is distant from the Republican Party of Donald J. Trump. In 2016, 55 percent of voters had an unfavorable view of the Republican Party, and just 40 percent were favorably disposed. This was in sharp contrast to opinions held about the Democrats: 49 percent unfavorable, 47 percent favorable.[26] Noting these trends, Kerbel writes:

> How does the right approach governance if it emerges as the dominant voice in a regime supported by a plurality segment of the electorate that does not represent the populace at large? Would questions arise about the regime's legitimacy, and to what degree might this constrain its ability to implement its agenda? In power, would it be able to avoid awakening voters whose disinterest enabled its ascendancy, or could it find a way to win over a large segment of the electorate? Would it tear itself apart trying to broaden its appeal or trying to broker differences between elites and the rank and file? Radicals generally do not support moderation; would they be able to temper their ideology in order to govern? If not, would their ascendancy be a false start?[27]

And yet, at the very moment both party establishments have been weakened, the party-in-the-electorate has been measurably strengthened. This is quite different from Reagan's 1980 win, when he recruited more than one in four Democrats to his cause. In 2016, a mere 8 percent of Democrats voted for Donald Trump, while an equal percentage of Republicans backed Hillary Clinton.[28] (Clinton's support among Republicans was confined to the party's elites, not the voters.) Indeed, for the past several elections, the number of Democrats and Republicans willing to cross party lines has shrunk to a precious few. As partisanship has become more rampant, the so-called Red States that voted Republican prior to the 2016 election, and the Blue States that voted Democratic have become even more partisan. In fact, much of Hillary Clinton's popular vote lead can be attributed to her overwhelming victories in the mega-states of New York and California where, taken together, she beat Donald Trump by nearly six million votes. Moreover, today's extreme level of partisanship has been magnified by social media, where voters increasingly obtain much of their political information. On the left, popular websites such as *The Huffington Post, Daily Kos,* and *MoveOn. org* serve to ratify existing points of view held by liberals and call them to action, while *Breitbart News, The Drudge Report, Townhall,* and *RedState* give information from a conservative standpoint and, like their liberal counterparts, often incite the committed to act upon their beliefs. In many ways, this reliance on partisan means for obtaining political information has deep roots in American history. Back in 1800, when the nation had its first truly contested presidential election, the two parties of the day—the Federalists and the Democratic-Republicans—controlled the major newspapers, particularly in Philadelphia, where citizens could choose either *The Gazette of the United States* (Federalist) or the *Aurora* (Democratic-Republican). These newspapers did not just tell the story of major events; they gave an undeniably partisan cast as to how voters should think about them.

But back in 1800, the franchise was limited to white, male property owners. Today's enlarged voting universe, with the increased partisanship that now characterizes our politics, has implications far beyond disagreements over policy and programs. A case in point: in 2016, 76 percent of voters who lived in counties with a Cracker Barrel restaurant cast ballots for Donald Trump, while only 22 percent who resided in counties with a Whole Foods Market did so.[29] This is just one indicator, among many, that our motto, "E Pluribus Unum," "out of many, one" is now more aptly described as "E Pluribus Duo"—"out of many, two"—two very different Americas, each standing separate and apart from each other. Americans were angry in 2016, and angry people vote. But this was anger with a difference: in 1980, Americans were angry at Washington, DC, and they voted in landslide proportions for Ronald Reagan. In 2016, Americans were angry with each other. Republicans were angry with Democrats who represented cultural values that were antithetical to their beliefs; Democrats were angry with Republicans who reflexively opposed a Democratic president regardless of the merits of his proposals; whites were angry with minorities whom they blamed for an economy that was eroding the American Dream by taking away their jobs; minorities were angry with police officers who seemed hellbent on incarcerating them and taking their lives in an unprovoked manner; gays were mad with people who wanted to deny them their rights, while some heterosexuals were angry with a Supreme Court that legalized gay marriage; Millennials were angry at seniors who benefitted from Social Security and Medicare (programs they believe they will never see), while seniors thought Millennials were quick to overturn centuries of traditional values, especially when it came to same-sex marriage. In 2016, there was no middle, no center, and virtually no swing constituencies. Nationwide landslides for either party were impossible to attain, even though Republicans won control of the federal government.

Following the 2016 election, both Donald Trump and Hillary Clinton called for unity. In his victory speech, Trump declared:

> Now it's time for America to bind the wounds of division; have to get together. To all Republicans and Democrats and independents across this nation, I say it is time for us to come together as one united people. . . . I pledge to every citizen of our land that I will be president for all Americans, and this is so important to me.[30]

Clinton echoed Trump's sentiments in her concession speech: "Donald Trump is going to be our president. We owe him an open mind and the chance to lead. Our constitutional democracy enshrines the peaceful transfer of power." At the same time, Clinton conceded the obvious: "We have seen that our nation is more deeply divided than we thought."[31]

Those divisions form the core of this textbook. How did we go from the Reagan era, where voters could easily transgress party lines to support a presidential candidate, to the Trump era, with its uncompromising partisanship? One reason is the perpetual arguments of U.S. politics, conversations begun by Alexander Hamilton and Thomas Jefferson two centuries ago. Back then, Hamilton and Jefferson asked, and answered very differently, questions that persist to this day:

- ♦ How do we limit our freedoms and still possess them?
- ♦ How much government should we have, and when is it too excessive?
- ♦ When do we need a national government to act in the interests of all of our citizens?
- ♦ When is it appropriate to leave matters to local customs and practices?

For more than two centuries, Democrats and Republicans have battled over Alexander Hamilton's concept of a national family of Americans who are inextricably tied to one another (which means a strong role for the federal government) and Thomas Jefferson's preference for lightly governed local communities (which necessitates a more modest role for the federal government). Our varied responses to this ongoing dispute between these two conceptions of America say much about who we are and what kind of government (and society) we want at any given moment. This book tells the roller-coaster story of political parties, once ironclad institutions that eroded over time to the point where they were counted out, only to revive and reemerge to face several new and different challenges. Chapter 1 describes the emergence of the arguments developed by Thomas Jefferson and Alexander Hamilton about the appropriate scope and nature of the federal government, which, as we will see, reverberated through the long history of political parties in America, and which provide the backdrop for the discussion in this book. Chapter 2 details the first century of that history, and explores how parties developed a uniquely American character while adapting to new times and technologies. Chapter 3 takes this history into the twentieth and twenty-first centuries, focusing on forces that molded party organizations into powerful institutions at the turn of the former century and on forces that eroded and then helped rebuild them at the turn of the latter. Chapter 4 describes the ongoing evolution in how parties choose their presidential candidates, with an emphasis on nomination politics in today's interconnected age and the rise of dominant personalities that overshadow formerly powerful party organizations. Chapter 5 notes how party loyalties can strengthen during periods of realignment (when a particular party can claim an enduring majority), and erode during periods of dealignment (when independent voters become decisive in elections). Chapter 6 explores the challenges parties face by the emergence of social media. Chapter 7 notes the importance of money in politics, explores the current state of campaign finance laws (or lack thereof), and examines how both the Internet and mega-wealthy individuals have revolutionized fund-raising. Chapter 8 examines the role of the party in government, including the importance of the national party organizations. Chapter 9 looks at the role of third parties in U.S. history, and notes that at key junctures they have captured public disillusionment with both major parties and helped them adjust to changing public demands. The conclusion notes the cumulative effect of these trends is a strengthening of national parties—a triumph for Alexander Hamilton in his eternal argument for a binding national force that could override Thomas Jefferson's preference for a more localized partisanship.

Individual presidential elections—be it Ronald Reagan's victory in 1980, or Donald Trump's 2016 win—may stand out because their results endure over time. (Reagan's did, but the lasting effects of Trump's victory are unknown at this juncture.) Nonetheless, the saga of the U.S. party system remains a fascinating story for more than these moments because parties are always evolving as institutions. With each election, we learn not only more about how the two major parties address the eternal questions of our politics, but how we, as Americans, give different answers to them at key moments in our history. The story of this evolution is the story of this book.

# NOTES

1. Edison Research, exit poll, November 8, 2016.

2. Other electoral votes cast were three for former secretary of state Colin Powell, one for Ohio governor John Kasich, one for former Texas congressman Ron Paul, one for Vermont Senator Bernie Sanders, and one for Native American activist Faith Spotted Eagle.

3. Edison Research, exit poll, November 8, 2016.

4. Quoted in Hugh Sidey, "The Presidency: A Conversation With Reagan," *Time*, September 3, 1984.

5. See *The Smoking Gun*, June 16, 2015. www.thesmokinggun.com/buster/donald-trump/donald-trump-voter-history-567920. Accessed January 6, 2017.

6. Steve Schmidt, *Meet the Press*, NBC News broadcast, October 9, 2016.

7.   Mitt Romney, "Remarks on Donald Trump," Salt Lake City, Utah, March 3, 2016.

8.   See Michael D'Antonio, "When Donald Trump Hated Ronald Reagan," *Politico*, October 25, 2015.

9.   Donald J. Trump, Republican Debate, Greenville, South Carolina, February 13, 2016. See www.washingtonpost.com/news/the-fix/wp/2016/02/13/the-cbs-republican-debate-transcript-annotated/?utm_term=.f9c427291ddd. Accessed January 6, 2017.

10.  See Ben Schreckinger, "Trump Attacks McCain: 'I Like People Who Weren't Captured,'" *Politico*, July 15, 2015.

11.  See David Sherfinski, "Donald Trump: Mitt Romney Choked Like a Dog in 2012," *Washington Times*, November 11, 2015.

12.  Donald J. Trump, *Crippled America: How to Make America Great Again* (New York: Threshold Editions, Simon and Schuster, 2015), p. 124.

13.  Quoted in Leigh Ann Caldwell, "A Party Divided: How Donald Trump Emerged From Decades of GOP Tension," NBC News, July 7, 2016.

14.  See especially Alan Ehrenhalt, *The United States of Ambition: Politicians, Power, and the Pursuit of Office* (New York: Times Books, 1991).

15.  Cited in Stephen Ambrose, *Nixon: The Education of a Politician, 1913–1962* (New York: Simon and Schuster, 1987), p. 71.

16.  Quoted in Chuck McCutcheon, "Populism and Party Politics," *CQ Researcher*, September 9, 2016, p. 723.

17.  Quoted in Frank Friedel, *Roosevelt: A Rendezvous with Destiny* (Boston: Little Brown and Company, 1990), p. 94.

18.  George W. Bush, "The True Goal of Education," Gorham, New Hampshire, November 2, 1999.

19.  Jonathan Rauch, "How American Politics Went Insane," *The Atlantic*, July/August 2016.

20.  David S. Broder, *The Party's Over: The Failure of Politics in America* (New York: Harper and Row, 1972), p. xvi.

21.  See John Podhoretz and Noah Rothman, "How Obama Wrecked the Democratic Party," *Commentary Magazine*, November 17, 2016, and Barbara Hollingsworth, "Republicans Now Control Record Number of State Legislative Chambers," CNSNews.com, November 16, 2016.

22.  Quoted in Philip Rucker and Marc Fisher, "A Drama King Never Lets Up," *Washington Post*, November 23, 2016, p. A-1.

23.  American Political Science Association, *Toward a More Responsible Two-Party System* (New York: Rinehart, 1950), p. 93.

24.  Harry S. Truman, Letter to Bertram M. Gross, in author's possession, September 14, 1951.

25.  Matthew R. Kerbel, "Sorting It Out (1 of 5)," *Wolves and Sheep*, blog, November 12, 2016. See www.wolvesandsheep.com/2016/11/12/sorting-1-5/. Accessed January 6, 2017.

26.  Edison Research, exit poll, November 8, 2016.

27.  Kerbel, "Sorting It Out."

28.  Edison Research, exit poll, November 8, 2016.

29.  See Kristen Powers, "Trumping the Liberal Elite," *USA Today*, November 10, 2016.

30.  Donald J. Trump, Victory Speech, New York City, November 9, 2016.

31.  Hillary Clinton, Concession Speech, New York City, November 9, 2016.

# 1

# Political Parties in an American Setting

The Framers of the U.S. Constitution were well versed in the writings of Aristotle, Locke, Montesquieu, and other democratic thinkers. From their extensive reading of history, they understood the dangers of unchecked ambition and the necessities of free speech and minority protections so vital in creating a representative democracy. The tripartite system of government they created—consisting of a president, Congress, and judiciary—has endured with only modest revisions to their original work. In the two centuries since the U.S. Constitution was ratified, those who have inhabited the presidential offices have sung its praises. For example, upon leaving the presidency in 1796, George Washington urged that the Constitution "be sacredly maintained—that its administration in every department may be stamped with wisdom and virtue."[1] Forty-two years later, Abraham Lincoln told the Springfield, Illinois, Young Men's Lyceum that the Constitution should become "the political religion of the nation."[2]

However, while the Framers realized great success in establishing political institutions, they struggled with how to organize elections. Popular, democratic elections were a novel experiment that many believed could not happen without widespread turmoil and violence. One Massachusetts delegate to the Constitutional Convention in Philadelphia contended that the "evils we experience flow from the excess of democracy."[3] Alexander Hamilton agreed: "The people are turbulent and changing; they seldom judge or determine right."[4] By the late twentieth century, however, the "excess of democracy" had become universal. The last time the U.S. Census Bureau counted in 1992, there were 513,200 popularly elected officials. Of these, 493,830 held local positions; 18,828 were state office-holders, with nearly half of them serving as administrative officials and judges.[5]

The Constitution's Framers were skeptical of political parties, thinking of them as factions to be avoided. So it was to their great astonishment that political parties proved to be the agents that made the document's provisions and the complex system of elections work. Parties afforded a way of organizing elections, legitimizing oppo-sition, and guaranteeing peaceful transitions of power. Once in office, they helped elected officials work together and bridged some of the differences between and among government institutions. One might assume, therefore, that political parties would be welcome instruments of governance. Quite the contrary. For more than 200 years, Americans have steadfastly refused to embrace party-led government—preferring instead that their leaders act in a nonpartisan manner. In 1956, John F. Kennedy wrote a Pulitzer Prize-winning book, *Profiles in Courage*, which extolled those who placed conscience above party.[6] Sixty years later, Republican presidential nominee Donald J. Trump took a different tack, this time underscoring the public's distaste for both major parties: "We look at politicians and think: This one's owned by this millionaire. That one's owned by that millionaire, or lobbyist, or special group."[7]

Given today's widespread public ambivalence directed at all political parties, it should come as no surprise that American parties have struggled to find their rightful place. The "solutions" to this dilemma have varied from place to place and time to time. For example, parties acquired a degree of public approval at the end of the nineteenth century as America entered the Industrial Age. After the first decade of the twenty-first century, parties have had to search for a place in a new, postindustrial, computer-centric era.

This book explores the evolution and role of political parties in America, and the remainder of this chapter sets the foundation for that discussion. We start by looking at the love-hate relationship Americans have with parties and how this has influenced party development. Next, we address what roles parties play and how they differ from other players in the political system. This chapter ends with a discussion of the disparate perspectives on political parties held by Hamilton and Jefferson, which will help to structure much of the discussion of this book.

# POLITICAL PARTIES: INSTITUTIONS AMERICANS LOVE TO HATE

The Founding Fathers were elitists who wanted to minimize the role citizens would play in choosing their officeholders. They were especially fearful of political parties, arguing that it was necessary, in Madison's words, to "break and control the violence of faction [meaning parties and other special interest groups]."[8] James Madison, George Washington, Alexander Hamilton, John Adams, and Thomas

Jefferson all believed that an enlightened citizenry would have no use for parties. Instead of parties, Madison hoped that other mediating institutions would

> refine and enlarge the public views by passing them through the medium of the chosen body of citizens, whose wisdom may best discern the true interest of their country and whose patriotism and love of justice will be least likely to sacrifice it to temporary or partial conditions.[9]

Madison believed that a multitude of interests would proliferate through continental expansion, thus making the development of large, mass-based parties virtually inconceivable:

> You make it less probable that a majority of the whole will have a common motive to invade the rights of other citizens; or if such a common motive exists, it will be more difficult for all who feel it to discover their own strength and to act in unison with each other.[10]

Madison's belief that parties were unsuited filters for mass expressions of public opinion was based on his reading of history. He thought that human beings were emotional creatures, embracing different religions and political leaders with a zealotry that usually resulted in chaos and violence. Most of Madison's contemporaries agreed, and they scorned political parties as vehicles that would, inevitably, ignite uncontrollable political passions. George Washington, for example, was especially critical of partisan demagogues whose objective, he claimed, was not to give people the facts from which they could make up their own minds, but to make them followers instead of thinkers. In an early draft of a 1792 speech renouncing a second term (it was never delivered when he had a change of heart), Washington maintained that "we are all children of the same country . . . [and] that our interest, however diversified in local and smaller matters, is the same in all the great and essential concerns of the nation."[11] Determined to make good on his intention to leave office in 1796, Washington issued his famous farewell address, in which he admonished his fellow citizens to avoid partisanship at any cost:

> Let me. . . warn you in the most solemn manner against the baneful effects of the spirit of party. . . . It exists under different shapes in all governments, more or less stifled, controlled, or repressed; but, in those of the popular form, it is seen in its greatest rankness and is truly their worst enemy. The alternate domination of one faction over another, sharpened by the spirit of revenge natural to party dissension, which in different ages and countries has perpetrated the most horrid enormities, is itself a frightful despotism. . . . [The spirit of party] agitates the community with ill-founded jealousies and false alarms; kindles the animosity of one part against another; ferments occasional riot and insurrection. It opens the door to foreign influence and corruption, which finds a facilitated access to the government through the channels of party passions.[12]

Washington was hardly alone in admonishing partisanship. In 1790, John Adams bemoaned the drift of the country's elites toward party politics: "There is nothing I dread so much as a division of the Republic into two great parties, each arranged under its leader and converting measures in opposition to each other."[13] Abigail Adams, observing the effects of partisan attacks on her husband during his presidency, wrote, "Party spirit is blind, malevolent, un-candid, ungenerous, unjust, and unforgiving."[14] James Monroe, the nation's fifth chief executive, urged his backers to obliterate all party divisions. When Abraham Lincoln sought reelection in 1864 under the newly created National Union banner, half a million pamphlets were published bearing titles such as "No Party Now but All for Our Country."[15]

Today's party leaders also seem skeptical about a place for parties in the American setting. In the keynote address that launched Barack Obama's national career at the 2004 Democratic National Convention, the future president spoke of the ills that stem from dividing the country into partisan groups:

> The pundits like to slice and dice our country into Red States and Blue States; Red States for Republicans, Blue States for Democrats. But I've got news for them. We worship an awesome God in the Blue States, and we don't like federal agents poking around our libraries in the Red States. We coach Little League in the Blue States and have gay friends in the Red States. There are patriots who opposed the war in Iraq and patriots who supported it. We are one people, all of us pledging allegiance to the stars and stripes, all of us defending the United States of America.[16]

Because this message resonates with so many people, political figures often find it advantageous to downplay political labels. Seeking reelection in 1972, Richard Nixon instructed his staff not to include the word Republican in any of his television advertisements or campaign brochures. Four years later, Gerald R. Ford was bluntly told by his advisors not to campaign for Republican candidates lest his support erode among independents and ticket splitters.[17] Campaigning for the presidency in 2016, Donald Trump mentioned the Republican Party just four times in his acceptance speech: twice to boast about the number of Republican primary votes he received; once to boast of his party's tax reduction plan; and finally, to scold the party after it applauded his pledge to defend LGBT (lesbian, gay, bisexual, and transgender) citizens after an Orlando, Florida, massacre.[18] For her part, Hillary Clinton mentioned the Democratic Party just three times: once to say that she will be a president for all people, regardless of party; second to brag that Democrats "are the party of working people," but then to scold her fellow partisans for not doing "a good enough job showing that we get what you're going through and that we're going to do something about it"; and finally to cite Franklin D. Roosevelt's famous 1933 inaugural address warning against the politics of fear.[19] In both instances, the partisan arguments put forth by the major-party candidates were tepid at best.

Students of political parties, however, have a much higher regard for them than do politicians and the public. In his book, *Constitutional Government*, published in 1908, Woodrow Wilson lauded political parties saying they were "absolutely necessary to hold things thus disconnected and dispersed together and give some coherence to the action of poltical forces." Without parties, Wilson argued, "it would have been impossible for the voters of the country to be united in truly national judgments upon national questions."[20] In a 1996 amicus curiae (friend-of-the-court) brief filed with the U.S. Supreme Court, the Committee for Party Renewal, a bipartisan group of political scientists, summarized the views held by most party scholars:

> Political parties play a unique and crucial role in our democratic system of government. Parties enable citizens to participate coherently in a system of government allowing for a substantial number of popularly elected offices. They bring fractures and diverse groups together as a unified force, provide a necessary link between the distinct branches and levels of government, and provide continuity that lasts beyond terms of office. Parties also play an important role in encouraging active participation in politics, holding politicians accountable for their actions, and encouraging debate and discussion of important issues.[21]

Without parties, the Committee for Party Renewal claimed that civic life would be reduced to

> a politics of celebrities, of excessive media influence, of political fad-of-the-month clubs, of massive private financing by various "fat cats" of state and congressional campaigns, of gun-for-hire campaign managers, of heightened interest in "personalities" and lowered concern for policy, of manipulation and maneuver and management by self-chosen political elites.[22]

Such statements buttressed the consensus that strong, vital parties are a prerequisite for a healthy democracy. Thus, political scientists measure the march toward democracy in such diverse places as Iraq, Afghanistan, and Libya in terms of those countries' capacities to develop strong party organizations that are the foundations for free, democratic elections—even as average Americans deplore what they see as the scourge of parties in their own country.

## THREE IMPORTANT PARTY DISTINCTIONS

One topic that bedevils any examination of parties in America is how one goes about defining them. What is a political party? What makes one organization more "party-like" than another? What are the differences among interest groups, campaign consulting firms, political action committees, and political parties? What are the various components of political parties? Are parties member-oriented, or are they simply tools for an office-seeking elite?

Scholars have wrestled with these and other related questions for some time. Many of these topics are discussed in the chapters that follow, but a few clarifications are in order. They center around three questions:

1. How do political parties differ from other organizations, particularly those concerned with the outcome of government activity?
2. What are the various elements that comprise American political parties?
3. What do parties seek to accomplish and how are their activities related to these goals?

These three questions have occupied the attention of scholars since the formal study of U.S. political parties began in earnest after World War II. But they have a renewed urgency in today's interconnected world. Even though the Internet allows individuals to access thousands of web pages dealing with politics, the major parties still retain their importance. Democrats and Republicans hold positions on a variety of issues, and identification with a particular political party provides vital cues to voters. In 2016, the Gallup poll found several large discrepancies on key issues between Democratic and Republican identifiers:

♦ Climate change: Democrats ranked this issue 48 percentage points higher in importance than Republicans.
♦ Size and efficiency of the federal government: Republicans ranked this issue 28 percentage points higher in importance than Democrats.
♦ The distribution of income and wealth in the U.S.: Democrats saw this as being more important by 26 percentage points over Republicans.
♦ Government regulation of Wall Street: Democrats viewed this issue 22 percentage points higher in importance than Republicans.
♦ The federal budget deficit: Republicans ranked this issue 21 percentage points higher in importance than Democrats.[23]

Simply put, on nearly every major issue confronting the United States today, Democrats and Republicans have two very different world views. In this environment, the strategic objectives of the two major parties matter a great deal because their partisans ascribe great weight to them.

# HOW PARTIES DIFFER FROM OTHER ORGANIZATIONS

At first glance, strangers to the American party system might find little distinction between parties and interest groups. Indeed, Madison's own discussion of "faction" is vague, and scholars have tangled with this issue for nearly two centuries. In the 1940s, for example, one student of political parties suggested that parties differ

from special interest groups in that the latter "promote their interests by attempting to influence the government rather than by nominating candidates and seeking
the responsibility for the management of government [as political parties do.]"[24]
Others disagreed, noting that interest groups and wealthy individuals who form
so-called Super PACs do influence nominations, elect favorite candidates, and
manage the government by influencing the appointment of officials and actual
decisions being made. So what, if anything, distinguishes a political party from, say,
the American Association of Retired Persons, the Environmental Defense Fund,
the National Rifle Association, or the National Association of Manufacturers? We
would point to three important distinctions:

1. Parties run candidates for office under their own label. Although interest
   groups may consistently back candidates of one party, such as the AFL-
   CIO's support of Democrats or the National Association of Manufacturers'
   support of Republicans, they do not have a party label and they do not
   officially nominate candidates for office.
2. When it comes to determining policy, parties have a broad range of concerns. A cursory reading of the 2016 Democratic and Republican Party
   platforms shows that both had something to say about every imaginable
   political issue. Democrats addressed the issues of income inequality, raising
   the minimum wage, protecting social security, criminal justice and healthcare reforms, terrorism, LGBT rights, gun violence, and even promoting
   arts and culture.[25] Republicans promoted smaller government; education,
   healthcare, and criminal justice reforms; drilling for more energy resources;
   and border security. Interest groups have a much narrower set of concerns.[26]
   The American Association of Retired Persons, for example, is keenly interested in policies affecting older Americans but pays scant attention to environmental legislation. The Environmental Defense Fund makes its views
   plain on modifications to the Endangered Species Act but offers little input
   on how to combat terrorism. Likewise, the National Rifle Association offers
   its unadulterated opposition to gun control but has little to say on other
   issues, such as reforming Social Security.
3. Political parties are subject to state and local laws, and the relationship
   between parties and the state is an intimate one. Interest groups, on the
   other hand, are private organizations operating under minimal state or federal regulations and with the aid of constitutional protections of free speech,
   assembly, and petition.

Interest groups and parties have worked together on numerous occasions. The
present-day merging of gun rights as advocated by the National Rifle Association
with the Republican Party is one example. The close ties between advocates of
dealing with the effects of climate change and the Democratic Party is another.
Today, there are so many overlapping activities between political parties and interest groups that the competition between the two has become especially intense—a
development that is discussed in greater detail in Chapter 2.

# THE COMPONENTS OF AMERICAN POLITICAL PARTIES

In ancient Greece, when the priestess of Apollo at Delphi made ready to deliver a prophecy, she positioned herself on a special seat supported by three legs, the tripod.[27] The tripod gave the priestess a clear view of the past, present, and future. Political scientists in the early 1950s likened political parties to the famous tripod of so long ago, contending that parties are supported by three legs: party in the electorate (PIE), party organization (PO), and party in government (PIG).[28]

*Party in the electorate* refers to those who identify with a particular party. In some countries, party organizations require active participation in order to be considered a member, which often means paying a membership fee. In the United States, however, party membership is not nearly as well defined. Here, the "party in the electorate" denotes a person's psychological attachment to a particular party. Some root for a political party the way others might cheer on their favorite baseball team. Attaching oneself to a political party in this fashion can manifest itself in a range of activities, although party identification may be weak and does not automatically translate into partisan behavior. Some people will vote exclusively or primarily for candidates of their party, although it is possible to identify with a party and still vote for the opposition or not vote at all. Some people choose to register as a Republican or Democrat when they sign up to vote, but formal registration is not a requirement for being included in the party in the electorate. Other formalized party activities may include participation in a party primary, raising money at a party fund-raiser, or making telephone calls to help get out the vote for a party's candidate.

*Party organization* refers to the formal apparatus of the party or the party bureaucracy. It encompasses physical assets like the party headquarters, collective activities like quadrennial national conventions, elites and rank-and-file workers, and regulations governing how activities are structured and how leaders and workers are to behave. When party meetings are held, members of the organization show up. When partisans pass out literature during a campaign, the party organization is responsible for delivering the pamphlets. The Republican National Committee (RNC) and the Democratic National Committee (DNC) each have headquarters in Washington, DC, and Democratic and Republican state party committees can be found in every state capital.

*Party in government* refers to those who have captured office under a party label. In 2017, Republicans in the Senate comprised one segment of the Republican Party in government led by majority leader Mitch McConnell (R-Kentucky), while Senate Democrats comprised one segment of the Democratic Party in government led by minority leader Chuck Schumer (D-New York). Similarly, in the House of Representatives, Speaker Paul Ryan spoke for the Republicans while minority leader Nancy Pelosi represented the Democrats. As president, Donald Trump is the overall head of the Republican Party in government. Branches of the party in government may be found in any legislative, executive, or judicial body that organizes itself along partisan lines, from the president and Congress down to states, counties, cities, and towns.

In the 1950s, the tripod model of political parties seemed both accurate and easy to comprehend. Partisanship was broad and fixed as tightly as one's religion. The public was divided between Democrats and Republicans, and they voted accordingly. What few "independents" there were generally did not vote and therefore placed themselves outside the political system. Legislative leaders were important figures. Party organizations were fixtures in nearly every community and controlled the nominations for most elective offices. Citizens were active in party organizations, either for ideological reasons or for the sense of belonging to the larger community that partisan activity engendered. Elected officials carried the party banner openly. In an age of black-and-white television, the tripod model nicely captured how the three party components neatly fit together.

## DOES THE TRIPOD MODEL WORK IN AN AGE OF TRUMP?

The rise in the importance and availability of information has changed the way parties operate. During the agricultural era, the key to production was land; in the Industrial Era, human labor; today, it is trained intelligence. In the early 1970s, sociologist Daniel Bell heralded the coming of a new postindustrial society that placed a premium on the gathering and dissemination of information.[29] In the subsequent four decades, American life has been transformed by several interrelated developments:

♦ Society has become wealthier and more affluent compared to earlier eras. Most workers are salaried professionals, whereas in the Industrial Era most employees were blue collar and were paid by the hour. Today, there are nearly 58 million workers who hold management, professional, and related occupations, while another 26 million workers are listed in service occupations. These numbers exclude the nearly 34 million Americans who hold sales and office jobs.[30]

♦ Brainpower has replaced manual labor as a key tool of productivity. A college degree, often followed by a postgraduate degree, has become the "union card" for employment in the Information Age.

♦ Technology that revolutionized mass communication has reshaped the way we interact with each other and diminished the once restrictive boundaries of time and space.

♦ New occupational structures, and with them new lifestyles and social classes, are creating new elites, including a self-selected political elite that works to influence political outcomes online through blogs and social networking.

♦ Modes of recreation have changed. More people find recreational outlets in their living rooms via television and the Internet. Social networking sites like Facebook, Instagram, Snapchat, and Twitter are what coffee socials were in a bygone era.

Even something as ubiquitous as email is a relatively new and transformational technology. In the years since 1971, when the first email was sent to a computer at the Pentagon,[31] an email evolution has changed the nature and form of voter contact. Today, both parties maintain an extensive email database they can access with a click of a mouse. In 2008, Barack Obama's presidential campaign was able to build an email list of *13 million* supporters who voluntarily joined his campaign through his website.[32]

# WHAT DO POLITICAL PARTIES SEEK TO ACCOMPLISH?

In one respect, the answer to this question is simple: parties seek to win elections. Winning means that parties seize power and can control one or more branches of federal, state, or local governments. Seizing power can also have material benefits, as parties collect the so-called spoils of office. Several notable political party definitions follow this logic:

♦ A political party is a group organized to gain control of government in the name of the group by winning election to public office (Joseph Schlesinger).[33]
♦ A political party [is] any group, however loosely organized, seeking to elect government officeholders under a given label (Leon Epstein).[34]
♦ Political parties can be seen as coalitions of elites to capture and use political office. [But] a political party is more than a coalition. A political party is an institutionalized coalition, one that has adopted rules, norms, and procedures (John Aldrich).[35]

Others argue that a party's true purpose is to implement its ideology by adopting a particular set of policies. Winning elections and controlling the government are means to larger ends—changing the course of government. Some definitions of party capture this objective:

♦ [A] party is a body of men [*sic*] united, for promoting by their joint endeavors, the national interest, upon some particular principle in which they are all agreed (Edmund Burke).[36]
♦ [A] political party [is] an organization that seeks to achieve political power by electing members to public office so that their political philosophies can be reflected in public policies (Jay M. Shafritz).[37]

The foremost problems with using the election-policy dimension to capture the essence of parties are that it is static and incomplete, and it discounts the diversity of party structures in the United States. The history of parties is continually evolving as new conditions arise. Suggestions that U.S. parties are "election driven," "policy oriented," or searching for the "vital center" assume that it has always been so, and that all party organizations scattered throughout the nation follow a similar pattern. A close reading of U.S. history suggests that party goals and activities have varied over time. As we will see shortly, sometimes parties have leaned toward the election-centered definition; at other times, they have been closer to the policy-driven perspective. Therefore, instead of defining party goals in any sort of concrete way, conceivably the best approach is to remain mindful of the dichotomy between winning elections or remaining true to one's principles, then trying to discern when each perspective best fits a given moment in history.

## ORIGINS: HAMILTON VERSUS JEFFERSON

After traveling what was then the breadth of the United States in 1831 and 1832, Alexis de Tocqueville remarked,

> All the domestic controversies of the Americans at first appear to a stranger to be incomprehensible or puerile, and he is at a loss whether to pity a people who take such arrant trifles in good earnest or to envy that happiness which enables a community to discuss them.[38]

In the twentieth century, Tocqueville's complaint was echoed in the oft-heard line: "There's not a dime's worth of difference between the Democratic and Republican parties."

Such ideological homogeneity has given rise to a belief that the United States is a special country set apart from its European origins. Addressing the Democratic National Convention in 2016, Barack Obama spoke about "what is right with America," adding:

> I see people working hard and starting businesses. I see people teaching kids and serving our country. I see engineers inventing stuff, doctors coming up with new cures. I see a younger generation full of energy and new ideas, not constrained by what is, ready to seize what ought to be. And most of all, I see Americans of every party, every background, every faith who believe that we are stronger together—black, white, Latino, Asian, Native American; young, old; gay, straight; men, women, folks with disabilities, all pledging allegiance, under the same proud flag, to this big, bold country that we love. That's what I see. That's the America I know![39]

Such expressions constitute what some have called American Exceptionalism.[40] The ideological consensus in the United States remains so pervasive that it even influences how Americans speak. Expressions such as "the American Dream" and "the American Way of Life" (along with the damning phrase "un-American") reflect the extraordinary self-confidence most Americans have in the experiment devised by the Framers. Historians have been struck by the rigidity of the American mind. As one has observed, "Who would think of using the word 'un-Italian' or 'un-French' as we use the word 'un-American'?"[41]

But such ideological rigidity does not mean that disagreements are lacking, either in the history books or in contemporary news accounts about politics. After the Constitution was ratified and George Washington took his place as the nation's first president, Alexander Hamilton and Thomas Jefferson began to act, as Jefferson recalled, "like two cocks."[42] The raging battle between these two stubborn and forceful men was personal and political. Both were staunchly committed to individualism, freedom, and equality of opportunity, yet they differed strongly on how these values could be translated into an effective form of governance.

Those disagreements came from the vastly different solutions each man devised to a vexing problem—namely, how liberty could be restrained such that it could be enjoyed. For his part, Hamilton preferred that liberty be coupled with authority: "In every civil society, there must be a supreme power, to which all members of that society are subject; for, otherwise, there could be no supremacy, or subordination, that is no government at all."[43] Jefferson, meanwhile, preferred that liberty be paired with local civic responsibility. It was on that basis that the enduring struggle between Hamiltonian nationalism and Jeffersonian localism began.

Hamiltonian nationalism envisions the United States as one "family," with a strong central government and an energetic president acting on its behalf. Addressing the delegates to the New York State convention called to ratify the Constitution, Hamilton noted,

> "The confidence of the people will easily be gained by good administration. This is the true touchstone." To him, "good administration" meant a strong central government acting on behalf of the national—or family—interest. Thus, any expression of a special interest was, to use Hamilton's word, "mischievous."[44]

But Hamilton had his own partialities, favoring the development of the nation's urban centers and an unfettered capitalism. His espousal of a strong central government aroused considerable controversy.

Unlike Hamilton, Jefferson had a nearly limitless faith in the ordinary citizen. To a nation largely composed of farmers, he declared, "Those who labor in the earth are the chosen people of God, if ever He had a chosen people."[45] Jefferson's devotion to liberty made him distrust most attempts to restrain it, particularly those of the federal government: "Were we directed from Washington when to sow, and when to reap, we should soon want bread."[46] In 1825, Jefferson warned of the expanding power of government and wrote that the "salvation of the republic" rested on the regeneration and spread of the New England town meeting.[47] The best guarantee of liberty in Jefferson's view was to restrain the mighty hand of government. Table 1.1 highlights several additional differences between Hamilton's

## Table 1.1 The Hamiltonian and Jeffersonian Models of American Governance

| Hamiltonian Nationalism | Jeffersonian Localism |
| --- | --- |
| Views the United States as one national "family." | Sees the United States as a series of diverse communities. |
| Prefers a concentration of power in the federal government so that it may act in the interest of the national family. | Prefers to give power to state and local governments so that they can act in deference to local customs. |
| Inclined to constrain liberty for the sake of national unity by marrying liberty with a strong central authority. | More inclined to favor liberty and wary of national authority. Prefers to concentrate governmental power at the state and local levels. |
| Trusts in elites to run the government. | Trusts in the common sense of average Americans to run their government. |
| Prefers a hierarchical party structure populated by "professional" party politicians. | Prefers a decentralized party structure populated by so-called amateur politicians, who often are local party activists. |
| Sees parties as vehicles whose primary purpose is to win elections and control the government. | Views parties as more ideologically based. Commitment to principles is viewed as even more important than winning elections. |

and Jefferson's view of government, with a special focus on how these differences might relate to the party system.

This debate between the political descendants of Alexander Hamilton and Thomas Jefferson is the touchstone for partisan conflict and party politics in America that continues to this day. Martin Van Buren, among many others, traces the evolution of parties to the factional disputes between Hamilton and Jefferson. According to Van Buren,

> The two great parties of this country, with occasional changes in name only, have for the principal part of a century, occupied antagonistic positions upon all important political questions. They have maintained an unbroken succession, and have, throughout, been composed respectively of men agreeing in their party passion, and preferences, and entertaining, with rare exceptions, similar views on the subject of government and its administration.[48]

Over time, the two parties, with changing names and roles, recast Hamiltonian nationalism and Jeffersonian localism to suit their evolving interests. During the Civil War and the Industrial Era that followed, Republicans stood with Hamilton, whereas Democrats claimed Jefferson as one of their own and promoted states' rights. Since the days of Franklin D. Roosevelt's New Deal, Democrats have consistently aligned themselves with Hamilton, likening the nation to a family. In a

2010 commencement address at the University of Michigan, Barack Obama channeled Hamilton by calling for a larger role for government to meet the challenges of the twenty-first century:

> There are some things we can only do together, as one nation—and our government must keep pace with the times. When America expanded from a few colonies to an entire continent, and we needed a way to reach the Pacific, our government helped build the railroads. When we transitioned from an economy based on farms to one based on factories, and workers needed new skills and training, our nation set up a system of public high schools. When the markets crashed during the Depression and people lost their life savings, our government put in place a set of rules and safeguards to make sure that such a crisis never happened again, and then put a safety net in place to make sure that our elders would never be impoverished the way they had been. And because our markets and financials systems have evolved since then, we're now putting in place new rules and safeguards to protect the American people. . . .
>
> Government is the police officers who are protecting our communities, and the servicemen and women who are defending us abroad. Government is the roads you drove on and the speed limits that kept you safe. Government is what ensures that mines adhere to safety standards and that oil spills are cleaned up by the companies that caused them. Government is this extraordinary public university—a place that's doing lifesaving research, and catalyzing economic growth, and graduating students who will change the world around them in ways big and small. . . . Government shouldn't try to dictate your lives. But it should give you the tools you need to succeed. Government shouldn't try to guarantee results, but it should guarantee a shot at opportunity for every American who's willing to work hard.[49]

Whereas Obama and his fellow Democrats espouse Hamiltonian nationalism, the Republican Party since the birth of the New Deal has immersed itself in the values cherished by Jeffersonian localism. Campaigning for the presidency in 1936, Alf Landon assailed the "folly" of Franklin Roosevelt's New Deal and denounced the "vast multitude of new offices" and the "centralized bureaucracy" from which "swarms of inspectors" swooped over the countryside "to harass our people."[50] Landon promised that his restrained and prudent management of the federal bureaucracy would result in an outpouring of freedom by a simple adherence to the following dictum: "I want the Secretary of the Treasury to be obliged to say to committees of Congress every time a new appropriation is proposed, 'Gentlemen, you will have to provide some new taxes if you do this.'"[51] Today's Republicans strike a similar theme. In their 2016 party platform, Republicans accused Obama and the Democrats of threatening personal liberty by vastly enlarging the powers of the federal government:

> The Constitution gives the federal government very few powers, and they are specifically enumerated; the states and the people retain authority over

all unenumerated powers. In obedience to that principle, we condemn the current Administration's unconstitutional expansion into areas beyond those specifically enumerated, including bullying of state and local governments in matters ranging from voter identification (ID) laws to immigration, from healthcare programs to land use decisions, and from forced education curricula to school restroom policies. We pledge to restore the proper balance and vertical separation of powers between the federal government and state governments—the governments closest to, and most reflective of, the American people. In a self-governing society, the only bulwark against the power of the state is the consent of the governed, and regarding the policies of the current government, the governed do not consent.[52]

Many historians believe that since the nation's founding, the character of the American people has not changed greatly. Though our values may be constant, the circumstances in which they are applied are not. The whiff of civil war, the onset of a depression, or the ravages of inflation inevitably cause Americans to take stock of their situation, alter their expectations of government, and choose a political party and a course of action in a manner consistent with the enduring values of freedom, individualism, and equality of opportunity. At critical junctures, Americans have shifted from Hamiltonian nationalism to Jeffersonian localism. Such shifts in public attitudes have usually been influenced by a dominant personality. Abraham Lincoln reasserted Hamilton's vision of a national family in order to save the Union; Franklin Roosevelt redefined Hamiltonian nationalism to meet the challenges of the Great Depression; and in the midst of the Great Recession, Barack Obama did the same. At other times, Jeffersonian localism has thrived, as when Ronald Reagan cited the federal government as the problem, not the solution to our problems.

Sometimes, Americans do not want to choose between Hamiltonian nationalism and Jeffersonian localism. Instead, they want to enjoy the fruits of both. So, for instance, "netroots" activists—people engaged in online-driven efforts to reform the Democratic party, whom we will discuss elsewhere in this book—align themselves with the first three Hamiltonian positions and the last three Jeffersonian positions in Table 1.1 without feeling any sense of contradiction. Thus, they view the United States as a national "family" (albeit made up of diverse communities), believe concentrated federal power is necessary to bring about a progressive agenda, and are willing to trade off a degree of liberty in exchange for greater government safety-net protections. At the same time, they trust the wisdom of average Americans—such as those who have chosen to engage in online political activism—over elite decision-making, oppose Democratic party professionals, and chafe when they perceive elected Democrats abandoning principle in order to win elections.

This melding of Hamiltonian nationalism and Jeffersonian localism is not unusual in American history. It reasserts itself during periodic swings from one faction to the other, when the parties test their ideas and battle for dominance amidst changing political and social problems. Over time, this enduring battle has produced surprising results. Hamilton would be astonished to learn that his concept of a national family is being used to promote the interests of have-nots, especially women and minorities, or as the basis for universal health insurance. But as this book suggests, political parties cannot escape the vineyards tilled by Hamilton and Jefferson, whose ideas give expression to American ideological impulses and serve as instruments to implement the constitutional designs of the Framers in a world they never could have envisioned.

After a period in the late twentieth century when it appeared political parties were dying, they remain an important part of the democratic process. For all their many deficiencies, parties afford average Americans the best avenue for speaking their minds and being heard; this remains true in today's networked age. As you read the chapters to follow, you are invited to assess for yourself the role and consequence of political parties in our system. You will find that despite the changes political parties have experienced through the centuries, it is still possible to find Hamilton's and Jefferson's fingerprints on the parties that dominate today's networked politics. Culturally, economically, geographically, and demographically, the United States has been a fluid work in progress since those two men fashioned organizations that would formalize the political divisions of post-Revolutionary War America. That these organizations would somehow evolve into the groups that now institutionalize the Red State/Blue State divisions of twenty-first century politics, and that they would continue to function in a world networked at the speed of light, is a testament to the enduring nature of a set of institutions that were not even imagined by the Constitution's authors. As they face each other across a steepening ideological divide, Republicans and Democrats, today's conservatives and liberals, party on, continuing a dialogue with deep historical and institutional roots.

# NOTES

1. George Washington, "Farewell Address," September 17, 1796. Reprinted at Senate Document Number 3, 102nd Cong., 1st sess., 1991.

2. Abraham Lincoln, "Address to the Young Men's Lyceum of Springfield, Illinois," in Don E. Fehrenbacher, ed., *Abraham Lincoln: Speeches and Writings, 1832–1858* (New York: Library of America, 1989), pp. 32–33.

3. Quoted in James MacGregor Burns, *Cobblestone Leadership: Majority Rule, Minority Power* (Norman: University of Oklahoma Press, 1990), p. 5.

4. Ibid.

5. See www.census.gov/prod/2/gov/gc/gc92_1_2.pdf. Accessed July 30, 2016.

6. John F. Kennedy, *Profiles in Courage* (New York: Harper, 1956).

7. Donald J. Trump, *Crippled America: How to Make America Great Again* (New York: Threshold Editions, Simon and Schuster, 2015), p. 98.

8. James Madison, "Federalist 10," in Edward Meade Earle, ed., *The Federalist* (New York: Modern Library, 1937), p. 77.

9.  Ibid., p. 59.

10.  Ibid., p. 61.

11.  Quoted in James Thomas Flexner, *Washington: The Indispensable Man* (New York: New American Library, 1974), p. 263.

12.  Washington, "Farewell Address."

13.  Quoted in David McCullough, *John Adams* (New York: Simon and Schuster, 2001), p. 422.

14.  Quoted in A. James Reichley, *The Life of the Parties: A History of American Political Parties* (New York: Free Press, 1992), p. 29.

15.  David Herbert Donald, *Lincoln* (New York: Touchstone Books, 1995), p. 537.

16.  Barack Obama, Keynote Address to the 2004 Democratic National Convention, Boston, July 27, 2004.

17.  President Ford Committee, "Ford Campaign Strategy Plan," August 1976. Courtesy of the Gerald R. Ford Library.

18.  Donald J. Trump, Acceptance Speech, Republican National Convention, Cleveland, Ohio, July 21, 2016.

19.  Hillary Clinton, Acceptance Speech, Democratic National Convention, Philadelphia, Pennsylvania, July 28, 2016.

20.  Woodrow Wilson, *Constitutional Government* (New York: Columbia University, 1908), p. 217.

21.  Amicus curiae brief filed by the Committee for Party Renewal in *Colorado Republican Federal Campaign Committee v. Federal Election Commission*, February 1996, p. 3. John K. White, personal copy.

22.  Committee for Party Renewal, "Statement of Principles," September 1977. John K. White, personal copy.

23.  Frank Newport, "Democrats, Republicans Agree on Four Top Issues for Campaign," Gallup press release, February 1, 2016. See www.gallup.com/poll/188918/democrats-republicans-agree-four-top-issues-campaign.aspx. Accessed July 30, 2016.

24.  V. O. Key Jr., *Politics, Parties, and Pressure Groups* (New York: Crowell, 1958), p. 23.

25.  Democratic Party Platform, 2016. See www.presidency.ucsb.edu/papers_pdf/117717.pdf. Accessed July 30, 2016.

26.  Republican Party Platform, 2016. See www.presidency.ucsb.edu/ws/index.php?pid=117718. Accessed July 30, 2016.

27.  See Everett Carll Ladd with Charles D. Hadley, *Transformations of the American Party System* (New York: W. W. Norton, 1975), p. 1.

28.  The PIE, PO, and PIG model was first developed by Ralph M. Goldman in 1951. See Ralph M. Goldman, *Party Chairmen and Party Faction, 1789–1900* (PhD diss.), University of Chicago, 1951, introduction; and Ralph M. Goldman, *The National Party Chairmen and Committees: Factionalism at the Top* (New York: M. E. Sharpe, 1990).

29.  Daniel Bell, *The Coming of Post-Industrial Society* (New York: Basic Books, 1973).

30.  U.S. Department of Labor, Bureau of Labor Statistics, 2015 report, "Labor Force Statistics From the Current Population Survey." See www.bls.gov/cps/cpsaat11.htm. Accessed July 30, 2016.

31.  See "Even More E-Mail?" *Opinion Wire*, October 18, 2001.

32.  Interview With Mitch Stewart, Organizing for America, Democratic National Committee, Washington, DC, May 27, 2010.

33.   Joseph A. Schlesinger, *Political Parties and the Winning of Office* (Ann Arbor, Michigan: University of Michigan, 1991).

34.   Leon D. Epstein, *Political Parties in Western Democracies* (New Brunswick, New Jersey: Transaction Books, 1990).

35.   John H. Aldrich, *Why Parties?* (Chicago: University of Chicago Press, 1995).

36.   "Thoughts on the Cause of the Present Discontents" (1770), in Paul Langford, ed., *The Writings and Speeches of Edmund Burke* (Oxford: Clarendon Press, 1981), p. 317.

37.   Jay M. Shafritz, *The Dorsey Dictionary of American Government and Politics* (Chicago: Dorsey Press, 1988).

38.   Alexis de Tocqueville, *Democracy in America*, Richard D. Heffner, ed. (New York: New American Library, 1956), p. 90.

39.   Barack Obama, Speech to the Democratic National Convention, Philadelphia, Pennsylvania, July 27, 2016.

40.   Seymour Martin Lipset, *American Exceptionalism: A Double-Edged Sword* (New York: W. W. Norton, 1996).

41.   Daniel Boorstin, *The Genius of American Politics* (Chicago: University of Chicago Press, 1953), p. 14.

42.   See William Nisbet Chambers, "Party Development and the American Mainstream," in William Nisbet Chambers and Walter Dean Burnham, eds., *The American Party Systems* (New York: Oxford University Press, 1975), p. 6.

43.   Quoted in Reichley, *The Life of the Parties*, p. 40.

44.   See Morton J. Frisch, ed., *Selected Writings and Speeches of Alexander Hamilton* (Washington, DC: American Enterprise Institute, 1985), p. 316.

45.   Quoted in Ted Morgan, *FDR: A Biography* (New York: Simon and Schuster, 1985), p. 38.

46.   Quoted in Richard Reeves, *The Reagan Detour* (New York: Simon and Schuster, 1985), p. 19.

47.   Quoted in Robert F. Kennedy, *To Seek a Newer World* (New York: Doubleday, 1967), p. 56.

48.   Quoted in A. James Reichley, "Party Politics in a Federal Polity," in John Kenneth White and Jerome M. Mileur, eds., *Challenges to Party Government* (Carbondale: Southern Illinois University Press, 1992), p. 43.

49.   Barack Obama, Commencement Address, University of Michigan, Ann Arbor, Michigan, May 1, 2010.

50.   1936 Republican National Platform, as reprinted in the *New York Times*, June 12, 1936, p. 1.

51.   Alfred M. Landon, "Text of Governor Landon's Milwaukee Address on Social Security," Milwaukee, Wisconsin, September 27, 1936.

52.   Republican Party Platform, 2016. See www.presidency.ucsb.edu/ws/index.php?pid=117718. Accessed July 30, 2016.

# 2

# The Rise, Fall, and Rebirth
# of Party Politics

The most frequently quoted lines in the study of political parties were penned in 1942: "It should be flatly stated," wrote political scientist E. E. Schattschneider, "that the political parties created democracy and that modern democracy is unthinkable save in terms of parties."[1] Schattschneider's proclamation is found in nearly every text on political parties written since the 1940s (you just read it here), and most political scientists still accept his assertion as a fact. Yet, to the average citizen, political parties are synonymous with corruption, gridlock, and elitism. Therefore, it should come as no surprise that political parties have had a tortured and tormented history. Although Americans, along with the British, can claim to have invented the modern political party, few take pride in this accomplishment. In 2013, the Gallup Organization found widespread public dislike of both political parties. Pluralities of those polled specifically called out the unwillingness of Democrats and Republicans to compromise and their desire to protect the rich at the expense of the middle class.[2] Thus, it should come as no surprise that for more than 200 years, political parties have searched for their rightful place in the American polity without ever quite finding it.

# THE COLONIAL EXPERIENCE

Contemporary political parties have their roots in colonial America, where pre-Revolutionary War parties were little more than extensions of rival family clans such as the Wards and Hopkins in Rhode Island and the DeLanceys and Livingstons in New York. The contests between these clans invariably centered on an ideological dispute over the reach of royal authority in the colonies, which began almost as soon as the British ships carrying settlers to Jamestown left port in 1607. On one side were those loyal to the Crown and the appointed royal governors; those opposed were faithful to the elected colonial assemblies. Those supporting the Crown were often wealthy, having received immense land grants from the king, whereas those who did not share these special privileges were tradesmen, small shop owners, and those who tilled the soil and had become accustomed to the hardships of the New World. These poor, adventurous outcasts were suspicious of authority figures, especially the king, and their political cynicism was deep-seated.

Although these divisions structured colonial politics, localism and diversity prevented mature parties from forming. In pre-Revolutionary America, each colony had its own customs, history, and political identity. Moreover, there was a great diversity of individual interests among small-freehold farmers, plantation slaveholders, merchants, ship owners and builders, emerging manufacturers, and others. In addition, there were numerous ethnic and religious groups, divided between those who desired an aristocratic and consolidated republic and those who preferred a more democratic regime with power concentrated in the states.

The American Revolution forged these cleavages into a debate about self-governance. Tradesmen and laborers despised King George III and favored severing ties with Britain. Dubbed patriots, many advocated violence to end what they saw as British subjugation. Increased taxation, coupled with royal disregard of their interests, prompted a number of high-profile protests, such as the Boston Tea Party of 1773 and the sinking of the *Gaspee* off the Rhode Island coast one year earlier. Edmund Burke, a member of the British House of Commons at the time, noted that "the state of America has been kept in continual agitation. Everything administered as [a] remedy to the public complaint, if it did not produce, was at least followed by, a heightening of the distemper."[3]

Colonial loyalists remained faithful to the British Crown, and they regarded the patriots as rabble-rousers. With the uprisings at Lexington and Concord in 1775, the contest between the patriots and loyalists became an outright civil war, with well-organized patriots winning control of state governments throughout the colonies. Through societies like the Sons of Liberty, they held rallies, sponsored "committees of correspondence" to spread their views, and recruited important community leaders to their cause. Patriot leader Thomas Paine espoused the virtues of self-rule in his 1776 pamphlet *Common Sense*, and John Adams organized his fellow Bostonians to fight against "foreign" influence in colonial affairs. Their activities were less focused on winning elections (there were few voters at the time) than on shaping public opinion.

Even before the Revolutionary War ended, Adams wrote to a correspondent, "There is nothing I dread so much as a division of the Republic into two great parties, each arranged under its leader and converting measures in opposition to each other."[4] But enduring conflict over the structure and scope of post-Revolutionary governing institutions moved the new nation inexorably in the direction of opposing camps. Differences that turned violent precipitated the collapse of the Articles of Confederation, the young republic's first governing document. For a brief time after the Revolution, a short-lived boom in imports from England pushed the cost of agricultural and manufactured goods downward. Money became scarce, resulting in a severe economic depression that began in the late 1770s and lasted nearly a decade. Working-class citizens and small farmers were hardest hit. Bank foreclosures skyrocketed. Most states levied heavy taxes in a largely unsuccessful attempt to eliminate their wartime debts. By the mid-1780s, the demands for action grew louder.

To avoid bloodshed, some states passed laws to postpone foreclosures and allow farmers to use agricultural products to help pay loans. But none of these actions eased the governing crisis, which came to a head when former army captain Daniel Shays led a mob of farmers against the state government of Massachusetts in 1787. Their purpose was to prevent foreclosures on their debt-ridden land by keeping the country courts of western Massachusetts from sitting until the next election. The state militia eventually dispersed the mob, but the uprising, which became known as Shays' Rebellion, galvanized the states to convene delegates in Philadephia for the purpose of drafting a new governing document.

The differences underlying Shays's Rebellion persisted during and after the Constitutional Convention. The Constitution's supporters, who became known as Federalists, and those who opposed its ratification, dubbed Anti-Federalists, carried their disputes from Independence Hall in Philadelphia to the various state capitals. Anti-Federalists contended that representatives in any national government must reflect a true picture of the people, possessing an intimate knowledge of their circumstances and needs. This could only be achieved, they argued, through small, relatively homogeneous republics such as those already constructed in the existing states. One prominent Anti-Federalist spokesperson asked, "Is it practicable for a country so large and so numerous . . . to elect a representation that will speak their sentiments? . . . It certainly is not."[5] Federalists believed that a representative republic was possible and desirable—especially if populated by those "who possess [the] most wisdom to discern, and [the] most virtue to pursue, the common good of society."[6]

## FEDERALISTS VERSUS REPUBLICANS

George Washington assumed the presidency in 1789 believing that parties were unnecessary and that he could bypass them by creating an "enlightened administration." To that end, Washington took into his Cabinet the leading political antagonists of his time: Alexander Hamilton as treasury secretary and Thomas Jefferson as

secretary of state. Less than a year after becoming president, Washington's experiment
of having a government without parties faltered. Hamilton and Jefferson vehemently
disagreed in the Cabinet councils over how to manage the growing economic crisis.

Hamilton offered a sweeping plan to revive the sagging economy—the
most controversial portion of which involved the complete assumption of debts
incurred by the states during the Revolutionary War. To Hamilton and his Federalist followers, this policy was not only sound economics but good politics: by
helping those who backed the revolt against King George III, confidence in the
national government would be restored and nearly $80 million would be put
in the pockets of those most likely to reinvest in the nation's tiny infrastructure.
The result would be an increase in the flow of goods and services accompanied
by a general rise in living standards.

To pay for full assumption, Hamilton proposed an excise tax on distilled
spirits that became known as the Whiskey Tax. Because most whiskey producers
were farmers in the South and West, this measure shifted the tax burden from
northeastern business owners to small farmers—in effect, punishing those most
likely to support Jefferson's Republicans. Additionally, to ensure that enough
money would fill the federal coffers, Hamilton advocated establishing a Bank
of the United States that would make loans and collect interest payments while
it curbed the diverse practices of state-chartered banks. The idea of a national
bank, not one of the powers specifically given to the Congress in the Constitution, created enormous animosity between advocates of states' rights and those
seeking a more powerful national government—a dispute that would not be
resolved until 1819 by the Supreme Court in the case of *McCulloch v. Maryland*.

Jefferson and the Republicans believed that federal assumption of state debts
would create a windfall for the monied class, especially those living in New
England. Opposition to Hamilton's scheme was led in the House of Representatives by James Madison. He agreed with Hamilton that the economy needed
strengthening, but he fretted about the shift of capital from the agricultural states
(including his native Virginia) to a few northeastern manufacturing states. Moreover, Madison thought the Whiskey Tax would be a financial disaster for small
farmers. His prediction came true in 1794, when farmers in western Pennsylvania caused an uprising that became popularly known as the Whiskey Insurrec-
tion. Madison corralled 17 House members to his side—about one-quarter of the
chamber. About the same number of legislators opposed him. At the conclusion of
the First Congress, an exasperated Hamilton exclaimed,

> It was not till the last session that I became unequivocally convinced that
> Mr. Madison, cooperating with Mr. Jefferson, is at the head of a faction
> decidedly hostile to me and my administration; and actuated by views, in my
> judgment, subversive to the principles of good government and dangerous to
> the union, peace, and happiness of the country.[7]

Vice President John Adams likewise bemoaned the "turbulent maneuvers" of
factions that could "tie the hands and destroy the influence" of those who desired

to promote the public interest. Adams told his son-in-law that the partisan battles between Hamilton and Jefferson had created a "division of sentiments over everything."[8]

The battle between Hamilton and Madison extended beyond the halls of Congress to the newspapers. In a move that foreshadowed the inextricable link that would develop between political parties and the mass media, Hamilton forged a close alliance with John Ward Fenno, publisher of the *Gazette of the United States*. Madison, not willing to let Fenno's editorials go unanswered, persuaded Philip Freneau to edit a rival newspaper, the *National Gazette*. These party-controlled newspapers, although having a small number of subscribers (the *Gazette of the United States* had only 1,500), quickly became the most popular method of communicating with the party faithful.[9] Together, they helped clarify this first battle between Hamiltonian nationalism and Jeffersonian localism, even as they exacerbated the animosity between these two leaders. The battle of epithets that played out in the country's young newspapers ensured that partisanship would overflow the Washington administration to capture much of American society.

Despite intense congressional opposition, Hamilton's economic plan won approval after some wily backroom maneuvering. Jefferson played a key behind-the-scenes role, endorsing the bill in exchange for assurances that the federal capital would be moved south from New York City to a new District of Columbia. But Jefferson's role in advancing Hamilton's initiative alienated his agrarian constituents. Seeking to mend political fences, Jefferson embarked on a tour with his ally James Madison during the spring of 1791 that was to have profound consequences for party development. Ostensibly, the duo set out on a nature tour to "observe the vegetation and wildlife in the region," but their real purpose was to sample public opinion. In effect, they were testing the waters for the formation of a new political party. In New York City, Jefferson and Madison met with Robert Livingston and George Clinton—two longtime rivals of Hamilton—as well as Senator Aaron Burr, who was attempting to broaden his political influence.

Two years later, in 1793, Jefferson and Hamilton renewed their struggle. This time, the issue was how to respond to the French Revolution. To Jefferson and his followers, the French cry for "liberty, equality, and fraternity" was an extension of the American Revolution. Thomas Paine was so moved by the French revolutionaries that he journeyed to France to help the cause. At the same time, the German Republican Society was formed in Philadelphia. Its members sympathized with the French revolutionaries and believed that the American Revolution was losing momentum because of Hamilton, who, they claimed, was endangering the promise of democracy contained in the Declaration of Independence. By 1798, there were 43 of these popular societies, organized in every state except New Hampshire and Georgia.

To Hamilton and his Federalist backers, the French Revolution signaled the emergence of anarchy and a rejection of traditional Christian values. They were horrified by the mob violence and feared that the emerging republican movement could lead America down the same path. Jefferson remarked that these different reactions to the French Revolution "kindled and brought forth the two [political] parties with an ardor which our own interests merely could never incite."[10] Jefferson dubbed Hamilton's party the "monocrats." For his part, Jefferson never referred to his party as the "Democrats," because the term conjured visions of mob rule; he preferred the name "Republicans" to describe his emerging political organization.

When the bloody beheadings of the Terror of 1793 became known, reservations about the French experiment became widespread. Seeking to cool the growing political passions in his own country, President Washington sent James Monroe to Paris and John Jay to London to obtain treaties that would protect American shipping interests and keep the United States out of the European political thicket. But when Jay returned with an agreement that many believed was partial to the British, a political firestorm erupted. The treaty was so controversial that Washington waited six months before submitting it to the Senate for ratification in 1795, where it barely received the two-thirds majority required for passage.

By 1796, Hamilton's controversial economic policies and the Jay Treaty divided public opinion and led to the creation of the nation's first official political parties. The Federalists took their name to signal their intention to create a strong, centralized government. (Note that this group of Federalists does not refer to the defenders of the Constitution crafted in Philadelphia in 1787.) The opposing Republicans wished to make clear that they were devoted to the people and "the republican principle" of representative governance. (This group later changed its name to the Democratic party and continues to function under that label today.) Most Federalists were affluent businessmen from the northeastern states, whereas Republicans won backing from small farmers in the mid-Atlantic and southern states. The division proved so powerful that in 1796, a presidential election was hotly contested for the first time. Thomas Jefferson was so opposed to the Jay Treaty that he accepted the Republican call to lend his name as a presidential candidate. The battle between Federalist John Adams and Republican Jefferson was a close one, with Adams winning 71 electoral votes to Jefferson's 68. Under the peculiar constitutional arrangements of the time—which did not anticipate or account for political party competition—runner-up Jefferson became vice president.

The 1796 Adams-Jefferson contest was more than a struggle between two men—it was a battle between two political organizations. Although there were scores of local groups, some even using the term *parties* before 1796, the election of 1800 saw the emergence of political organizations as we know them today. Propelled by a strong conviction that the Federalist-controlled U.S. government was abandoning sacred "republican principles," Jefferson and the Republicans formed a party replete with grassroots supporters, which ran slates of candidates for numerous offices on a platform of issues that appealed to the American sense of limited government and a prevailing fear of placing too much authority in one individual.

In what proved to be a futile attempt to stem the growing Republican tide, John Adams and his Federalist followers in Congress sought to emulate Jefferson's organizational skills. Because they had less grassroots support—there were no Federalist clubs to speak of—organizing proved difficult. Yet, by virtue of the fact that they ran the government, they could use their positions to press their advantage, in the process confirming some of the Founders' fears about the factional dangers of partisanship.

Thus, the Federalist-controlled Congress passed the 1798 Sedition Act, which made it a misdemeanor to publish false or malicious information and provided that anyone convicted of conspiring to hinder the operations of the federal government would be subject to heavy fines and possible imprisonment. The Alien Acts, which became law in the same year, made it easier to deport political adversaries who were not citizens—especially the growing Irish population, which was pro-Republican, as well as any migrating French revolutionaries. Fourteen indictments were issued between 1798 and 1800. One Republican was jailed because he carried a placard protesting the acts; another was sentenced to six months for attempting, in the words of a Federalist-appointed judge, to "mislead the ignorant and inflame their minds against the President."[11]

Jefferson worried that these new laws might make it possible for the Federalists to install one of their own as a president-for-life. Thus, the organizing efforts of Jefferson and Madison became a whirlwind of activity as the election of 1800 approached. Republican members of Congress met in Philadelphia and formally endorsed Jefferson for president and Aaron Burr for vice president. The Federalists responded by nominating a ticket consisting of John Adams of Massachusetts and Thomas Pinckney of South Carolina—the first of many North-South pairings.

As in 1796, the Adams-Jefferson contest was hard fought. Hamilton warned his Federalist followers that no defections would be tolerated in the Electoral College. But Hamilton's admonition notwithstanding, Jefferson prevailed. As in the first Adams-Jefferson race, the southern states backed Jefferson while most of the Northeast sided with Adams. But the switch of New York from Adams to Jefferson—the culmination of Jefferson's courting of New Yorkers that began with his 1791 "nature tour"—paid off. Clinton and Livingston, together with Burr's New York City organization, rallied the troops on Jefferson's behalf. New York's electoral votes gave Jefferson an eight-vote plurality in the Electoral College. The Republican victory, which had to be ratified in the House of Representatives, extended to both houses of Congress. As Jefferson later recalled, "The Revolution of 1800 was as real a revolution in the principles of our government as that of 1776 was in its forms."[12] That revolution, as John Adams later observed, was the rejection of what Adams called "the monarchial principle"—a reference to his belief that those in power would do what is right for the country regardless of partisanship. After Jefferson's victory, future presidents would be party leaders. Adams himself blamed his lack of party standing for his defeat: "Jefferson had a party; Hamilton had a party; but the commonwealth [a reference to Adams] had none."[13] Jefferson replied that political parties had become an inevitable part of public life that had separated the two founding brothers.

## JACKSON AND MASS-BASED PARTIES

In the two decades following Thomas Jefferson's election, Republicans strengthened their hold on the government and overcame an abortive attempt by the

Federalists to lengthen their stay. But this did not stop the partisan bickering between Jeffersonian localists and Hamiltonian nationalists and their successors. One of the very first, and most bitter, partisan battles Jefferson faced involved the "midnight appointments" of loyal Federalists to the federal judiciary made by John Adams upon leaving the presidency in March 1801. The Federalists hoped that by making these appointments, they could limit the damage done by the Republicans until the next election in 1804. One of those appointed by Adams was William Marbury, who was slated to become a justice of the peace. The incoming Republican secretary of state, James Madison, refused to deliver Marbury's nominating papers after the outgoing Federalist secretary of state, John Marshall, failed to deliver them in time. In response, Marbury and seven others sued the government, claiming that Madison had defaulted on his duty to serve his appointment papers. The Supreme Court heard the case of *Marbury v. Madison* in 1803. In a landmark ruling, Chief Justice John Marshall (the same former secretary of state who had been appointed to the Court by John Adams) wrote that Marbury was entitled to his appointment, but Congress had exceeded its authority when it gave the Court the power to order Madison to surrender the papers, which it had in a provision of the Judiciary Act of 1789. Marshall thus wormed his way out of a certain confrontation with President Jefferson while expanding the Federalist principle of strong central government by claiming for the Court the authority to declare acts of the other branches unconstitutional, an authority known as judicial review.[14]

The next 20 years saw what historians sometimes call the Era of Good Feelings because of the apparent lack of political disagreement. In truth, the Republicans were so powerful and organized that for the only time in American history, there was essentially a one-party government with no serious electoral competition. The trio of Jefferson, Madison, and Monroe established a Virginia dynasty that controlled the White House; in the five elections held between 1804 and 1820, Republicans won between 53 and 92 percent of the Electoral College votes and held between 61 and 85 percent of the seats in Congress.

Meanwhile, the Federalists had started down a path to political obscurity, sealed by their reaction to the War of 1812. Federalists, who retained a strong base of support in the New England states, vehemently opposed the war, believing that it would seriously impede vital trade with England. They dubbed the conflict "Mr. Madison's War," and New Englanders continued to illicitly trade with the British, sometimes even withholding money and militia from the war effort. Republicans, in turn, stoked popular outrage at the British impressment of American sailors— the removal of British-born sailors from American vessels and forced entry into the British navy—and believed that the rampant nationalism would unify their diverse party. Partisan passions escalated after Congress declared war on Great Britain in 1812. When the *Federal Republican*, a Federalist newspaper located in Baltimore, editorialized against the war, an angry mob razed the building where it was printed. Elsewhere, Federalist sympathizers were beaten, stabbed, and even tarred and feathered. Two years later, the Federalists met in Hartford, Connecticut, and proposed generous peace terms. Rumors persisted that the Federalists favored the secession of the New England states from the Union, and the party, already weakened by its antiwar stance, fell into disrepute. By 1820, the Federalists had become political dinosaurs, not even bothering to nominate a token candidate to oppose James Monroe in that year's presidential contest. Hamilton's party faded into the history books; however, Hamilton's ideas did not.

The strength of the Republicans ultimately was their undoing. By 1810, the House of Representatives was filled with a variety of Republicans. Some were traditional states' rights advocates; others wanted an enlarged role for the federal government to enhance westward expansion. Thus, even though most elected officials were Republicans, the label became increasingly ambiguous. By 1824, the divisions within the party had widened into a chasm. Five candidates, each representing a different Republican faction, aggressively sought the presidency: Henry Clay, the powerful Speaker of the House and champion of westward expansion; John C. Calhoun, secretary of war and supporter of states' rights; Andrew Jackson, the hero of the Battle of New Orleans; John Quincy Adams, son of the former president and secretary of state under Monroe; and William Crawford, former treasury secretary and, like Calhoun, a doctrinaire states' rights advocate. The Congressional Caucus (the means by which Republican nominees had been chosen since 1800) convened in Washington, DC, in February and selected Crawford to be the party's standard-bearer with Calhoun as his running mate. The remaining three candidates boycotted the caucus and persuaded their respective state legislatures to place their names in contention.

On Election Day, Jackson led in the popular votes cast, winning 153,000 more than the combined votes cast for Adams and Crawford. But Jackson failed to win an electoral majority. The all-important Electoral College vote split, with Jackson receiving 99 votes; Adams, 84; Crawford, 41; and Clay, 37. Under such conditions, the Constitution turns the matter over to the House of Representatives for a final decision among the top three contenders. Clay, excluded from consideration, backed Adams, who reciprocated by promising to make Clay secretary of state in the new administration. Because he was the powerful Speaker of the House, Clay was able to clinch the House vote, and the presidency, for Adams.

Jackson's supporters were outraged by what they believed was a corrupt bargain between Adams and Clay. They considered Adams a usurper in the White House, and in several state capitals they plotted a comeback, with New York senator Martin Van Buren providing the organizational muscle. Van Buren correctly suspected that his home state could be decisive in the 1828 election, and he formed an alliance with Jackson that would help put "Old Hickory" over the top and avenge his 1824 defeat.

By 1826, several states had changed their laws allowing voters to choose delegates to the Electoral College rather than leaving the task to the various state legislatures. A general loosening of voter qualifications also greatly enlarged the size of the potential electorate. Meanwhile, the Republican Party continued fracturing. On one side were the Adams-Clay followers who were determined to implement internal improvements to the nation's infrastructure. Like the Federalists of two decades earlier, they were convinced that national prosperity necessitated an active government. On the other side were the so-called traditional Republicans whose ranks included Van Buren. They opposed internal improvements, including road and canal construction, because they believed such projects would violate state sovereignty. Jackson had managed to keep his distance from both factions, remaining a popular figure without an official party organization—until Van Buren took charge of his campaign.

Van Buren's first step toward involvement in national politics was to solidify his following in Congress. He quickly became leader of the Democratic-Republicans, a name chosen to express solidarity with the more egalitarian agrarian wing of the Republican Party. Van Buren undertook scores of trips around the country, campaigning for Jackson wherever he went. His goals were to arouse public indignation against the Adams-Clay deal, conduct door-to-door canvasses in every town, and make sure that Jackson supporters went to the polls on Election Day. Adams's forces derided Jackson as a military butcher and even called the chastity of his wife into question. Nonetheless, Jackson handily beat Adams, winning all of the South, the new western states, and Van Buren's New York. Just as significant, voter turnout doubled from 25 percent in 1824 to 50 percent in 1828. Jackson and Van Buren were the first to understand the power of mass-based party politics. Political parties were now firmly established as a primary vehicle for translating public sentiments into governing policies. Henceforth, parties became a mainstay of American political life.

With his victory, Jackson's Democratic-Republican Party, which shortened its name to the Democratic Party, had overtaken Jefferson's Republican Party. Henry Clay, John C. Calhoun, and others banded together as the opposition Whigs. Their name was intended to summon up the spirits of those who composed the patriot party during the heyday of the American Revolution and the British Whigs of the eighteenth century. Whigs stood for restrained executive powers, westward expansion, and protective tariffs. Thus, by the mid-1830s, a two-party system had taken root on American soil. But unlike the earlier political skirmishes between Hamilton and Jefferson, ideological differences were gradually supplanted by a "politics of personality," as people decided they either loved or hated Jackson. In addition, by raiding the federal treasury, Van Buren purchased an additional degree of party unity. The bargain was straightforward: state and local Democrats would be given dollars from the national treasury as long as they called themselves Democrats, supported Jackson on most matters, and took no controversial policy stands. As for issues of local concern, they were free to do as they saw fit. This move established a pattern of reciprocal deference characterized by both linkages and autonomy between levels of the party system. In this case, local party organizations would be linked to the state and national organizations, but they were also free to run their own shows.

By forming a political machine capable of winning elections, Van Buren won the grudging admiration of his opponents. Parties had moved beyond a collection of like-minded followers to organizations seeking the control of government. Indeed, organization has been a watchword in party politics ever since. As we will see in subsequent chapters, the resource-driven nature of party organizations and policy independence defines much of contemporary politics and is determining the role parties play in the twenty-first century.

During Jackson's presidency, power shifted from the affluent to the common citizen. Jacksonian Democracy had a number of consequences—the most significant of which was an immense increase in both the number of officials chosen by election and the number of people allowed to participate in electoral politics. Between 1824 and 1848, voter turnout increased from 25 percent to 79 percent—and in some states was as high as 92 percent. State and national party conventions emerged as important decision-making bodies in selecting candidates for office. A partisan press flourished, as parties used newspapers to communicate with their expanding ranks of followers—a low-tech precursor to the partisan weblogs of the twenty-first century.

To Van Buren, this new political environment posed both challenges and opportunities. Could the ever-increasing range of political voices be harmonized into consistently supporting one political party? Could issues attract new backers, or would appealing personalities be the key to winning new supporters? Van Buren maintained that the answers to these questions lay in building a party organization that was committed to principles even as it dispensed political favors. But jobs, not principles, formed the basis of politics in the 1830s and 1840s. The emergence of the spoils system (as in, "to the victor belong the spoils of the enemy"[15]) had a single purpose: to fill government jobs with loyal party workers. Even the mailman was a party loyalist. The spoils system meant that those filling these so-called patronage jobs would work diligently for the party or risk being bounced from the payroll. Because a job was based on one's party activity, giving time and money to the party became a means of ensuring economic security.

Over time, the spoils system changed the essence of politics. Elections were no longer solitary affairs confined to the affluent. Instead, they were community events, as issues and candidates were debated over the "cider barrel." Party organizations sponsored picnics, socials, and dinners, and held rallies, demonstrations, and conventions. By immersing themselves in the social fabric of civic life, parties kept citizens involved and inspired their loyalty on Election Day. Many voters proudly displayed their party affiliation by wearing political buttons on their lapels. Indeed, party devotion affected more people and reached more deeply than ever considered possible. The result was a stable pattern of voting; true independents and vote-switching between elections were rarities.

Parties reached their zenith by the late nineteenth century. They organized politics by affording social outlets, presenting tickets of candidates, drafting platforms, and initiating meaningful cues and symbols to voters. In short, American politics was party politics. Parties provided coherence to political thought, even as they created a politics of "us versus them," which reached its height during and immediately following the Civil War.

Although sectionalism had been a factor in American politics since 1796, the growing economic disparities between North and South during the first decades of the nineteenth century heightened those regional differences. The North was increasingly urban and ethnically pluralistic as it developed a strong industrial-based economy, whereas the South remained mostly agricultural. This economic gulf led each region to see its political interests differently.

The politics of the two regions became increasingly irreconcilable. In 1846, Democratic congressman David Wilmot from Pennsylvania introduced legislation prohibiting slavery in any territory acquired from the Mexican War. The Wilmot Proviso passed in the House, where representatives from states prohibiting slavery were in the majority, but pro-slavery Southerners blocked it in the Senate. Bitter animosities ensued, splitting the Democrats and Whigs in half. Northern Democrats moved toward establishing a new abolitionist party while Southern Democrats defended slavery. The Whig Party split into two factions: Conscience Whigs supported the Wilmot Proviso while Cotton Whigs believed that the federal government had no business outlawing slavery. When the Whig Party refused to consider the Wilmot Proviso during the 1848 election, many Conscience Whigs left the party in disgust.

By 1854, any remnant of party unity was shattered when the Kansas-Nebraska Bill became law and annulled the Missouri Compromise of 1820 by permitting slavery if voters in these two states approved. The Kansas-Nebraska Bill created a political firestorm and ignited violence between supporters and opponents in the two states. Pro-slavery Democrats backed the new law and excluded abolitionist Democrats from party councils. Opposition to the new law was widespread in the North, resulting in protests that led to the creation of the Republican Party. After an 1854 Republican gathering in Ripon, Wisconsin, one participant observed, "We came into the little meeting held in a schoolhouse Whigs, Free Soilers, and Democrats. We came out of it Republicans."[16] Four years later, the Republicans attained major-party status when Democrats lost 40 percent of their northern seats in the House of Representatives, enabling the Republicans to win control—an extraordinary achievement. In 1860, Republicans nominated Abraham Lincoln for president; in a four-way race, he won every free state except New Jersey. Democrats had become the party of the South, and Republicans the party of the North; the Whigs collapsed from their inability to reconcile the incompatible demands of their Conscience and Cotton factions.

Slavery sealed the Whigs' fate, but the question of immigration also contributed to their demise. Powerful nativist, anti-Catholic sentiments buffeted northern Whigs following a huge influx of Irish immigrants. The failure of the Irish potato crop in 1840 and the death from famine of over a million people prompted more than 750,000 Irish to emigrate to the United States from 1841 to 1850, eroding Anglo-Saxon Protestant denominations of many northern cities. Anti-Catholic riots erupted in Boston, Philadelphia, and New York.

As anti-immigrant fervor spread, an organization called the Know-Nothings gained influence. Their name derived from members' statements that they "kn[e]w nothing" about this secret society's existence. Adopting the name American Party, the Know-Nothings believed that "foreigners ha[d] no right to dictate our laws, and therefore ha[d] no just ground to complain if Americans see proper to exclude them from offices of trust."[17] Their contempt for the foreign-born was directed at Roman Catholics, who, they believed, owed their primary allegiance to the pope rather than the Constitution—a prejudice that was not fully expunged until John F. Kennedy became the first Catholic president in 1961. The Know-Nothings enjoyed their greatest success in 1854 when they successfully competed in Massachusetts, New York, Maryland, Kentucky, and California. In Massachusetts, where Irish Catholic immigrants had been pouring into the state at a rate of more than 100,000 per year, the Know-Nothings won all but three seats in the more than 350-seat state House of Representatives, every congressional seat, and all statewide offices, including the governorship. One despondent Whig declared, "This election has demonstrated that, by a majority, Roman Catholicism is feared more than American slavery."[18]

In 1856, the Know-Nothings attempted to capitalize on their victories by selecting former president Millard Fillmore to be their presidential candidate. Fillmore and Republican candidate John C. Fremont split the anti-slavery vote, resulting in Democrat James Buchanan's victory. The schism was eventually repaired as the Know-Nothings became subsumed into the ranks of an insurgent Republican Party, which retained its popular majority from its inception until the Great Depression of the 1930s. Republicans benefitted from having been the party that saved the Union and emancipated the slaves. Civil War veterans were minded by GOP leaders to "vote as you shot," and their partisan loyalties were reinforced by generous benefits allocated by Republican-controlled Congresses. Later, Republicans became associated with industrialism and economic prosperity. They appealed to farmers by supporting the Homestead Act, which offered cheap land in the East, and won support from business and labor by advocating high protective tariffs and land grants designed to develop transcontinental railroads. Only when the Republicans were divided, or nominated weak candidates, were Democrats able to win the presidency—as happened with Grover Cleveland in 1884 and 1892, and with Woodrow Wilson in 1912 and 1916.

## POLITICAL MACHINES

European immigration exploded between 1890 and 1930, when more than 15 million left Europe—roughly the same number who had emigrated to the United States from all countries during the period 1820 to 1890. For those stepping from the steerage ships, confusion about where to stay and find employment predominated. The Industrial Revolution provided jobs, but at low wages and under insufferable conditions. Few services existed to help the downtrodden. In this make-it-on-your-own atmosphere, political party machines helped ease the transition for many immigrants and in the process cemented one-party rule in large American cities. By 1900, robust party machines ruled in New York, Chicago, St. Louis, Boston, Pittsburgh, Philadelphia, Kansas City, and Minneapolis. At the state level, machines controlled Pennsylvania, New York, Ohio, Illinois, Michigan, and Wisconsin.

In exchange for a job, food, and occasional help with the law, party "bosses" asked for votes on Election Day. George Washington Plunkitt, one-time head of New York's Tammany Hall machine, was infamous for his candid portrayal of how the machine worked, and he won the undying loyalty of those who benefitted from it. The more people the machine helped, the greater was its grasp of the reins of power. State political bosses, mayors, and other ward leaders doled out thousands of patronage jobs to loyal party workers. Awarding jobs after a campaign was a top priority. One party leader reputedly met with his director of patronage every week to pursue every application for every city job down to the lowliest ditch digger's. In fact, patronage was an important party tool that continued to be widely used until the dawn of today's networked age.

The machines were also aided by local election laws that ensured that voting was not a private matter, permitting party machines to exercise a corrupt hold on power. Prior to 1888, each party printed its own ballot, usually in a distinctive color. Voters chose a party ballot and placed it in the ballot box. Split-ticket voting was not possible under this system, and the public selection of a ballot made it no secret whom the voter preferred. Moreover, election "inspectors" were appointed by the party machine to view the proceedings, sometimes even getting their supporters to vote more than once or to vote under the name of a deceased person. Characteristically, the bosses required firms doing government business to pay a kickback fee. The same held true to secure favorable health and safety inspections and zoning regulations. Overt corruption was tolerated because party leaders had such a devoted following. If someone's house burned, a child was arrested, or there was no food in the pantry, it was the boss who came to the rescue. As Chicago resident Jane Anderson wrote in 1898,

> If the Boss's friend gets drunk, he takes care of him; if he is evicted for rent, arrested for crime, loses wife or child, the Boss stands by him and helps him out. . . . The Boss gives presents at weddings and christenings; buys tickets wholesale for benefits, provides a helping hand at funerals, furnishing carriages for the poor and a decent burial for the destitute when they are dead, keeping his account with the undertaker and never allows a county burial. To ask where the money comes from which the Boss uses this way would be sinister.[19]

The period from the 1830s to the 1890s can be described as America's true party period; parties shaped the government and the way average citizens thought about politics. Some have even described this period as the "cult of parties," meaning that voters felt a lifelong commitment to a particular party. During the twentieth century, however, the party tale took a number of interesting twists and turns—once again, peculiarly American ones. Starting with the Progressive Era at the turn of the twentieth century, parties began to lose their strength and entered into a long period of decline, only to emerge, reinvented and revived, as something quite different than they were during the era of the party machine. We'll consider that part of the story in Chapter 3.

Throughout their history, however, the rivalry between Alexander Hamilton and Thomas Jefferson persisted, as party leaders split over how much influence the federal government located in Washington, DC, should have in local affairs. In the nineteenth century, Democrats supported Jeffersonian limits on the national government; in the twentieth century, this would become the Republican Party's position. But so deeply embedded is the ongoing debate between Hamilton and Jefferson that it persists in the twenty-first century. In an era defined by instantaneous communication, debates about the role of government persist on the major parties' websites, on ideological blogs, and on Facebook and Twitter. These debates echo the Hamilton–Jefferson divide and, far from making old divisions obsolete, strengthen age-old philosophical differences. It is not uncommon to find, on the pages of conservative and progressive blogs, Hamilton and Jefferson used to justify or explain current political divisions. For instance, this entry appeared on the conservative blog RedState in 2010:

> If Mr. Jefferson were alive today, he would no doubt approve greatly of the great American spirit that remains alive and well, while simultaneously fearing that Americans have so allowed government to dominate their lives as risking extinguishment of that flame. . . . As we work to stop the explosive growth of government and the corrosion of our deeply held American values, we must remember what the founders sacrificed and risked to give this gift to us. We furthermore must remember, and not run away from, the righteousness of our cause, . . . as Mr. Jefferson wrote.[20]

This entry, in turn, appeared on the progressive blog Daily Kos:

> What provokes me to write this is the Tea Party idea that they represent the vision of the founders. They wear t-shirts that read "Jefferson, Madison, Hamilton: Right-Wing Extremists." Poppycock! Balderdash! Liberals represent the vision of the founder far more than conservatives do, and we need to let Americans know it.[21]

Thus, remnants of nineteenth-century partisan habits have been revived in the very partisan and highly networked twenty-first century, manifesting themselves not just in the wearing of political buttons or attending party functions, but in the 24/7 world of online communication.

# NOTES

1. E. E. Schattschneider, *Party Government* (New York: Rinehart, 1942), p. 1.

2. Gallup poll, March 20–21, 2013. Text of question: "Next, please tell me one or two specific things you dislike about the Republican Party?" Inflexible/unwilling to compromise, 21 percent; for the rich/protecting the wealthy not the middle class, 12 percent; don't stand up for their positions/give in too easily, 9 percent; inconsistent/dishonest/say

one thing and do another, 5 percent; choice of candidates/party leaders, 4 percent; positions on social issues, 4 percent; abortion/women's policies, 3 percent; only worry about themselves, 3 percent; spend too much money/increased budget deficit, 3 percent; too conservative, 3 percent; favor big business/corporations too much, 2 percent; influence of religion on party, 2 percent; economic policies, 2 percent immigration policies, 2 percent; foreign policy/war issues, 1 percent; gun policies, 1 percent; position on gay marriage, 1 percent; not conservative enough, 1 percent; other, 10 percent; everything, 2 percent; nothing, 17 percent; no opinion, 17 percent.

3.   Howard Bement, ed., *Burke's Speech on Conciliation with America* (Norwood, MA: Ambrose and Company, 1922), pp. 45, 54–55, 61.

4.   Quoted in David McCullough, *John Adams* (New York: Simon and Schuster, 2001), p. 422.

5.   "Essays of Brutus, October 18, 1787," in Robert Ketcham, ed., *The Anti-Federalist Papers and the Constitutional Convention Debates* (New York: Signet Classic, 2003), p. 277.

6.   Alexander Hamilton, James Madison, and John Jay, "Federalist 57," in Edward Mead Earle, ed., *The Federalist* (New York: Modern Library, 1937), p. 370.

7.   Quoted in A. James Reichley, *The Life of the Parties: A History of American Political Parties* (New York: Free Press, 1992), p. 42.

8.   Quoted in McCullough, *John Adams*, p. 422.

9.   Cited in Thomas E. Patterson, *The American Democracy* (New York: McGraw-Hill, 1990), p. 350.

10.   Quoted in James Thomas Flexner, *Washington: The Indispensable Man* (New York: New American Library, 1974), p. 276.

11.   Quoted in Reichley, *The Life of the Parties*, p. 52.

12.   Ibid., p. 64.

13.   Quoted in Joseph J. Ellis, *Founding Brothers: The Revolutionary Generation* (New York: Vintage Books, 2000), p. 204.

14.   *Marbury v. Madison*, 1 Cr. 137 (1803).

15.   See A. James Reichley, "Party Politics in a Federal Polity," in John Kenneth White and Jerome M. Mileur, eds., *Challenges to Party Government* (Carbondale: Southern Illinois University Press, 1992), p. 44. The originator of the phrase was New York governor William Marcy, a close Van Buren ally.

16.   Quoted in Reichley, *The Life of the Parties*, p. 120.

17.   Quoted in Elinor C. Hartshorn, "Know-Nothings," in L. Sandy Maisel, ed., *Political Parties and Elections in the United States: An Encyclopedia* (New York: Garland, 1991), p. 549.

18.   Quoted in William E. Gienapp, "Formation of the Republican Party," in Maisel, *Political Parties and Election in the United States*, p. 399.

19.   Quoted in James Albert Woodburn, *Political Parties and Party Problems in the United States* (New York: Putnam, 1903), pp. 416–417.

20.   "Happy Birthday, Mr. Jefferson," posted by Hogan on RedState, April 13, 2010.

21.   "Jefferson, Madison, Hamilton: Left-Wing Radicals," posted by Doc Dorango on Daily Kos, December 22, 2010. See www.dailykos.com/story/2010/12/22/931076/. Accessed August 2, 2016.

# 3

# Party Organizations in the Twenty-First Century

O
ne hundred years ago, had you walked up to someone and asked whether the two-party system was necessary, you likely would have received a puzzled expression—and not just because you were talking to a stranger. Americans had forged connections to public officials through parties, and they spent much of their leisure time involved in party-related activities. To paraphrase James Madison, "Eliminating parties from politics would be like separating air from fire; how could the latter exist without the former?"

Shortly after the presidential race of 1840, where some 80 percent of eligible voters came to the polls, Charles Dickens traveled to the United States. While riding on a train, he made the following observation:

> Quiet people avoid the question of the presidency, for there will be a new election in three-and-one-half years, and party feelings run very high: the great constitutional feature of this institution being, that [as soon as] the acrimony of the last election is over, the acrimony of the next begins; which is an unspeakable comfort to all strong politicians and true lovers of their country: that is to say, to ninety-nine men and boys out of every ninety-nine and a quarter.[1]

In many ways, twenty-first century politics resembles that of the 1840s. Partisan polarization is very high. In the last three presidential elections (2008, 2012, and 2016), the major-party candidates have won nearly 90 percent support (or more) from their respective partisans—a far cry from the mid- and late-twentieth century, when voters often crossed party lines to support a preferred candidate. Today's voters are reluctant to split their tickets—often voting for candidates of the same party for President, Congress, and at the state and local levels. One reason for the greater party loyalty is that Americans tend to live in like-minded communities and they adopt cultural values that reinforce their partisan loyalties. For example, gun owners are far more likely to vote Republican, while those voters who don't own a weapon often support Democrats. Church attendance is another example: those who go to a church frequently (whatever their denomination) often vote Republican; those who don't, vote Democratic. Finally, demography has become a crucial factor in determining voter choice: nonwhites are far more likely to support the Democrats, whereas white voters prefer Republicans by large margins. In short, Red (Republican) States have become redder, while Blue (Democratic) States have become bluer.

In many ways, the party decline of the mid-twentieth century has been replaced by a party revival in the twenty-first. As we conclude our saga of parties in U.S. history, we'll confront a number of issues related to the decline and resurgence of parties. What caused parties, once vital players in politics at the close of the nineteenth century, to decline in influence during the twentieth? When and why did these changes occur? Were they intentional or the by-products of other developments unrelated to politics? What factors caused the party system to revive in the twenty-first century? And have these transformations shifted what remains of the party system in a Jeffersonian or Hamiltonian direction?

## THE PROGRESSIVE ERA

Party machines reigned in an America that, by the turn of the twentieth century, had become a place of great inequalities brought about by the Industrial Revolution. Colossal fortunes were made by the likes of John D. Rockefeller, Cornelius Vanderbilt, and J. P. Morgan, industrial giants who controlled the production and delivery of everything from oil to sugar, copper to beef, tobacco to rubber, and candy to locomotives. But many urban residents huddled in tiny tenements after working long hours in unsightly factories and sweatshops. Farmers suffered from falling prices for their goods, low inflation, and the private ownership of railroads. Appalachian coal miners were forced to accept insufferable working conditions because the government did little to help and there was no other work available. Poverty-stricken 12- and 13-year-old children were often pressed into work because their small bodies could fit more easily into the tiny mine shafts.

Calls for reform abounded but went largely unheeded, as the U.S. government and most states pursued a laissez-faire policy on economic matters. Many Republicans, who were the majority party at the time, believed the federal government should confine itself to those explicit powers given the president and the Congress in the Constitution. That meant virtually no government intervention in ending child labor, alleviating horrendous working conditions, and improving the poverty-level wages paid by the industrial giants. Frustrated by government inaction and gridlock, the working class mobilized. Labor unions, such as the Federation of Labor and the Knights of Labor, quickly expanded. But they were no match for a government aligned with corporate interests. When the unions decided to strike, government injunctions were issued to summon workers back to the factories. Union leaders were jailed for conspiracy and contempt for not obeying the injunctions. Labor riots ensued—notably the Pullman Car Strike in May 1894 following a cut in workers' wages. The American Railway Union, led by Eugene Debs, authorized a sympathy strike that spread from Chicago to the Northwest. After several outbursts of violence, President Grover Cleveland sent thousands of federal troops and marshals into Chicago in August 1894 under the pretense of protecting mail deliveries. With that, the strike came to a screeching halt.

It was of no small consequence that many upper-class citizens felt the corruption of party machines. Gas, water, and electric companies faced little competition and gouged customers at every turn. Residents could either pay the prices set by the company or go without lights, heat, or fresh water. By the early 1880s, the reformers banded together, calling themselves mugwumps—a name that became synonymous with independent or nonpartisan voters. They were less concerned with the substance of public policy than with the allegedly corrupt manner in which it was made. The winds of change were blowing, and the party machines were about to confront a storm.

But ending corruption was easier said than done, as legions of workers continued to owe their livelihoods to the city jobs and contracts provided them by party machines through the spoils system. By the second decade of the twentieth century, reformers had organized as Progressives, forming a third party aimed at upending corrupt Democratic and Republican Party bosses. The Progressive Party platform of 1912 described how the party machines controlled by both the Democrats and Republicans had become a threat to liberty:

> Political Parties exist to secure responsible government and to execute the will of the people. From these great tasks both of the old parties have turned aside. Instead of instruments to promote the general welfare, they have become the tools of corrupt interests which use them impartially to serve their selfish purposes. Behind the ostensible government sits enthroned an invisible government owing no allegiance and acknowledging no responsibility to the people. To destroy this invisible government, to dissolve the unholy alliance between corrupt business and corrupt politics is the first task of the statesmanship of the day.[2]

Former President Teddy Roosevelt carried the Progressive Party banner that year, despite his early association with the Republican Party establishment. Roosevelt began his political career after returning as a hero from the Spanish-American War in 1898. He was elected governor of New York, thanks to the backing of the

GOP boss Senator Thomas C. Platt, but was quickly sickened by the graft that characterized New York politics. Rather than abandoning party politics, however, Roosevelt attempted to remake the Republican Party into an agent of reform. His efforts did not sit well with the party chiefs, and they vowed to get rid of their nemesis. Platt engineered Roosevelt's nomination as the Republican vice presidential candidate in 1900, believing the obscurity of the vice presidency would surely bury Roosevelt. That plan backfired when, within a few months of his inauguration, McKinley was assassinated and Roosevelt became the 26th president of the United States. Almost overnight, Vice President Roosevelt was catapulted from obscurity to prominence.

Roosevelt's reform agenda was relatively modest. Besieged by conservative, business-minded congressional Republicans on the one hand, and reform-minded Progressives on the other, Roosevelt chose a middle-of-the-road course. He declined to seek reelection in 1908, opting to support his longtime friend, Secretary of War William Howard Taft, who easily defeated Democrat William Jennings Bryan. Frustrated by Taft's lackluster performance as president and by his failure to espouse Progressive reforms, Roosevelt once again sought the presidency in 1912. But wresting the Republican nomination from an incumbent president whom he had virtually anointed proved impossible, so Roosevelt accepted an invitation to join with like-minded renegade Republicans who had organized as Progressives. This new party adopted the nickname "Bull Moose" (following Roosevelt's declaration that he was "as strong as a bull moose"), and the name stuck. The Bull Moose platform called for the direct election of U.S. senators, women's suffrage, restricting the president to a single six-year term, a constitutional amendment allowing an income tax, the institution of a minimum wage, the prohibition of child labor, the creating of a Department of Labor, and even the overturning of some judicial decisions.

Roosevelt finished second, winning more votes than the Republican Taft—the best performance for a third-party presidential candidate in the twentieth century. But the Republican split enabled Democrat Woodrow Wilson to enter the White House. These results proved to be a high-water mark for the Progressives and marked only an interlude in GOP control of the White House. The Progressive Party faded from the scene in 1916, after Roosevelt refused its nomination and most of its followers returned to the Republican ranks. Robert M. La Follette Sr. was the Progressive Party's presidential nominee in 1924 and attracted 16 percent of the popular vote, but he won only his home state of Wisconsin. In retrospect, though, the 1912 election had a decisive impact on the Progressive struggle. Democrats, as well as conservative Republicans, could no longer withstand the power of the reform wave, as both parties were vulnerable to insurgent candidacies. President Wilson won enactment of several Progressive planks, as did most state and local governments. By attacking political parties so vehemently and scoring so solidly with the voters, the Progressives ensured that the remainder of the twentieth century would be an anti-party age.

However, it had taken decades of gradual and persistent reform efforts for Progressives to change how political parties operated. Reform initiatives began in 1870, shifted into high gear during the 1890s, and finally slowed after the 1912 elections. One reason why the Progressive movement was successful was this slow forward movement. Once a state or city was "cleaned up," residents elsewhere took notice and demanded reform in their own communities. Almost like an avalanche, the Progressive movement gathered more followers as it pushed ahead, until nearly all in its path were engulfed.

The media also aided the Progressive cause. Facing an entrenched party structure fueled by patronage, Progressives turned to the press to expose some of the conditions made possible by government neglect. Journalists called "muckrakers" (a term attributed to Teddy Roosevelt) graphically exposed the inhuman conditions permitted to flourish in sweatshops and on farms by a government that turned a blind eye to the suffering of the working classes. Newspapers and magazines found an audience for these lurid and disturbing accounts, and over time, with the assistance of charismatic leadership, Progressives were able to chip away at machine control by successfully promoting a set of legal reforms, eventually changing not only the character of party politics but the nature of government itself. Key Progressive reforms included the introduction of the Australian ballot, direct primary elections, a merit system to replace the spoils system, municipal ownership of utilities, ballot initiatives, nonpartisan municipal elections, direct election of U.S. senators, and women's suffrage.

***The Australian Ballot.*** When each party was allowed to print its own ballot on distinctly colored paper, machine politicians could keep track of how people voted and take retribution against anyone who voted against them. Bribery in the form of vote buying was also easy. The Australian ballot, named after its country of origin, curbed these abuses. It required that election ballots be prepared by the states, not party organizations. Ballots were to be identical and include the names of all candidates seeking office, thereby enabling voters to cast a secret ballot. It did not eliminate intimidation and bribery, but party henchmen could now lose an election and never know whom to blame. The new ballot also enabled citizens to split their tickets—that is, to vote for candidates of opposing parties running in the same election. The Australian ballot was first introduced in Kentucky in 1880; by 1896, most states had followed suit.

***Direct Primary Elections.*** Existing election laws made it easy for party bosses to keep reform-minded candidates off the ballot by controlling the nominating process. To qualify for the ballot, candidates had to receive the party's nomination, which was cleared by party leaders in private and subsequently ratified at local or state party conventions. A civic-minded reformer might consider running for office under a third-party label, but most state election laws were written with the consent of both Democrats and Republicans, thereby prohibiting insurgent candidates and parties from participating in the election process. Direct primary elections provided a solution to this dilemma. Instead of a small group of party leaders choosing a nominee, all party supporters would be given the opportunity. Nominations would be made through elections, called primaries, where the entire party membership had a say.

*The Merit System.* Supported by generally well-to-do urban mugwumps, the idea of filling government posts on the basis of merit rather than favoritism posed a direct threat to the patronage relationships at the heart of political machines. Attacking the patronage system denied party machines the ability to provide government jobs to faithful subordinates, while assuring that government positions would be filled with qualified people—a novel idea at the time. Thus, the merit system (later termed the civil service) became a pillar of the Progressive platform, favored by reformers weary of lackluster government services. The idea was not initially well-received by party leaders, but following the assassination of President Garfield by a disappointed job seeker in 1881, Congress established the Civil Service Commission to set standards for employment by the federal government and create thousands of permanent federal jobs that would continue regardless of which party controlled the White House. By the turn of the twentieth century, most states followed the federal government's example, dealing a decisive blow to party leaders.

*Municipal Ownership of Utilities.* At the turn of the twentieth century, utility companies that had been awarded their franchises by the party machines charged exorbitant rates even as they continued to provide poor service. The companies were guaranteed huge profits, raising the cost to customers who had no choice but to pay. Party leaders kept profits high because they were receiving huge kickbacks from the companies in exchange for franchise rights. Reformers realized that breaking this cozy relationship meant that public regulation of utility companies was necessary, and they pushed measures to do so through state and local governments. Many of these businesses remained privately owned, but in exchange for the franchise they agreed to allow a public board or commission to set rates. Other services, such as garbage collection, sewage removal, and transportation, would be assumed by government under new agencies administered by employees who got their jobs through the merit system.

*Ballot Initiative, Referendum, and Recall.* One way to link voters to their government is to give average citizens a direct say in what government does. Another is to dismiss elected officials should they lose voter confidence. In an era of partisan corruption, Progressives championed these reforms. The ballot initiative requires a legislature to consider specific measures. The referendum gives voters a voice on policy matters by gathering enough signatures to place a measure on a ballot. The recall allows voters to remove elected officials in a special election before their term of office is over. South Dakota was first to authorize ballot initiatives in 1898; Oregon was first with referenda in 1902 and with recalls in 1908. After California instituted ballot initiatives in 1910 under outspoken Progressive Republican Governor Hiram Johnson, these measures earned national attention, and by the 1920s about three-fourths of the states allowed initiatives, referenda, and recalls. Today, these forms of direct popular participating are commonplace. In 2003, California voters recalled unpopular Democratic Governor Gray Davis and replaced him with Republican Arnold Schwarzenegger. In 2012, Wisconsin voters rejected a recall of controversial Republican Governor Scott Walker after he successfully sought legislation limiting the collective bargaining rights of public unions. In recent years, voters in various states have been permitted to voice their preferences on a host of policy questions including gay rights, campaign finance reform, gambling, and the legal use of marijuana.

*Nonpartisan Municipal Elections.* Progressives generally believed that the problems facing most municipalities were technical and could be solved by a combination of professional administration and scientific principles. Following this logic, Progressives pushed for nonpartisan city elections, where candidates were not identified by party label. Boston was the first to implement this reform in 1909; two decades later, 26 of the nation's largest cities had followed suit. Like the direct primary, however, this reform has been only modestly successful. Although the party labels of these mayoral candidates may not be printed on the ballot, it is generally no mystery which candidates are sponsored by a particular political party.

*Direct Election of U.S. Senators and Women's Suffrage.* Two additional Progressive measures helped reduce the influence of party machines: the direct election of U.S. senators and extending the vote to women. Under Article I of the Constitution, the election of senators was left to state legislatures. Progressives argued that this provision, combined with a six-year term and staggered elections, insulated the upper chamber from public opinion. They provided the impetus for the Seventeenth Amendment (ratified in 1913) that allowed citizens to cast a ballot for individual senatorial candidates. Women's suffrage was another Progressive cause. In 1890, Wyoming was the first state to grant women the right to vote, followed by Utah and Idaho in 1896. Even though the women's suffrage movement was centered in the East (primarily New York and Massachusetts), change did not come to that region until 1919—the year the Nineteenth Amendment to the Constitution was ratified, giving women everywhere the right to vote. Credit for passage of the amendment lies with the grit and determination of women demanding equality, especially Susan B. Anthony and Elizabeth Cady Stanton. But Progressive reformers also lent their voices to the cause because they believed that once women were enfranchised, corrupt party machines would suffer at the polls.

Over a long period of time, Progressives fundamentally altered the party system by changing politics from a private affair to a public concern. During the 1800s, parties conducted their business free from government interference, operating as private organizations. Progressives demanded public oversight and regulation of most party activities, transforming the parties into quasi-public agencies subject to legislative control. This meant eliminating most "mediating institutions," especially the party machines. The direct primary stripped party leaders of their ability to completely control nominations; the secret ballot reduced voter intimidation and election fraud; the merit system lessened patronage opportunities; and public control of utility companies drained party coffers. The direct election of U.S. senators and women's suffrage were the icing on the cake.

Placed on the defensive by disclosures of corruption and a growing sense of public outrage, party bosses yielded to the inevitable and accepted reform. But this did not mean that they were willing to commit suicide. In fact, many reform measures that reduced corruption inadvertently worked to strengthen the two-party system. Although the direct primary precluded complete control over nominations by party leaders, a candidate's ability to get on a state primary ballot required a massive number of signatures. This labor-intensive process was something parties were well-suited to accomplish. Senators were subject to direct popular election, but they needed a party nomination to win a place on the ballot and initially relied on party organizations to run their campaigns. The merit system reduced patronage, yet there remained scores of "exempt" and "temporary" positions to be filled. Utilities might be controlled by boards and commissions, but the city government-corporate nexus was far from broken. Party war chests continued to overflow with contributions from businesses.

Some Progressive reforms ironically strengthened the major parties' legal standing. The new laws curtailed the worst abuses of the machine era, but also made independent and minor-party candidacies more difficult. Instead of adhering to the Australian practice of omitting party designation on the ballot, most states adopted a general election ballot that required party labels to be placed alongside a candidate's name. It was easy for the two major parties to keep this official ballot recognition because state law reserved a place for whichever two parties received the most votes in the last election. Any remaining parties would have to circulate petitions before the next election to gain ballot access—a difficult and extremely time-consuming chore.

Another change during the Progressive movement that has come under scrutiny is voter registration. In a provocative book entitled *Why Americans Still Don't Vote, and Why Politicians Want It That Way*, scholars Frances Piven and Richard Cloward argue that voter registration requirements, implemented around the turn of the twentieth century, were designed to shrink the size of the electorate. For leaders of both parties, demobilization created a more manageable and controlled system. They write,

> A system of registering voters seems at first glance a reasonable development. It was, after all, simply a means of compiling a list of those who were eligible to vote, a procedure that became more necessary as the population grew, and as the vote fraud perpetrated by the clientelist political parties became more common. In practice, however, the way the lists were compiled had a great deal to do with who was likely to be on them, and who was likely to be omitted.[3]

Nonetheless, Progressive reforms directly attacked the Jeffersonian style of local governance by shifting governing responsibilities to nonpartisan administrative agencies in order to fight corruption at the local level. Jeffersonian localism was then dealt a second blow one generation later, when Franklin D. Roosevelt's

New Deal politics called on the national government to take an unprecedented role in protecting its citizens.

## THE NEW DEAL AND PARTY POLITICS

Other than Wilson's upset victory in 1912 and his narrow reelection victory four years later, Republicans controlled the federal government during the first third of the twentieth century. By decisive margins, Warren Harding won in 1920, Calvin Coolidge in 1924, and Herbert Hoover in 1928. This Republican trifecta profited from a strong national economy, and as long as the economy prospered, Republicans would retain their natural majority. But everything changed on October 24, 1929, when the stock market crashed and the Great Depression began. Stock values dropped nearly 75 percent overnight, and two years later unemployment reached 25 percent. Farmers were especially hard hit, seeing prices for commodities drop to their lowest levels since 1910. Thousands of children were unable to attend school due to a lack of shoes.

In 1932, Franklin Delano Roosevelt, the popular governor of New York and cousin to Teddy, won the presidency in a landslide. Roosevelt won 42 states to President Hoover's 6, and Democrats carried both houses of Congress by overwhelming margins. In the Senate, Democrats won 59 seats to the Republicans' 37; in the House, Democrats had 312 members to the Republicans' 123. Roosevelt moved rapidly to take advantage of these majorities, proposing a flurry of legislation designed to provide immediate relief to those he described as "ill-housed, ill-clad, and ill-nourished."[4] During his first term, Congress approved the Tennessee Valley Authority (TVA), the National Recovery Administration (NRA), the Works Progress Administration (WPA), the Public Works Administration (PWA), the Civilian Conservation Corps (CCC), and the Social Security Act. The first hundred days of Roosevelt's administration, which saw the creation of so much of what came to be known as the New Deal, set a standard against which Roosevelt's successors have been measured ever since.

Roosevelt's New Deal drastically transformed both the national government and the political parties. Abandoning its laissez-faire posture, the federal government became an active player whose primary responsibility was to ensure the economic well-being of the people. The New Deal signaled the emergence of a system whereby the federal government regulated some elements of the economy; elevated the cause of organized labor, farmers, and the elderly; and redistributed wealth through a progressive income tax. It also transformed the relationship between citizens and government. Prior to Roosevelt, a rugged individualism prevailed. But the Great Depression made it possible for Roosevelt to construct a foundation for economic security. The inalienable rights secured by the Constitution—speech, press, worship, due process—were supplemented by a new bill of rights "under which a new basis of security and prosperity can be established for all—regardless of station, race, or creed."[5]

The president became the center of the governing process—in effect, a guarantor of economic rights granted by the New Deal. To ensure a more efficient and enlightened administration, Roosevelt proposed the 1939 Executive Reorganization Act, which gave the president extraordinary powers and created a personalized White House bureaucracy known as the Executive Office of the President—an agency that has epitomized the personalization of presidential power.

The rise of executive-centered government was a serious blow to local party organizations. Local and state powers diminished as Americans looked to the federal government, especially the president, for leadership. Surprisingly, the two parties had not established ongoing national party organizations until the late 1920s. Under Roosevelt, Democrats established a permanent national headquarters in 1932, and Republicans quickly followed suit. Since then, the Democratic National Committee and the Republican National Committee (and their congressional counterparts) have vastly expanded their money-gathering abilities even as local party organizations have withered. Together, they constitute the focal points of the two-party system.

The cumulative effects of the Progressive and New Deal reforms on political parties were apparent by the 1950s. The rise of nonpartisan administration was so complete, and the concentration of power at the federal level so entrenched, that the last vestiges of the spoils system had been removed and party-centered politics had begun to disappear. By 1964, Jeffersonian localism—which concentrated power at the state and local level, instead of the federal government and especially the presidency—was viewed as a radical departure from the norm. Presidential nominee Barry Goldwater sought to combat this new reality, telling the Republican Convention: "Extremism in the defense of liberty is no vice. Moderation in the pursuit of justice is no virtue."[6] He lost 44 states to Lyndon B. Johnson.

## TELEVISION AND CANDIDATE-CENTERED POLITICS

Aside from Progressivism and the New Deal, the cold war deeply affected party politics. Initially, the rise of communism was a boon to Republicans, who had been shut out of the White House in five consecutive elections from 1932 through 1948. From 1952 to 1988, Republican presidential candidates benefitted from increased cold war tensions between the United States and the Soviet Union. Promising America "peace through strength," Dwight D. Eisenhower, Richard M. Nixon, Ronald Reagan, and George H. W. Bush won the presidency because they projected the right combination of steadiness and toughness. In the ten presidential elections held between 1952 and 1988, Republicans won seven.

But as a party, Republicans paid a high price for their presidential victories. Eisenhower, Nixon, Reagan, and the first President Bush were "plebiscitary presidents"—winning personal victories without increasing the number of people who called themselves Republicans. Thus, although the cold war served the interests of Republican presidential candidates, the growing personalization of political campaigns weakened the Republican Party. Democrats also grew weaker, as their congressional incumbents ran increasingly personal campaigns, often emphasizing their own local accomplishments rather than broad party themes. Accordingly, voters came to view politics in terms of individual rather than party competition.

At the same time, party activists, who had conducted campaigns throughout most of U.S. history, were pushed aside by professional campaign consultants who used mass-based voter contact techniques to reach large numbers of voters through television and direct mail. These people learned their craft in marketing firms rather than in the trenches of partisan political warfare, and turned electioneering into a professional contest between strategists and handlers. Today, nearly every congressional candidate, most state legislators, and a growing number of municipal officials hire campaign consulting firms, who provide a breathtaking range of services necessary to waging mass campaigns: polling, conducting focus groups, fund-raising, direct mail, radio and television production, event planning, demographic research, and message development. Volunteer-based and party-run campaigns are a rarity, as candidates prefer to let hired professionals run things.

More than any other factor, television turned campaigns into exercises in consumer marketing and candidates into clay to be molded and sold to the public as reflections of what people tell pollsters they want in their politicians. As an entertainment medium that plays directly to people's emotions, television is an ideal vehicle for reaching voters at a gut level, and smart candidates managed by savvy handlers have used it to great effect to connect with voters on a large scale—without actually forming the direct associations characteristic of the era of patronage politics. In the television age, politics became an exercise in manipulating mass public opinion.

Acquiring a party's nomination by abandoning the party in favor of personalized voter outreach dates back to when television was an infant medium in the 1950s. Dwight D. Eisenhower was the first presidential candidate to employ television advertising, and, not coincidentally, he was the first of several "citizen politicians" to seek and win the presidency on the strength of their personal biographies and with the help of a carefully calibrated television campaign. On February 2, 1952, Citizens for Eisenhower opened its doors, managed not by Republican partisans, but by a mortgage banker and the president of the Ford Foundation, and propelled by advertising executives who had run successful television campaigns for consumer products like aspirin.[7] They presented Eisenhower as a nonpartisan office seeker who was simply renting the top slot on the Republican ticket, selling the public on the idea that the likable World War II hero with humble Midwestern roots was a natural for the presidency. For their part, voters could support Eisenhower without making a partisan commitment. It was a marriage of convenience.

Richard M. Nixon emulated Eisenhower's approach in 1968, but took it a giant step further by using television to reinvent himself after his failed 1960 presidential campaign and an unsuccessful run for governor of California in 1962. In the parlance of hired image consultants, Nixon suffered from "high negatives" among voters who didn't trust him after a checkered career clouded by ethical questions. In an age of candidate-centered campaigns, it was unlikely that Nixon could have been elected without an image makeover; however, in the previous era of strong party organizations, it would have been equally unlikely that party leaders would have given him their blessing to try. At least in the age of candidate-centered politics, Nixon was free to try to transform his image, and he found in television the perfect vehicle for creating what his consultants cleverly called the "New Nixon": honest, open, sympathetic, and accessible.

However, Nixon's efforts were at their core quite cynical, because in order to project an image of openness, his handlers understood that they had to run a closed campaign from inside a television studio, limiting access to reporters and calibrating the candidate's every move in order to avoid spontaneous exchanges that might undermine the campaign's carefully crafted message. And they recognized that resuscitating the candidate's image didn't mean really changing anything about Nixon, who remained aloof and enigmatic to the people around him.[8] As long as they could get enough people to *believe* Nixon to be more embraceable, they could solve his electability problem, so they staged a performance for voters using a medium known foremost for its ability to tell a story.

# INSTITUTIONAL RETRENCHMENT

Just as presidential campaigns were becoming candidate-centered affairs, the national political parties engaged in efforts to reinvent themselves so as to become relevant in changing political times. The Republican Party went first. Even though Richard Nixon won the presidency in 1968, Democrats maintained their control of both houses of Congress and most state and local offices. By 1973, the GOP was in serious trouble as the economy soured; then, in 1974, the Watergate scandal forced Nixon's resignation. The 1974 midterm elections proved disastrous for Republicans, when a large class of Democratic freshmen, dubbed "Watergate babies," was elected in heretofore safe Republican districts. Following Jimmy Carter's 1976 victory, some prognosticators predicted that the GOP was headed for extinction.

Given the prevailing pessimism, leaders in the Republican National Committee (RNC) decided to reconfigure the party. The task fell to the newly appointed chair, William Brock, a former U.S. senator from Tennessee. To enhance the party's electoral prospects, Brock opted to centralize power within the RNC. He initiated a four-part strategy to accomplish this goal: (1) aggressive fund-raising, (2) organizational improvements, (3) better candidate recruitment, and (4) changing the party's image.

***Fund-Raising*** Believing that Republicans needed more money to win more elections, Brock decided to solicit it from ordinary voters, using some of the same techniques for party building that campaign consultants used on behalf of electing candidates. Large computerized lists of potential prospects were sent letters asking for small contributions. Although the response rate to these direct-mail solicitations was low, those who gave were placed on a donor list and asked every six months or so to contribute more money. Brock argued that direct mail had two advantages: (1) by seeking small individual contributions, the party could shatter its image of catering to the rich; and (2) if successful, direct mail could raise large sums. Brock's bet paid off. In 1977, the RNC expanded its base of contributors from 250,000 to 350,000. Three years later, a phenomenal 1.2 million Republicans were sending in checks payable to the RNC. Even though the average contribution was small—just $25—total receipts grew from $12.7 million in 1976 to more than $26 million in 1980.[9]

*Organizational Improvements.* Brock revamped the organizational structure of the national committee by installing 15 regional directors to help plan strategy and bolster the state parties; establishing task forces to encourage states to develop long-range plans; providing regional finance directors to help raise money; and sending one organizational expert to help each state committee. Brock also initiated a program whereby state and local party organizations could use RNC-owned equipment and sophisticated technologies at a minimal cost. A massive computer network enabled the state and local Republican parties to download a variety of software programs to expedite accounting, word processing, direct mail, get-out-the-vote drives, mailing list maintenance, and political targeting. Finally, the RNC provided GOP candidates with low-cost polling services. In 1980, it supplied 130 campaigns with discounted polling, sometimes for as little as $250.[10] Thus, Brock reconfigured the RNC to meet the demands of modern-day political organizations where high technology, survey research, computer-driven targeting, television advertisements, and direct mail are all essential tools.

*Candidate Recruitment.* Brock also realized that these tools meant nothing without good candidates. He instituted a "farm team" approach to candidate development by recruiting prospective Republicans to seek lesser offices. Once these rising stars got a taste for public life, Brock reasoned, they would seek higher office, and thanks to their previous political experience, they would win. Toward that end, the RNC created the Concord Conferences that permitted young professionals, party leaders, and prospective candidates to discuss strategy, tactics, and the importance of political involvement. In 1980, more than 600 men and women attended these events. Brock also developed other forums for would-be candidates that included training seminars on issue development, public speaking, managing the inevitable stresses of a campaign, and media relations. Between 1977 and 1980, more than 10,000 Republicans, mostly state and local candidates, attended these sessions.[11]

*Image Repair.* Finally, Brock sought to refurbish the Republican Party's tattered image. Prior to his tenure, the Republican Party was likened to a country club inhabited by older, white, well-to-do men. Brock wanted these "country club Republicans" to make way for more women and minorities. To accomplish this, he spent $640,000 in 1977 to attract more African Americans to the Republican ranks, largely without success. A few years later, Brock organized a similar effort to recruit women. To help these efforts along, he began publication of a lively opinion journal. Entitled *Commonsense*, it included articles from prominent conservative Democrats, independents, and Republicans—providing an intellectual breath of fresh air to replace what had become stale party doctrine. By 1980, new ideas had become the hallmark of the GOP.

The Democratic Party's reaction to the Brock reforms was to say, in effect, "Stop until we can catch up!" Disgruntled Democrats pointed to Brock's success at fund-raising and wondered how they could match it. In 1978, for example, the RNC disbursed more than $2.7 million to state and local candidates, whereas the Democratic National Committee (DNC) contributed just $107,000.[12] After Democrats took a drubbing at the polls in 1978 and 1980, the grumbling grew louder. The head of the Association of State Democratic Chairs complained, "The 1980 election was a referendum on national party structure. We were outspent, out-targeted, and out-polled. The RNC did a superlative job. The Democratic Party should hang its head in shame."[13]

But the Democratic Party found itself unable to match the organizational sophistication of the Republican National Committee during a time when Republicans were regularly winning presidential elections and, eventually, would take control of Congress while making deep inroads at the state and local level. Under the leadership of Charles Manatt, who was chosen in 1981 to serve as chair of the Democratic National Committee, the DNC was reorganized to provide stronger managerial leadership and fund-raising prowess. Manatt tripled the number of DNC staffers, began a series of training seminars for state and local candidates, organized a State Party Works program that allowed state parties access to state-of-the-art campaign techniques and strategies, devised a massive voter registration program, and copied the RNC's successful direct-mail efforts.[14] Although these changes resulted in more prolific fund-raising, that didn't translate into success at the ballot box. In 1984, Democratic presidential nominee Walter F. Mondale lost 49 states against incumbent President Ronald Reagan.

Institutional retrenchment also involved greater institutional specialization, notably the development of branch organizations designed to finance and manage legislative contests. At the national level, these organizations are called the Hill committees because of their origins within the halls of Congress. There are four units, one for each party in each house of Congress: the Democratic Congressional Campaign Committee (DCCC), the Democratic Senatorial Campaign Committee (DSCC), the National Republican Congressional Committee (NRCC), and the National Republican Senatorial Committee (NRSC).

In one respect, campaign committees are a very old invention. The NRCC was established in 1866 by Radical Republicans from the Northeast to protect against political retaliation from their rival, Andrew Johnson of Tennessee, who had become president after Abraham Lincoln's assassination and controlled the RNC by virtue of his holding the presidency. Not to be outdone, a group of pro-Johnson Democrats created the DCCC. Senators had little need for these legislative party organizations until the Seventeenth Amendment was passed in

1913, instituting direct election of senators. Senate campaign committees were established by both parties shortly thereafter.

However, these committees were unimportant players until the 1970s, serving as little more than fund-raising apparatuses for incumbents to collect money in Washington and channel it back to local districts. No professional staff or permanent headquarters existed for these "poor sisters" in the party hierarchy. All that began to change in the 1960s, as the cost of campaigning began to escalate, television became an integral part of political campaigns, partisan loyalties weakened, and progressive reformers stripped local parties of much of their patronage, resulting in fewer volunteers showing up at party headquarters. Accordingly, members of Congress turned to the congressional campaign committees for help. Once again, Republicans were the first innovators. Taking their lead from Bill Brock, the Senate and House Republican campaign committees devised extensive direct-mail programs. Other "inside the Beltway" fund-raising schemes were pursued, including holding extravagant dinner parties in Washington, DC. The result was an avalanche of cash: NRCC receipts quintupled from nearly $12 million in 1978 to $58 million in 1984, while NRSC receipts ballooned from $2 million in 1978 to $82 million in 1984. At the start of the 2016 election cycle (from January 1, 2015, to June 30, 2016), the combined receipts for both GOP committees totaled more than $188 million.[15]

Democrats followed a similar path. Under the aggressive leadership of California congressman Tony Coelho, the DCCC implemented scores of new fund-raising programs. Coelho made it a practice to visit hundreds of business and trade associations asking for contributions. According to then-Representative Barney Frank, "Tony Coelho was very good at explaining the facts of life to PACs: if you want to talk to us later, you had better help us now."[16] Similarly, Hill committees began playing a brokerage role, serving as intermediaries between special interest groups and needy candidates. At meet-and-greet events, candidates and PAC representatives commingle, as if on a blind date, to help candidates hit it off with the PAC representatives and convince would-be donors that the candidates stand a good chance of winning and will not forget their friends after Election Day. Time only made the Democratic campaign committees more powerful. At the start of the 2016 campaign (from January 1, 2015, to June 30, 2016), the Democratic congressional committees raised more than $226 million to help their party's congressional candidates.[17] Although vastly different in form and capacity from their earlier incarnations, political party organizations found ways to reinvent themselves and reestablish their relevance in the political process.

# PARTIES AND THE ADVENT OF THE INTERNET

Richard Nixon's success at reinventing himself became the template for how to run a campaign in the television era, and it was emulated by other successful candidates who, with the help of media professionals, crafted biographical appeals that resonated with iconic American lore: Jimmy Carter as the Lincolnesque figure who would never lie to you; Ronald Reagan as the cowboy who came to town to clean up the mess made by others; Bill Clinton as the everyman from a small town with a name that could have been created by a screenwriter (Hope, Arkansas); Barack Obama as the candidate of "hope" and change; and Donald Trump as the successful businessman of the television show *The Apprentice* whose catchphrase was "You're fired."

But the advent of the Internet as a political tool has moved us into a new age when politics is not driven exclusively by television. As we will discuss in Chapter 6, Internet-based politics is heralding a public re-engagement comparable to what we saw prior to the ascendancy of television. Today, Internet activism has infiltrated the mainstream as sizable "blogospheres" have emerged on the left and right of the political spectrum, and social media engage countless numbers in politics. The voluntary endeavors of politically engaged citizens now fuel serious efforts to influence elections, policy outcomes, and media narratives.[18] In many ways this began with the 2004 presidential campaign of former Vermont governor Howard Dean, who shocked the political world by taking an obscure, long-shot candidacy to the verge of the Democratic nomination on the strength of hundreds of thousands of supporters who self-organized on the Internet. Four years later, Internet supporters made the difference in Barack Obama's unlikely run against Hillary Clinton for the Democratic nomination and the presidency. Obama updated his online presence in 2012 to incorporate social media that were in their infancy during his first campaign. In 2016, Democratic presidential candidate Bernie Sanders nearly overcame overwhelming odds by garnering supporters and dollars via the Internet in his battle to wrest the Democratic nomination away from the favorite, Hillary Clinton. As for Clinton, she included many of Obama's web-savvy advisors, while her general election opponent, Donald Trump, elevated Tweeting into a campaign art form.

This leads us to the question we posed at the start of the chapter: Was the increased involvement and excitement surrounding the 2008 Obama campaign the start of a party resurgence in the emerging Internet era? The evidence is not at all clear. The Obama campaign was candidate-centered rather than party-centered, continuing a key twentieth-century trend. Obama's election brought with it large Democratic congressional majorities, but how many of the new voters who also pulled the lever for down-ballot Democrats were Obama loyalists first and Democrats second? Many of them did not turn out two years later to vote in congressional elections where Obama was not on the ballot, and Obama's active support of fellow Democrat Hillary Clinton as his chosen successor could not carry her to victory despite passionate appeals to his supporters. Donald Trump's 2016 campaign was even more candidate-centered than Obama's, with a large number of establishment Republicans refusing to endorse their party's nominee. So Trump relied on social media to communicate his message to supporters and build a brand that was independent of the Republican Party.

These observations suggest what while Internet politics may revitalize participation, it may not have the same effect on parties. Instead, the Internet promises to create more customized relationships between candidates and supporters that could strengthen their political bonds. The success of Obama's Internet campaign rested in part on a web presence that users could tailor to suit their needs and wishes so that they could take the initiative, if so inclined, to organize events, write testimonials, give money, volunteer, or persuade friends and neighbors about the strengths of the candidate. We will discuss this operation in more detail in Chapter 6. Unlike television, Internet communication is individualized and personalized, and candidates who know how to use it can do so to create a loyal following. It is an open question whether the social networking tools made possible by technological advances and effectively employed by the Obama campaigns will continue to engage voters when other candidates try to use them, or whether 2008 and 2012 will stand alone as campaigns featuring a charismatic candidate who understood how to present himself online. Hillary Clinton's struggle to reach Millennial voters speaks to the importance of the messenger over the medium.

Consider also that the 2010 election restored divided government only two years after a Democratic sweep, brought about in part by a segment of the electorate that continues to swing between Republicans and Democrats—sometimes with such rapidity that it can almost cause whiplash. This result also continues a trend from the weak-party television era. And divided government in recent years has facilitated polarization and paralysis, in part through the emergence of Tea Party voters who largely identify with the Republican Party and have mobilized to vote in Republican primaries, successfully moving Republicans to assume a hard-core anti-government Jeffersonian position. This, too, could be a sign of the weakening of parties, as members of the party in government are hamstrung by the intense wishes of their base in the electorate. On the other hand, it could be evidence of a partisan revival, as Tea Party supporters thrust themselves into political discourse in a manner reminiscent of nineteenth-century party politics, using the Republican Party as their vehicle.

Simultaneously, on the left, progressives have been organizing online in an attempt to move Democratic Party elites to embrace their positions on wealth inequality, prodding Democrats to challenge rather than acquiesce to the demands of large banking and corporate interests in such policy areas as healthcare, energy, taxes, and economic stimulus. Philosophically aligned with the Progressive movement of the early twentieth century, online progressive organizations and blogs affiliate with the Democratic Party but are also among the party's harshest critics. Like the Tea Party movement, the emergence of online progressives may signal a weakening of party influence if their efforts make bipartisan compromise more difficult. Or their push to reshape the Democratic Party, if successful, may prove to be evidence of a revival in the importance of party organizations. Certainly, Bernie Sanders' surprisingly strong challenge to Hillary Clinton in the 2016 primary campaign demonstrated how an insurgent who hadn't even considered himself a

Democrat before running for the Democratic nomination could shift the center of gravity of a major party by resonating with a large share of the party base.

Then there are questions about what happens to the relationship between new media campaign operations and the political parties when campaigns are successful. Upon taking office, President Obama fine-tuned his campaign web presence, re-christened it Organizing for America, and folded it into the every-day operations of the Democratic National Committee—effectively remaking the national party in the image of his successful Internet campaign. With that, the rela-tionship between party and politician had completed a 180-degree shift from the turn of the twentieth century, even as party activity returned to the community level. Whereas the party of 100 years earlier had aided candidates by organizing campaigns and government, recruiting grassroots workers, and providing a social outlet for community activities, now an Internet campaign run by a candidate was performing these functions in the name of the party.

Americans have never fully embraced political parties. As we have seen, public distaste for parties lingered throughout the nineteenth and twentieth centuries, even as they became more deeply rooted in the political system. Parties were tolerated because they helped create an efficient means of organizing mass-based politics. Just when they reached their zenith, a reform wave swept the nation and systematically dismantled much of the leverage party machines held on the system. Progressives stripped party organizations of their institutional strengths and helped change public attitudes toward them. Direct primaries reduced the capacity of party leaders to control who got on the ballot. Referenda allowed average citizens to go over the heads of elected officials to change public policy. Franklin D. Roo-sevelt continued the movement away from parties by nationalizing governance. The cold war, television, and the emergence of candidate-centered campaigning accelerated the personalized presidency, which shows no signs of subsiding even as the Internet becomes more prevalent in our politics.

Through it all, though, political parties have proved to be resilient. The prin-cipal difference between the major parties at the onset of the twenty-first century from their predecessors lies not in their relative standing but in their charac-ters as players in the process. The Progressive movement and other phenomena that have contributed to party decline might best be described as a shift from Jeffersonian-style local parties to more nationally based parties in the Hamiltonian tradition. Now the Internet promises to engage Hamiltonian mass parties in the business of Jeffersonian-style local politics, while planting the locus of control over political operations more firmly in the hands of politicians. We will consider the possibilities in Chapter 6.

After decades of change, candidates still seek office using a party label, elected officials of the same party still caucus together, and voters still rely heavily on party identification when voting. But as the centuries change, these Hamiltonian-style organizations continue to meet with widespread skepticism as they did a hundred years before; they remain an integral but often unwelcome part of the family of American politics.

# NOTES

1.   Charles Dickens, *American Notes* (London: Chapman & Hall, 1842), p. 149, as cited in Howard L. Reiter, *Parties and Elections in Corporate America*, 2nd ed. (New York: Longman, 1993), p. 6.

2.   "Progressive Platform, 1912," in Kirk H. Porter and Donald Bruce Johnson, eds., *National Party Platforms, 1840–1968* (Urbana, IL: University of Illinois Press, 1970), p. 173.

3.   Frances Fox Piven and Richard A. Cloward, *Why Americans Still Don't Vote, and Why Politicians Want It That Way* (Boston: Beacon Press, 2000), p. 8.

4.   Franklin D. Roosevelt, Second Inaugural Address, Washington, DC, January 20, 1937.

5.   Franklin D. Roosevelt, Address to the Commonwealth Club, 1932. Quoted in Sidney M. Milkis, "Programmatic Liberalism and Party," in John Kenneth White and Jerome M. Mileur, eds., *Challenges to Party Government* (Carbondale: Southern Illinois University Press, 1992), p. 111.

6.   Barry M. Goldwater, Acceptance Speech, Republican National Convention, San Francisco, California, July 16, 1964.

7.   Edwin Diamond and Stephen Bates, *The Spot: The Rise of Political Advertising on Television* (Cambridge, MA: MIT Press, 1988).

8.   See Joe McGinniss, *The Selling of the President, 1968* (New York: Trident, 1969).

9.   Philip A. Klinkner, *The Losing Parties: Out-Party National Committees, 1956–1993* (New Haven, CT: Yale University Press, 1994), p. 39.

10.   Ibid., p. 144.

11.   A. James Recihley, *The Life of the Parties: A History of American Political Parties* (New York: Free Press, 1992), p. 356.

12.   John F. Bibby, "Party Renewal in the National Republican Party," in Gerald M. Pomper, ed., *Party Renewal in America: Theory and Practice* (New York: Praeger, 1980), p. 113.

13.   Anne Campbell quoted in Klinkner, *The Losing Parties*, p. 157.

14.   See Paul S. Herrnson, *Party Campaigning in the 1980s* (Cambridge, MA: Harvard University Press, 1988), p. 37.

15.   See www.fec.gov/disclosure/committeeDetail.do. Accessed August 10, 2016.

16.   Quoted in Reichley, *The Life of the Parties*, p. 365.

17.   See www.fec.gov/disclosure/committeeDetail.do. Accessed August 10, 2016.

18.   Matthew R. Kerbel, *Netroots: Online Progressives and the Transformations of American Politics* (Boulder, CO: Paradigm Publishers, 2009).

# 4

## Nominating Presidents in a Time of Trump

The year 2016 was one of political disenchantment for voters and candidates alike. As for the voters, 57 percent said they were dissatisfied with making a selection between Donald Trump and Hillary Clinton.[1] The reasons for their dissatisfaction were clear: 58 percent described the real estate mogul as "not qualified" for the presidency,[2] while 66 percent said the former secretary of state was "not honest and trustworthy" following disclosure of her using a private email server while serving in the Obama administration.[3] On Election Day, an unhappy electorate cast ballots for one of the two major-party candidates, each side hoping the other's candidate would not become the 45th president.

The two major-party candidates were almost as unhappy as the voters. For more than a year, they were subjected to a physical endurance test, running in a gauntlet of primaries and caucuses, all the while placed in a protected bubble. There is a well-known story from 2008 when first-time presidential candidate Hillary Clinton complained about having to endure meeting the same people over and over again at the first-in-the-nation caucus in Iowa. Clinton staffers reported that their candidate derided a system that gave the first-in-the-nation Iowa caucus such power in selecting the nominees, recalling her as saying: "This is so stupid. So unfair."[4] For his part, Donald Trump complained about living inside a web of Secret Service protection, saying, "It's not like a normal situation."[5] One Trump biographer described how "a drive of a few blocks was a precision-choreographed paramilitary operation," with Trump himself adding:

> I get into a car, thousands of people. . . . They close the street and thousands of people form on the corner, waving, going crazy, and all this Secret Service. And my wife gets in, and she looks at me, and we're in this car with windows that are *this* thick, with steel walls. . . . And she says to me, "Are you sure this is what you want for the rest of your life?"[6]

How did we get here? This chapter will answer how the nominating process has vexed both the constitutional Framers and modern-day reformers. After 2016, there is widespread agreement that the nominating system needs to be reformed—again. But how to do that so Americans can make happier choices between candidates they perceive as qualified and honest remains unclear. In short, what kind of president do we want, and how do we devise a nominating process that can reliably produce that person?

## WHAT KIND OF PRESIDENT?

In 1962, a reporter asked President John F. Kennedy this question: "Somewhere in our land today there is a high school or college student who will one day be sitting in your chair. If you could speak to this future president, what advice and guidance would you give him or her?" Kennedy wisely replied, "It will help you to know the country you seek to lead," adding, "If you find the opportunity to know and work with Americans of diverse backgrounds, occupations, and beliefs, then I would urge you to take eagerly that opportunity to enrich yourself." Kennedy also advised his successor to see the world because "the future of your own country is bound to your capacity to exercise leadership and judgment on a global scale."[7]

Nearly six decades later, most Americans agree with Kennedy's assessment of the qualities they would like their potential presidents to have, but, unsurprisingly, they have added even more qualifications to his short list. These include some prior executive experience (such as serving as a governor or mayor), being of sound character, and serving as an effective advocate of policies deemed to be in the "public interest." But how to find such persons remains elusive. In the nearly 60 years since John F. Kennedy issued his presidential job description, would-be presidents have bemoaned the fact that to be a *successful candidate*, one must foreswear any other occupation, abandon one's family, and single-mindedly devote every waking hour to seeking the presidency. And none of this matters when it comes to being a *successful President*. The year 2016 was no different. One can make the case that Hillary Clinton never stopped campaigning after losing the Democratic nomination to Barack Obama in 2008—devoting full-time to the task after stepping down as secretary of state in 2013. As for Donald Trump, seeking the presidency was hardly a new idea. In 2000, he made an abortive bid for the nomination of the Reform Party (the third party created by Ross Perot after his 1992 campaign).[8] Trump seriously contemplated a run on the Republican ticket in 2012, later bowing out and (reluctantly) endorsing Mitt Romney. Soon after Mitt Romney lost to Barack Obama, Trump copyrighted his 2016 slogan "Make America Great Again"—a sure sign that he would spend the next four years seeking his ultimate goal.[9] In 2016, Trump was joined by *16* other Republican aspirants who themselves had spent years devoted to the task of seeking the presidency, as the word "former" that was so often affixed to their first names attests.[10] The list of Republican "formers" included former Florida governor Jeb Bush, former Virginia governor Jim Gilmore, former Texas governor Rick Perry, former New York governor George Pataki, former Arkansas governor Mike Huckabee, and former Pennsylvania senator Rick Santorum—all once having held elective office. On the Democratic side, the "formers" included former senator and secretary of state Hillary Clinton, former Maryland governor Martin O'Malley, and former Rhode Island senator and governor Lincoln Chafee.

To limit prospective presidents to those willing to sacrifice their families and devote four, eight, or more years of their lives to seeking the presidency often excludes those who might be good chief executives but lack either the time, money, or determination to compete in today's grueling presidential selection process—including a willingness to cede all privacy to inquiring reporters and subject themselves to round-the-clock Secret Service protection. In a 2006 meeting, David Plouffe, who would become Barack Obama's campaign manager, told the putative candidate he had two stark choices:

> You can stay in the Senate, enjoy your weekends at home, take regular vacations, and have a lovely time with your family. Or you can run for president, have your whole life poked at and pried into, almost never see your family, travel incessantly, bang your tin cup for donations like some street-corner beggar, lead a lonely, miserable life.[11]

Time is a precious resource for would-be presidents. To have even a chance of victory, first-time candidates must invest vast quantities of both time and money introducing themselves to the party faithful. Barack Obama's 2008 candidacy is a case in point. After announcing his candidacy in 2007, the junior senator from Illinois practically relocated himself to the state next door, Iowa. Since 1976, the Iowa caucuses have been a first-run test of the potential strength the major candidates might have among the party faithful. Obama realized that winning Iowa was vital to his success, and he practically lived in the state for more than a year. From February 10, 2007 (the date Obama declared his candidacy), until January 3, 2008 (the date of the Iowa caucuses), Obama held *174* campaign events in the Hawkeye State. One witness described the effects such a backbreaking schedule had on Obama personally:

> The schedule was killing him. The fatigue was all-consuming. The events piled up on top of one another, making his temples ache. He tried not to bitch and moan too much, except when it got out of hand—meaning almost

every day. Once, at five in the afternoon on the bus in Iowa, he turned to his body guy, Reggie Love, and asked, "How many more things do I have today?" Reggie: "Three." Barack: *"Are you kidding me?"*[12]

Yet thanks to his constant presence on the hustings, Obama won the Iowa caucuses, but paid a price in time lost with his family, and was subsequently entrapped in a physical endurance contest with the ever-ready Hillary Clinton, who matched Obama in nearly every race and took the contest all the way to the Democratic Convention. Eight years later, Clinton was herself in a tit-for-tat match with Vermont senator Bernie Sanders, whose fiery rhetoric about economic inequality fueled his candidacy to near-success, making Clinton relentlessly work for each vote in a contest that spanned more than a year.

## FROM JOHN ADAMS TO DONALD TRUMP: THE PROBLEMS OF PRESIDENTIAL SELECTION

Today's backbreaking process for selecting presidents is relatively new, but changes to our nominating system are not. In fact, ever since the Constitution was ratified in 1789, the United States has had no consistent method for choosing its presidents. The failure to devise a selection system that recognizes the national character of the presidency, yet also provides some role for states and localities, has had enormous implications. For how a president wins an election will directly influence the direction of the federal government in Washington, DC, and the ability of any given president to govern. Yet most Americans seem content to leave the definition of the electoral process to the whims of 50 state legislatures and the ambitions of countless would-be presidents. As a result, two questions that perplexed the Founding Fathers still remain largely unanswered: (1) What kind of president do we want? and (2) How do we devise a nominating system that produces "good" presidents?

The Framers understood that the challenge of consistently finding a good president was the single most conspicuous failure of the Constitutional Convention. Convening in Philadelphia in 1787, the delegates considered a myriad of schemes before finally settling upon the Electoral College. As devised by the Framers, each state would have a prescribed number of electors equaling its congressional delegation, based on the number of senators (two) plus the number of representatives (which varies from state to state based on its population). Under the Electoral College system, each elector would cast *two* votes for president. The Framers believed that state loyalties would determine the first vote (i.e., votes would go to "favorite sons"), but that the second vote would be for someone of national stature. Alexander Hamilton wrote in *The Federalist* that the electors' "transient existence" and "detached situation" made the Electoral College a wise instrument for choosing the right kind of president.[13] In effect, the Electoral College would act as a presidential search committee.

However, the Electoral College only worked as planned in the first two elections of George Washington in 1788 and 1792. In those elections, Washington won unanimous victories—the only president ever to receive such a distinction. But by 1796, the Federalist and Democratic-Republican parties were more organized and vigorously competing for votes—thereby negating the Electoral College's role of finding the best person with the greatest national standing to serve as president. In 1800, the system broke down completely when Thomas Jefferson recruited Aaron Burr to run with him as vice president. Burr broke his promise to defer to Jefferson and have him become president in the event of a tie vote. Instead, Burr sought the presidency outright, with the result being a deadlock in the House of Representatives that was broken by the leader of the opposition party, Federalist Alexander Hamilton. By 1804, the Electoral College that had once been the object of Hamilton's effusive praise was completely overhauled when Congress and the states approved the Twelfth Amendment—that part of the U.S. Constitution creating "tickets" of presidential and vice presidential candidates.

Today, the Electoral College remains one of the most flawed parts of the original Constitution (the other being how the Framers treated the issue of slavery), and two of that document's 27 amendments mention it directly. Each time it appears that a presidential candidate could win the Electoral College and fail to capture a majority of the popular vote—something that happened in 1828, 1876, 1888, 2000, and 2016, and nearly happened in 1960, 1968, 1976, and 2004—calls for abolishing the Electoral College mount. In 2013, 63 percent told the Gallup Organization that they favored doing away with the Electoral College and making the selection of the next president solely dependent on the winner of the popular vote.[14] Other proposals to change the Electoral College include (1) prohibiting electors from voting for anyone other than the candidate who won their state; (2) having states cast their electoral votes on a more proportionate basis—for example, the winner of a particular congressional district (as is the case in Maine and Nebraska[15]); (3) creating bonus electors that would be awarded to the candidate who won the national popular vote; (4) allocating electoral votes on the basis of proportional representation; and (5) resorting to a popular vote count altogether with the proviso that if a candidate fails to win a majority, a runoff would take place between the top two finishers.[16] Yet for all of its flaws, none of these proposed reforms has captured either much public or congressional attention.

So the riddle that confronted the Framers still remains: How do we select the next president? Clearly, the president must be a national leader who can articulate issues and solutions that are in the public interest. Seeking the presidency in 1960, John F. Kennedy famously declared: "[O]nly the President represents the national interest. And upon him alone converge all the needs and aspirations of all parts of the country, all departments of the Government, all nations of the world."[17] Yet even as presidents assert that only they represent the "national interest," it is also true that the United States consists of a myriad of interests, both special and regional. And as more money is needed to wage a successful presidential

campaign—with major candidates and their supporters raising close to *two billion dollars* in 2016,[18] Americans increasingly resent the influence exercised by the
so-called special interests. On the eve of the 2016 presidential campaign, majorities
thought it would be "effective" to reduce the "influence of money in politics"
by placing limits on how much an outside group could spend on a candidate's
campaign, or how much a political party could spend, or how much an individual
candidate could spend regardless of where the money came from.[19]

But congressionally imposed limits on any presidential candidate's source of
money presently runs afoul of a controversial 2010 Supreme Court case entitled
*Citizens United v. Federal Election Commission*. In it, the Court affirmed that political speech and money went hand in hand, and both are protected by the First
Amendment—therefore allowing corporations and individuals to spend unlimited sums of money supporting their respective candidates, including those running for president.[20] The impact of the decision was fully evident in the 2016
Clinton-Trump race. Hillary Clinton raised over $700 million, while billionaire
Donald Trump spent millions on behalf of his own campaign. Outside sources—
including political action committees (PACs) and independent groups formed to
advocate for one candidate or the other—also spent hundreds of millions of dollars. Over $200 million of Hillary Clinton's fund-raising haul came from outside
groups.[21] These actions, born out of necessity and the unwillingness of any party
to forego substantial contributions, were unpopular with the public. Vermont senator Bernie Sanders premised his presidential bid on the notion that Wall Street
wields too much power and elected officials are beholden to the outsized role
of money in politics. In his announcement speech, Sanders declared: "Today, we
stand here and say loudly and clearly that enough is enough. This great nation and
its government belong to all of the people, and not to a handful of billionaires,
their Super-PACs, and their lobbyists."[22] Meanwhile, Republican nominee Donald Trump maintained that his personal wealth meant that he couldn't be bought,
while other, less wealthy, politicians could: "We look at politicians and think: This
one's owned by this millionaire. That one's owned by that millionaire, or lobbyist,
or special group."[23] Both candidates' appeals resonated with voters, and each saw
himself as a tribune acting on behalf of the "people," not the special interests.

The vast amounts of time and money required to become president have
created a strong public impression that the presidential selection system is broken. Accordingly, ideas for fixing it have flourished. But the various instruction
manuals differ. When it comes to selecting a chief executive, Americans want
the process to be fair, yet provide for majority rule; deliberative, as well as
quick; representative, but with some having a greater voice than others. Those
in the national party establishments have tried unsuccessfully over the years to
resolve these contradictory impulses. Their discussions have centered around
abstract details that have little to do with how best to pick a president, including (1) which state or states should go first in selecting presidential candidates;
(2) when the national party conventions should be held (and where); (3) how
many party officeholders should be permitted to attend the national convention and in what capacity; and (4) what proportions of men, women, blacks,

Latinos, Asians, Native Americans, and other minority groups should comprise the various state delegations. This chapter focuses on the alternate roads taken in search of the best method for choosing a presidential candidate. Once again, the debates between Alexander Hamilton and Thomas Jefferson play a prominent role in the disagreements about which is the best path to take.

# HAMILTON'S FAMILY VERSUS JEFFERSON'S COMMUNITY

Legendary party boss William Marcy Tweed once remarked, "I don't care who does the electin' as long as I do the nominatin'."[24] The issue of who should "do the nominatin'" has vexed the American polity for more than 200 years. This argument, like so many others in American politics, is rooted in the dispute between Alexander Hamilton and Thomas Jefferson as to how best to implement the American ideology of classical liberalism. As we discussed in Chapter 1, Hamilton preferred to wed liberty to national authority—preferring a strong central government that could act on behalf of a national family. Jefferson, meanwhile, wanted to marry liberty with local civic authority, believing that America was a series of diverse communities and deference should be paid to local customs.

*The King-Making Caucuses.* The struggle between these two perspectives informs the controversy surrounding how presidents should be chosen. Throughout history, American political parties have at one time or another adopted either a Hamiltonian or a Jeffersonian approach to the exercise of power. Initially, they thought they had a solution in the Congressional Caucus. The caucus consisted of House and Senate members who belonged to the same party. They would meet, discuss the pros and cons of various candidates, and emerge with a nominee. As a national institution that represented state and local interests, it was thought that a gathering of congressional party leaders to choose a president made sense given the failure of the Electoral College. Moreover, it was generally assumed that presidents would come from the national legislature, so it seemed only natural that Congress would choose from among the prospective candidates.

The Congressional Caucus never functioned well, and the system completely broke down in 1824 after the last of the Founding Fathers, James Monroe, ended his presidency. That year, the caucus nominated William Crawford, who commanded little support outside the caucus and was badly beaten in the election. A five-way scramble for the presidency ensued, and John Quincy Adams, the son of John Adams, became president. By the late 1820s, the caucus system became a target of supporters of defeated candidate Andrew Jackson, who vehemently argued that the entire nominating process epitomized aristocratic rule and thwarted the popular will.

***Enter the Party Conventions.*** When the Congressional Caucus collapsed, the search for another mode of making presidential nominations began. Initially, the youthful parties gravitated toward a convention system that took local sensibilities into account. Thomas Ritchie, editor of the *Richmond Enquirer*, urged a national convention, in a letter addressed to Martin Van Buren dated January 2, 1824:

> Vain is any expectation found upon the spontaneous movement of the great mass of the people in favor of any particular individual, the elements of this great community are multifarious and conflicting, and require to be skillfully combined to be made harmonious and powerful. Their action, to be salutary, must be the result of enlightened deliberation, and he who would distract the councils of the people, must design to breed confusion and disorder, and to profit by their dissensions.[25]

In Ritchie's view, party conventions allowed for a successful fusion of Hamiltonian nationalism and Jeffersonian localism. The convention spoke with an authoritative voice in selecting the nominee, but individual states maintained their sovereignty in choosing the delegates. In 1831, the Anti-Masonic Party held the first political convention in Baltimore. A year later, the Democratic Party followed suit. The Democrats were driven toward the convention system not only because it seemed more "democratic," but because President Andrew Jackson wanted to replace Vice President John C. Calhoun, who had become an outspoken administration critic. One key Jackson operative pointed out

> the expediency, indeed absolute necessity, of advising our friends everywhere to get up a national convention to convene at some convenient point, for the purpose of selecting some suitable and proper person to be placed upon the electoral ticket with General Jackson, as a candidate for the vice presidency.[26]

Eventually, the convention was held and the delegates chose a Jackson loyalist, Martin Van Buren, for the vice presidential slot.

Over the years, nominating conventions became a vital party instrument—providing a forum for making key decisions about who would head the presidential ticket, what issues might be stressed, and how to support those persons once elected. Today, conventions are held in mid-summer before the general election, usually in one of the nation's largest cities in an important electoral state, like Philadelphia, Pennsylvania, the site of the 2016 Democratic convention, and Cleveland, Ohio, the Republicans' 2016 choice.

Until the 1970s, convention delegates were chosen by state and local party leaders. Party leaders ran the show, instructing delegates what platform planks to support and which candidates to back. Still, conventions were exciting affairs. Prior to the Progressive Era during the early twentieth century, when party bosses wielded their greatest power, Democrats usually took ten ballots to select their nominees; Republicans, five. As boisterous and contentious as these gatherings could get, conventions were a way of aggregating the interests of local party leaders with the concerns of the national party to nominate a winner.

But the fusion of national party authority and states' rights was not completely harmonious and differed for each party. Initially, it was the Republican Party of the late nineteenth century that was most hospitable to Alexander Hamilton's notion of a national family. When it came to governing, Republican presidents paid attention to state concerns. But when it came to nominating, they viewed their party as a national organization that was all-important in choosing their presidential ticket. During a credentials fight at the 1876 Republican Convention, one delegate asked "whether the state of Pennsylvania shall make laws for his convention; or whether this convention is supreme and shall make its own laws?" The delegate answered his own question, saying, "We are supreme. We are original. We stand here representing the great Republican Party of the United States."[27]

Democrats adopted a wholly different approach, believing they should adhere to the traditions of their progenitor, Thomas Jefferson. At their first convention in 1832, the party adopted the two-thirds rule under which no candidate could be nominated for president unless two-thirds of the delegates agreed. Whigs and Republicans eschewed calls for a supermajority, nominating their presidential candidates instead by a simple majority. Democrats also invented the unit rule, a device that allowed a state to cast all of its votes for one candidate if a majority so desired. These changes presented considerable difficulties in getting the southern and northern wings of the party to agree on a nominee. Thus, it took 49 ballots to nominate Franklin Pierce in 1852, and 17 to select James Buchanan four years later. Yet, the two-thirds rule and the unit rule accentuated the federal character of the Democratic Party's nominating process—something the party desperately sought to protect. Rising to defend the unit rule, a delegate to the 1880 Democratic Convention excoriated the Republicans as

> a party which believes. . . that the states have hardly any rights left which the Federal Government is bound to respect. . . [and] that the state does not control its own delegation in a national convention. Not so in the convention of the great Democratic Party. We stand, Mr. President, for the rights of the states.[28]

At the beginning of the twentieth century, the debate over which approach to take in nominating presidents—one rooted in Hamilton's idea of nationalism, or Jefferson's preference for localism—intensified. The struggle took place not only between the two parties, but within them. During the first years of the twentieth century, the Republican Party developed a growing Progressive faction that wanted to nationalize party affairs since local politics was often rife with corruption. Progressive leader Theodore Roosevelt advocated the creation of a national presidential primary in 1912. Failing that, Progressives wanted state parties to establish a direct primary, believing that Teddy Roosevelt would dominate them. Fourteen states followed this route, and Roosevelt beat incumbent William Howard Taft in all of the primaries. But Republican stalwarts, led by Taft, preferred having state GOP leaders retain their decisive voice in selecting presidential candidates. Taft's dismal third-place finish in 1912 resulted in a further nationalization of the nominating process. Progressive advocacy of the direct primary was extended to most elective offices, including the presidency. By 1916, 23 states with 65 percent of the delegates had adopted presidential primaries, though the party bosses still retained their power to decide the party nominee. Even so, the process had begun where slowly, but surely, party regulars were being shown to the convention exits.

Democrats, meanwhile, continued to support a Jeffersonian-like approach in choosing their presidents. Although Woodrow Wilson backed Theodore Roosevelt's call for a national primary, the 1912 Democratic platform upheld the rights of the states and condemned as a "usurpation" Republican-inspired efforts "to enlarge and magnify by indirection the powers of the Federal Government."[29] Thus, any attempt to nationalize the party's rules would be turned aside. In fact, southern leaders blocked the nomination of Speaker of the House Champ Clark, who was unable to obtain the two-thirds support from the delegates needed to win the nomination. Seeking a compromise, the delegates turned to New Jersey Democratic governor Woodrow Wilson, whose birthplace was Staunton, Virginia.

But not all was harmonious within the Democratic ranks. The coming of the immigrant—beginning with the Irish in the 1840s and eastern, central, and southern Europeans in the 1890s—wrought havoc in Democratic Party councils. These foreign-tongued Americans, mostly Roman Catholics, gravitated to the Democrats early and sought a voice in their state and national conventions. Most supported New York governor Alfred E. Smith in his quest for the Democratic presidential nomination in 1924. But the two-thirds rule prevented Smith from capturing the nomination. After 103 ballots, an exhausted convention finally turned to John W. Davis, a well-known lawyer whose views on race were acceptable to the South.

These internal party squabbles—and the many attempts to quell them—did not solve the nominating dilemma. This is because the argument between the Hamiltonian and Jeffersonian perspectives became linked to the ongoing debate about what kind of president we should have. Those advocating a national-centered system suggested leaders make the best presidents, not party bosses. As Theodore Roosevelt espoused, the true test of leadership rests in an ability to reason with followers in an open, public fashion. Therefore, a national system of presidential selection is preferable because it provides an environment in which candidates can test their mettle in such a way that successful contenders will maximize their ability to govern. Those who subscribe to a Jeffersonian approach hold that the selection of a presidential nominee must be consensual, and to accomplish this the deliberations must necessarily be private. Candidates should be judged by their peers, even if that verdict is rendered in a smoke-filled room. From these deliberations, a candidate will emerge with sufficient institutional backing to make the party instrumental in mounting a winning campaign and crucial in forming a successful administration.

# THE RISE OF HAMILTONIAN NATIONALISM

During the nineteenth century, the youthful parties zigzagged between the Hamiltonian and Jeffersonian approaches to presidential nominating—never quite sure how to balance the two. But during the twentieth century, Hamiltonian nationalism gained the upper hand. Two individuals, both Democrats, were largely responsible: Franklin D. Roosevelt and George S. McGovern.

The movement toward a national-centered model was given its first push during the Progressive Era. A principal goal of this movement was to create a more open and democratic electoral process. One means to accomplish this was to allow average voters a say in nominations. By 1912, a dozen states adopted presidential primaries, and a few years later, about one-half followed suit. Back then, however, the outcome of these primaries was only advisory, making them little more than political "beauty contests." The results provided information to party leaders as to which candidates were popular, but the delegates were not bound to support these "beauty contest" winners. This gave local party leaders bargaining leverage at the conventions. So although the growth of presidential primaries at the turn of the twentieth century appeared to shift the nomination process in a national direction, the change was mostly symbolic.

Beginning with Franklin D. Roosevelt, the Democratic Party adopted a Hamiltonian approach to picking its presidential candidates. In 1936, Roosevelt succeeded in having the Democratic Convention strike down the two-thirds rule, despite the vigorous resistance from southerners. Former navy secretary and ambassador to Mexico Josephus Daniels spoke for the administration: "The Democratic Party today is a national party, and Northern, Southern, and Western states would have greater representation in the party conventions under a majority rule."[30] Southerners argued that revoking the two-thirds rule would drastically reduce the role of individual states in the nomination process. On the surface, it was a call to a Jeffersonian-like system. Below the surface, southerners realized that as long as a two-thirds majority was needed for the nomination, they could veto any nominee by acting in unison. Even in the 1930s, racial issues divided the Democratic Party and the country, so the end of the two-thirds rule was a blow to southern party leaders.

Following Roosevelt's four terms in the White House, Democrats continued in the Hamiltonian tradition as their nominating process became increasingly nationalized. In 1952, a Democratic National Committee member lost his seat because he supported Republican Dwight D. Eisenhower for president. Four years later, the Democratic Convention passed a resolution that required a state to list the party's presidential nominee on its ballot in order for its delegates to be seated in the convention hall. (Some southern states, in a protest to the Democratic Party's pro-civil rights stance, refused to list Democratic nominee Adlai Stevenson on the ballot in 1952.) A major step toward nationalizing the parties occurred in 1964, when the so-called Mississippi Freedom Democratic Party claimed to be more representative of that state's Democratic voters than the "regulars" who ran the state Democratic Party. Asked to settle the dispute between the two factions, the 1964 Democratic Convention passed a resolution forbidding discrimination in choosing delegates. Henceforth, delegates would be chosen without regard to their race, creed, or national origins. If a state delegation did not comply with the new rule, it could be ejected from the convention hall. A committee chaired by New Jersey governor Richard Hughes would be responsible for implementing the rule. On July 2, 1967, Hughes wrote to the DNC and all state Democratic Party chairs outlining six requirements each state must meet in order to comply with the charge of the 1964 convention. Failure would mean that the seats would be vacated and filled by the convention—an unprecedented act at that time.

## THE MCGOVERN-FRASER COMMISSION

Not all states met Governor Hughes's criteria. In 1968, the Democratic Convention tossed out all of the Mississippi and half of the Georgia delegations for violating the Hughes resolution. In addition, the delegates abolished the 146-year-old unit rule that permitted a state to cast all of its votes for a presidential candidate even if other candidates had support within the delegation. The unit rule was a favorite among southerners, who used it to maximize their power at Democratic conventions. But the pendulum toward a Hamiltonian-like nationalization of party affairs swung even further with the creation of the McGovern-Fraser Commission following the disastrous 1968 convention.

The year 1968 was perhaps the worst year in the history of the Democratic Party. At first, it appeared that the convention would be a dull affair because Lyndon B. Johnson, the sitting Democratic president, gave every indication of seeking renomination. Not since Chester Arthur in 1884 had a party denied an incumbent president renomination. One lone Democrat had the temerity to challenge Johnson: a little-known U.S. senator from Minnesota, Eugene McCarthy. Propelled to oppose Johnson because of the Vietnam War, McCarthy had few resources and even less backing from party leaders. But with a battalion of antiwar activists drawn from several college campuses, McCarthy campaigned in New Hampshire, site of the first primary. Johnson defeated McCarthy, but the margin of victory was much smaller than expected—50 percent to 42 percent—an extremely poor showing for an incumbent president. In a dramatic turn of events, Johnson told a nationwide television audience, "I shall not seek, and I will not accept, the nomination of my party for another term as your president."[31]

Johnson's departure did not mean that most Democratic Party leaders were ready to back McCarthy—quite the contrary. If Johnson was out, their choice was Vice President Hubert H. Humphrey. Given the relative unanimity of party leaders supporting his candidacy, Humphrey did not need to campaign in any of the 17 states holding primaries in 1968. This infuriated anti-Vietnam War demonstrators within the Democratic Party, who charged that Humphrey was a member of the Johnson administration that had escalated U.S. involvement in Vietnam. Robert F. Kennedy, the brother of the late president and a U.S. senator from New York, entered the primaries and, along with McCarthy, fueled an anti-Humphrey movement. For a while, it looked as though Kennedy had a chance to win the nomination. He drew large crowds at every stop, received substantial media attention, and won most of the primaries he entered. Whether he would have been nominated is left to historical debate—on the night Kennedy won the California primary, an assassin ended his life. Needless to say, the nation was in a state of shock and the Democratic Party was essentially leaderless.

By the summer of 1968, the Democratic Party was in tatters. So deep were the divisions that two conventions were held: one in the hall, another in the streets of Chicago. Mayor Richard J. Daley, the Democratic boss of Chicago, refused to grant the crowds of young college students who descended upon the city a permit to demonstrate against the Vietnam War. Daley's police attacked the demonstrators with clubs and tear gas, creating what authorities subsequently described as a "police riot." Inside the hall, party leaders nominated Vice President Hubert H. Humphrey amid the usual hoopla and floor demonstrations. The jarring contrasts between these scenes led presidential chronicler Theodore H. White to describe Humphrey as "being nominated in a sea of blood."[32]

The protests in the streets, a widespread perception that Humphrey won his party's nod unfairly (because he did not compete in a single primary), and raucous dissent within the Democratic ranks led to the creation of the McGovern-Fraser Commission. As George McGovern, then a U.S. senator from South Dakota, recalled,

> Many of the most active supporters of Gene McCarthy and Robert Kennedy and later of me, believed that the Democratic presidential nominating process was dominated by party wheel horses, entrenched officeholders, and local bosses. They believed that despite the strong popular showing of McCarthy and Kennedy in the primaries, a majority of the convention delegates were selected in a manner that favored the so-called establishment candidates.[33]

The McGovern-Fraser Commission arrived at a similar conclusion. In evocative language, it urged Democrats to change their ways:

> If we are not an open party; if we do not represent the demands of change, then the danger is not that the people will go to the Republican Party; it is that there will no longer be a way for people committed to orderly change to fulfill their needs and desires within our traditional political system. It is that they will turn to third and fourth party politics or the anti-politics of the street.[34]

First chaired by McGovern and later by Minneapolis mayor Donald Fraser, the commission was officially called the Committee on Party Structure and Delegate Selection. The McGovern-Fraser Commission adopted several recommendations that further nationalized presidential politics, including the following:

◆ A reaffirmation of the abolition of the unit rule, an action already approved by the 1968 Democratic Convention;
◆ Refusing to seat delegates chosen in back rooms;
◆ Prohibiting certain public or party officeholders from serving as delegates to county, state, and national conventions by virtue of their official position;

- Banning proxy voting, a practice used by party bosses to cast votes on behalf of absent delegates, often without their knowledge;
- Ordering states to choose delegates during the calendar year in which the convention is held;
- Requiring states to post public notices announcing the selection of a delegate slate that would be committed to a particular candidate, and inviting the rank and file to participate in the selection process;
- Creating a Compliance Review Division within the DNC to ensure that states obeyed the McGovern-Fraser recommendations.

In effect, the McGovern-Fraser Commission told the party establishment to "reform or else." As McGovern recalled:

> In public statements, speeches and interviews, I drove home the contention that the Democratic Party had but two choices: reform or death. In the past, I noted, political parties, when confronted with the need for change, chose death rather than change. I did not want the Democratic Party to die. I wanted our party to choose the path of change and vitality. That was the function of the reforms.[35]

But behind the reforms lay another agenda: removing the so-called Old Democrats—mostly white, middle-aged, establishment types who supported the Vietnam War—and replacing them with New Politics Democrats—younger, college-educated professionals, females, and minorities who were antiwar, anti-establishment, and anti-party. The commission exceeded all expectations in achieving this objective. At the 1968 Democratic Convention, just 14 percent of the delegates were women, 2 percent were under age 30, and only 5 percent were black. Four years later, women accounted for 36 percent of the delegates; those under age 30, 23 percent; blacks, 14 percent. But these increased numbers of women, blacks, and young voters came with a high price tag. In an unprecedented act, the 1972 Democratic Convention voted to exclude the delegates from Cook County, Illinois (including Chicago), led by Chicago Mayor Richard J. Daley, and replace them with pro-McGovern delegates led by a young, black civil rights activist named Jesse Jackson. In a subsequent legal action, the U.S. Supreme Court affirmed the convention's decision using decidedly Hamiltonian language: "The convention serves the pervasive national interest in the selection of candidates for national offices and this national interest is greater than any interest of any individual state."[36]

Establishment Democrats were astounded at the convention's actions and their ratification by the Supreme Court. Daley delegates had won the Illinois primary, whereas Jackson's slate had not even competed. Moreover, Daley was still viewed as key to winning this electoral vote-rich state in the fall. As it turned out, McGovern lost Illinois (and 48 other states) to Republican Richard M. Nixon. But by removing the Daley delegation on the grounds that it had less than the desired number of women, young voters, and blacks, the convention opened a Pandora's box to what became a virtual quota system for choosing delegates. As McGovern later acknowledged, "Whatever the commission originally intended, in administering the guidelines on minorities, women, and young people, it eventually moved very close to adopting a de facto quota system."[37]

Along with mandating specifics of the composition of each state's delegation, the commission also sought changes in how they were to be selected. The 1968 fiasco suggested that party regulars were excluded from the process in favor of party bosses who picked the president in smoke-filled rooms. The commission's proclamation that delegate selection must be "open, timely, and representative" was considered somewhat vague, but few states wished to jeopardize their role at the next convention. Most state Democratic Party leaders shrugged their shoulders and abandoned their state conventions in favor of primaries and caucuses, where the rank and file would make their presidential preferences known. As compensation, however, Democratic leaders would retain a decisive voice in selecting their own candidates for state and local offices. The shift from party leaders deciding who would be the next president to primary voters has been significant. In most of the states that hold primaries, voters choose how many delegates will go to the nomination convention for each of the various aspirants. A candidate who nets 50 percent of the primary votes, for instance, will receive 50 percent of the state's delegation. The actual delegates themselves are usually selected by state party meetings and conventions, but, unlike the "advisory" primary system of the Progressive Era, they are bound to support the candidate they were sent to support, at least on the first ballot. Other states have a "pure" primary system whereby voters directly elect delegates to the national convention. Each would-be delegate's candidate preference is listed on the ballot. A delegate who has no preference is listed as "uncommitted." Delegates chosen under this system are duty-bound to support the candidate listed on the ballot.

# REPUBLICANS FOLLOW THE MCGOVERN-FRASER LEAD

Although not subject to the recommendations of the McGovern-Fraser Commission, Republicans felt its effects when state legislatures passed laws mandating state presidential primaries. The gusts of change blowing through Democratic convention halls rattled Republican windows, too. Several state legislatures, largely controlled by Democrats, passed laws mandating presidential primaries for both parties. Republicans also engaged in a modest effort to alter their rules in the name of fairness. The 1972 convention authorized the creation of a Delegate-Organization (DO) Committee. The purpose of the DO Committee (called the "Do-Nothing Committee" by critics) was to recommend measures for enhancing the numbers of women, youth, and minorities at future Republican conventions. The committee proposed that traditional party leaders be prohibited from serving as ex-officio delegates; that party officials should better inform citizens how they could participate in the nomination process; and that participation should be increased by opening the primaries and state conventions to all qualified citizens. But the 1976 Republican Convention rejected several of the committee's more important recommendations, including (1) allowing persons under 25 years of age to vote in "numerical equity to their voting strength in a state"; (2) encouraging equal numbers of male and female delegates; and (3) having one minority group on each of the convention's principal committees. Later, the RNC rejected a recommendation that it review state affirmative action plans, and the GOP has refused to abolish winner-take-all primaries such as the one in California. Winner-take-all primaries helped John McCain wrap up the Republican nomination on March 4, 2008, even as Barack Obama and Hillary Clinton were still slugging it out in the Democratic primaries and caucus contests.[38]

# THE UNINTENDED CONSEQUENCES OF THE MCGOVERN-FRASER REFORMS

Despite its intentions, the McGovern–Fraser reforms unleashed several unintended consequences, including the proliferation of primaries and caucuses, the emergence of outsider candidates, and a power shift from party elites to media elites.

# A PROLIFERATION OF PRIMARIES

One unintended consequence of the McGovern–Fraser reforms has been a substantial increase in the number of presidential primaries. In 1960, John F. Kennedy ran in only three state primaries: West Virginia, Wisconsin, and New Hampshire. In 2016, Democrats held primaries in 41 states and territories, while Republicans held primaries in 39 states and territories. A large number of these contests were held on March 1, 2016, a date known as "Super Tuesday" (see Table 4.1). Under the current system, successful candidates have to run virtually everywhere, meaning that they often must be in two (or three) places at once.

As Table 4.1 demonstrates, the primary calendar is complicated. Both national party committees provide that four states go first: Iowa, New Hampshire, South Carolina, and Nevada. In 2016, these states were given the month of February to hold their contests. Other states were allowed to begin their contests in March, with Republicans dictating that these states allocate only a portion of their delegates to the winner. Republicans then allowed other states to allocate their delegates on a winner-take-all basis beginning on April 1, 2016, and extending to the end of the primary season in June. The intention of the Republican National Committee in setting these rules was to prolong the presidential contest and thereby generate more public interest in it. Thus, Donald J. Trump did not secure the Republican nomination until May 3, 2016, when he claimed victory in the Indiana primary. Democrats continued to use a proportional representation rule

## Table 4.1  2016 Schedule of Primaries and Caucuses

| Date | Democratic Primary/Caucus | Republican Primary/Caucus* |
|------|---------------------------|----------------------------|
| February 1 | Iowa | Iowa |
| February 9 | New Hampshire | New Hampshire |
| February 20 | Nevada | South Carolina |
| February 23 | | Nevada |
| February 27 | South Carolina | |
| March 1 | Alabama | Alabama |
| March 1 | | Alaska |
| March 1 | American Samoa | |
| March 1 | Arkansas | Arkansas |
| March 1 | Colorado | |
| March 1 | Georgia | Georgia |
| March 1 | Massachusetts | Massachusetts |
| March 1 | Minnesota | Minnesota |
| March 1 | | North Dakota |
| March 1 | Oklahoma | Oklahoma |
| March 1 | Tennessee | Tennessee |
| March 1 | Texas | |
| March 1 | Vermont | Vermont |
| March 1 | Virginia | Virginia |
| March 1–8 | Democrats Abroad | |
| March 5 | Kansas | Kansas |
| March 5 | | Kentucky |
| March 5 | Louisiana | Louisiana |
| March 5 | Maine | Maine |
| March 5 | Nebraska | |
| March 6 | | Puerto Rico |
| March 8 | | Hawaii |
| March 8 | | Idaho |
| March 8 | Michigan | Michigan |
| March 8 | Mississippi | Mississippi |
| March 10 | | Virgin Islands |
| March 12 | | District of Columbia |
| March 12 | Northern Marianas | |
| March 12 | | Wyoming |
| March 15 | Florida | Florida |
| March 15 | Illinois | Illinois |

(continued)

**Table 4.1** *(continued)*

| Date | Democratic Primary/Caucus | Republican Primary/Caucus* |
|------|---------------------------|----------------------------|
| March 15 | Missouri | Missouri |
| March 15 | North Carolina | North Carolina |
| March 15 | | Northern Mariana Islands |
| March 15 | Ohio | Ohio |
| March 22 | Arizona | Arizona |
| March 22 | Idaho | |
| March 22 | Utah | Utah |
| March 26 | Alaska | |
| March 26 | Hawaii | |
| March 26 | Washington | |
| April 1 | | North Dakota |
| April 5 | Wisconsin | Wisconsin |
| April 9 | Wyoming | |
| April 19 | New York | New York |
| April 26 | Connecticut | Connecticut |
| April 26 | Delaware | Delaware |
| April 26 | Maryland | Maryland |
| April 26 | Pennsylvania | Pennsylvania |
| April 26 | Rhode Island | Rhode Island |
| May 3 | Indiana | Indiana |
| May 7 | Guam | |
| May 10 | | Nebraska |
| May 10 | West Virginia | West Virginia |
| May 17 | Kentucky | |
| May 17 | Oregon | Oregon |
| May 24 | | Washington |
| June 4 | Virgin Islands | |
| June 5 | Puerto Rico | |
| June 7 | California | California |
| June 7 | Montana | Montana |
| June 7 | New Jersey | New Jersey |
| June 7 | New Mexico | New Mexico |
| June 7 | North Dakota | |
| June 7 | South Dakota | South Dakota |
| June 14 | District of Columbia | |

*Two territories held a Republican Convention to select their delegates: Guam on March 12, and American Samoa on March 22.

based on winning a 15 percent threshold, meaning that Hillary Clinton did not secure the Democratic nomination until the near-end of the primary season on June 7, 2016, when she won California.

The complicated primary and caucus calendar and the rules established by the major parties means that candidates must know the dates of the scheduled contests and plan their calendars accordingly. But candidates must do more than be in multiple places at once. They and their staffs have to know the state laws that govern the primaries and caucuses. In 2016, 14 states held closed primaries in both parties in which voters were required to declare their party affiliation before voting.[39] Often this declaration is done when one registers to vote. The idea behind a closed primary is to ensure that only loyal party members participate in selecting the nominee. Thirteen states took a different route in 2016 and conducted completely open primaries, where voters could choose in which party's presidential primary they would cast a ballot. Other states have a mixed system that allows for registered party members and those not enrolled in a political party (the so-called independents) to participate. The rules for each state's primary are set by the different state legislatures (since the states absorb the cost of the election), but they must be in compliance with the guidelines established by the Democratic and Republican National Committees.

# PARTY CAUCUSES ALSO BECOME POPULAR

Caucuses are another popular means for selecting delegates. Instead of voting at one's leisure during the primary day, caucuses require the party's rank and file to appear at an organized meeting and publicly declare one's support for a candidate. The process is similar to a town hall meeting or a mini-convention, as people gather alongside neighbors and strangers to voice their support for a candidate. In 2016, Democrats held caucuses in 14 states and in American Samoa, the Northern Mariana Islands, and the Virgin Islands; Republicans held caucuses in 12 states and in Puerto Rico, the Virgin Islands, and the Northern Mariana Islands. For both parties, the most prominent of these is the Iowa caucuses, which provide the first test of a candidate's strength. On February 1, 2016, Democrats and Republicans gathered at libraries, town halls, and church basements across Iowa to declare their support for their preferred candidate. If a candidate failed to garner a threshold level of support, caucus-goers had to regroup and make another choice. In addition, Iowa caucus-goers took positions on important issues of the day and forwarded them to the state party committees and the national convention. Not surprisingly, only the very committed from both parties resolved to come out on a cold, snowy night and remain at their caucus locations for several hours.

Since it is committed party members who often attend the caucuses and are willing to publicly state their support for a preferred candidate, it is often the candidate who appeals to hard-core partisans who comes out on top. In 2016, many Democrats were passionate about Bernie Sanders, and he won 11 of the 16 caucuses held, nearly besting Clinton in the first-in-the-nation caucus in Iowa (49.9 percent to 49.6 percent).[40] On the Republican side, Texas senator Ted Cruz won five caucuses; Donald Trump, six; and Florida senator Marco Rubio, two.[41]

## A SURGE IN OUTSIDER CANDIDACIES

The McGovern-Fraser Commission facilitated a surge in outsider candidacies, beginning with McGovern's anti-Vietnam War candidacy in 1972. George McGovern admitted that the new rules spawned by the commission he led would fuel ideologically inspired candidacies: "My successful bid for the nomination in 1972 was based in part on the opportunity which the new rules offered to a candidate willing to take his case directly to rank-and-file voters rather than depending on big-name endorsements."[42] In fact, many who worked for the commission played key roles in McGovern's successful drive to win the Democratic nomination. But the exclusion of "big-name endorsements" has contributed mightily to a weakening of parties as institutions. By removing the most important function party leaders have—making the party's choice for president—what remained of the old establishment found itself with almost nothing to do. In the years since 1972, successful insurgent candidacies have included Donald Trump for the Republicans and Jimmy Carter for the Democrats. Other insurgencies have made establishment candidates work harder than expected to win their nominations— including Bernie Sanders in 2016, who fought the highly favored Hillary Clinton to a near-draw at the Democratic Convention, and Ronald Reagan, who in 1976 nearly beat incumbent President Gerald Ford for the Republican nod. Today, no one can say with any assurance that an establishment-backed candidate is highly favored to win their party's nomination, as the voters have often eschewed such candidacies in favor of those outsiders who capture a political moment in time.

## THE MEDIA PLAY AN IMPORTANT ROLE

The ongoing arguments about whether the rank-and-file or party leaders should exercise a dominant role in selecting presidential candidates are virtually meaningless today, given the presidential nomination system engendered by the McGovern-Fraser Commission—one that is dominated by primaries and where most voters learn about politics through television and on the Internet. A key unanticipated result of the party reform process is that instead of shifting control over the nominating system from party elites to the rank and file, reform efforts made individual candidates free agents of sorts, who campaign for primary votes through traditional media and on the Internet. This development has thrust journalists foursquare into the selection process, replacing party elites with media elites who have become unwitting king-makers, often running elections on their terms. Collectively, reporters exercise a form of "peer review," acting as political analysts and talent scouts.

Political reporters are fascinated with two things: who has raised the most money and from what sources, and how the various candidates fare in the public opinion polls. In fact, it can be said that even before the primaries begin, there is a pre-presidential primary whose criteria include how the candidates stand in the national polls, how much money they have raised, and the strength of their organizations. Making these judgments and declaring a winner is often the sole province of the national media.

Once the primaries begin, the press frequently plays a determinative role as to what constitutes a "win" or a "loss." In 2016, Donald Trump's first-place finish in New Hampshire gave him an extra-added bump in media coverage and campaign donations. Similarly, Bernie Sanders' near-first-place finish in Iowa and his subsequent trouncing of Hillary Clinton in New Hampshire meant that he was squarely in the media bull's-eye. Candidates who fared poorly in the early contests were written off by the press, and quickly dropped out of the race. Limited media resources often means that journalists and their editors must make crucial decisions about which candidates they will cover and which ones they will not. In making these choices, journalists and their bosses are exercising a role once reserved for the party bosses.

# THE MIKULSKI, WINOGRAD, HUNT, AND UNITY COMMISSIONS

The unintended consequences of the McGovern-Fraser reforms have not stopped Democrats from continuously tinkering with their presidential nominating system. The 1972 Democratic Convention authorized the creation of a Commission on Delegate Selection and Party Structure to be chaired by then-Baltimore city councilwoman Barbara Mikulski. The Mikulski Commission reaffirmed the idea of choosing convention delegates through direct primaries and state party caucuses, and having a delegate's presidential preference clearly expressed on a state ballot. But even more radically, the commission recommended that anyone receiving 10 percent of the primary or caucus votes receive a proportionate share of the delegates. The DNC agreed with the basic thrust of the recommendation, but raised the threshold to 15 percent. Together, the McGovern-Fraser and Mikulski Commissions represented a revolution in the nominating process. Old bosses became extinct, and individuals motivated more by ideology than pragmatism in both parties seized the reins of power.

As Democrats continued to lose presidential elections in the 1970s and 1980s, reform commissions continued. In 1975, Democratic National Chairman Robert Strauss created the Commission on the Role and Future of Presidential Primaries, chaired by Morley Winograd, the Michigan state Democratic chairman. The Winograd Commission recommended that each state Democratic Party "adopt specific goals and timetables" to carry out affirmative action programs, citing women, blacks,

Hispanics, and Native Americans as groups for which remedial action was needed to overcome the effects of past discrimination. Upon receiving the commission report, the DNC immediately ordered that state delegations comprise equal numbers of men and women.

Taken together, these changes banished much of the Democratic Party establishment from the convention proceedings. Before the McGovern-Fraser Commission, 83 percent of Democratic governors, 68 percent of senators, and 39 percent of representatives attended the 1968 Democratic Convention as delegates or alternates; by 1976, only 76 percent of Democratic governors, 14 percent of senators, and 15 percent of representatives were delegates.[43] Proportional representation was introduced and soon engendered disputes among prospective nominees. The *New York Times* columnist Tom Wicker wrote that the Democratic Party's obsession with the purity of the process had overcome its desire to win presidential contests: "[Democrats have become] *a party of access* in which the voiceless find a voice while Republican control of the presidency has permitted them to maintain enough coherence and unity to become a *party of government*."[44]

Jimmy Carter's landslide 1980 loss to Ronald Reagan prompted the creation of the Hunt Commission, chaired by North Carolina governor James Hunt, which undertook to restore some modicum of federalism to the nominating process. It called for the creation of superdelegates—that is, Democratic officials and party officeholders who would be automatic convention delegates. In 2008, these so-called superdelegates cast nearly 20 percent of the total votes at the Democratic National Convention. Not officially bound to any candidate per se, these 795 delegates could, if they wished, reverse the verdict issued by the rank-and-file primary voters. At first, many of these superdelegates assumed that Hillary Clinton had a lock on the nomination. But as Barack Obama began to win many of the primary and caucus contests, it became evident that the superdelegates confronted two political dilemmas: (1) vote for Clinton, even if she lost the total primary and caucus vote, and be saddled with a nominee whose legitimacy would be questioned from the start; or (2) change their publicly stated support for Clinton and throw their weight behind Obama. If the superdelegates ignored the primary and caucus voters and backed the popular vote loser, a sizable 37 percent of registered voters said they would consider such a nominee to be illegitimate; only 31 percent said the nomination would have been won fair and square.[45] In the end, the superdelegates moved toward Obama, and the roll call at the Democratic Convention was shortened when Hillary Clinton asked the delegates to make Obama's nomination unanimous.

Eight years later found Hillary Clinton seeking the presidency, and once again her candidacy won strong support from the superdelegates to the Democratic National Convention. Of the 716 superdelegates to the convention (about 15 percent of the total), Clinton had the support of 609 superdelegates, while her opponent, Bernie Sanders, garnered a mere 47.[46] Many superdelegates were reluctant to support Sanders, given his distance from the Democratic Party and the fact that he never once sought elective office as a Democrat before running for President. Sanders supporters cried foul, saying that the overwhelming superdelegate support for Clinton was unfair, since primary voters and caucus-goers never elected these delegates in the first place. At the 2016 convention, Clinton and Sanders struck a deal to create a new Unity Commission that would dramatically reduce the number of superdelegates, and bind them to the results of their respective state primaries and caucuses. While the details will be worked out over the next few years, the Unity Commission will require that superdelegates "be required to cast their vote at the [2020] Convention for candidates in proportion to the vote received for each candidate in their state."[47]

# LOOKING TO 2020

Americans are ambivalent about political parties. That ambivalence stems, in part, from the accent on individualism that permeates the American polity. When it comes to choosing a president, a focus on the individual, not the party, has prevailed. This post-1968 emphasis on personalities has complicated the selection process. The Framers' attempt to devise a presidential selection system that would create a presidency free of partisan constraints resulted in the creation of the Electoral College, which many judge to have failed. By the mid-1800s, political parties became more firmly rooted in American tradition, and the party convention, which emphasizes group activity rather than individual choice, supplanted the Congressional Caucus. The party convention has enjoyed a long life, in part because it fused federalism with nationalism, and also because it became a source of social activity in an era when parties were an important socializing force. But the convention as a collective decision-making entity is no more—a victim of party decay, reform, and the ambitions of would-be presidents.

Today, conventions exist to ratify the choices made by voters in the party primaries and caucuses—choices that are made by a candidate's own desire to place his or her name into presidential contention. Observers could see the first inkling of this phenomenon as early as 1960, when reporter Richard Reeves wrote that the most important feature of John F. Kennedy's political career was his own ambition:

> He did not wait his turn. He directly challenged the institution he wanted to control, the political system. After him, no one else wanted to wait either, and few institutions were rigid enough or flexible enough to survive impatient ambition-driven challenges. He believed (and proved) that the only qualification for the most powerful job in the world was wanting it. His power did not come from the top down nor from the bottom up. It was an ax driven by his own ambition into the middle of the system, biting to the center he wanted for himself. When he was asked early in 1960 why he thought he should be president, he answered: "I look around me at the others in the race, and I say to myself, well, if they think they can do it why not me? 'Why not me?' That's the answer. And I think it's enough."[48]

Ever since John Kennedy uttered those words, every other presidential candidate in the decades since has said, in effect, "Why not me?" In presenting themselves to the public, these ambitious contenders have relied on their own personas, rather than their party affiliations, to help them get elected. Celebrity politics is entertaining, but it is not party politics. This point was highlighted in 2016 when Donald Trump morphed from a culture figure, who dominated Nielson television ratings in shows such as *The Apprentice* and *Celebrity Apprentice*, into a serious candidate for president. Trump's ties to the Republican Party were, at best, nominal, as he had previously given campaign contributions to many *Democrats*, including Senate minority leader Harry Reid, New York senators Chuck Schumer and Kirsten Gillibrand, and even Hillary Clinton's 2008 campaign for president. In sum, Trump leveraged his celebrity status to engineer a hostile takeover of the Republican Party—all the while promising to "Make America Great Again." Meanwhile, Bernie Sanders came within a whisker of winning the Democratic nomination, despite having had no previous affiliation with the party.

In an era of empty sloganeering, it is no wonder that party conventions hardly resemble the days of yore. In the 1965 edition of *The World Book Encyclopedia*, conventions were described as allowing "all citizens an opportunity to observe one of the processes of representative government. And when two strong candidates seek nomination, a national convention is more exciting than a World Series."[49] But it has been years since a convention has been more exciting than any World Series. The last gathering to take more than one ballot was 1952, when Democrats nominated Adlai E. Stevenson on the third ballot.

In a sense, we have never left square one, seeking to "fix" what many Americans see as a broken nominating system. Besides wondering about what kind of president we want, future tinkerers must also ask, "How do we get a president who can govern effectively?" The answers to both of these questions are harder to find as political parties become less able to control the selection process and in many ways have lost the ability to award the greatest prize in politics: the nomination of a major party for the presidency of the United States.

# NOTES

1.  ABC News/*Washington Post*, poll, August 1–4, 2016. Text of question: "How do you feel about a choice between (Hillary) Clinton and (Donald) Trump as the (2016) major party candidates for president—are you very satisfied with this choice, somewhat satisfied, somewhat dissatisfied, or very dissatisfied?" Very satisfied, 13 percent; somewhat satisfied, 28 percent; somewhat dissatisfied, 26 percent; very dissatisfied, 31 percent; no opinion, 1 percent.

2.  Quinnipiac University Polling Institute, poll, August 18–24, 2016. Text of question: "Regardless of whether or not you'd vote for him (in 2016), do you think Donald Trump is or is not qualified to serve as President?" Yes/qualified, 40 percent; no/not qualified, 58 percent; don't know/no answer, 2 percent.

3.   Fox News, poll, August 28–30, 2016. Text of question: "Do you think Hillary Clinton is honest and trustworthy, or not?" Yes, 31 percent; no, 66 percent; don't know, 3 percent.

4.   Quoted in John Heilemann and Mark Halperin, *Game Change: Obama and the Clintons, McCain and Palin, and the Race of a Lifetime* (New York: HarperCollins, 2010), p. 94.

5.   Quoted in Michael Kranish and Marc Fisher, *Trump Revealed: An American Journey of Ambition, Ego, Money and Power* (New York: Scribner, 2016), p. 331.

6.   Ibid. Trump responded to his wife saying he was sure.

7.   Quoted in Fred Blumenthal, "How to Prepare for the Presidency," *Parade Magazine*, 1962. Reprinted in *The World Book Encyclopedia* (Chicago: Field Enterprises Educational Corporation, 1965), pp. 678–679.

8.   See Kranish and Fisher, *Trump Revealed*, pp. 285–287.

9.   Ibid., p. 292.

10.   The lengthy list of Republican candidates included former Florida governor Jeb Bush, neurosurgeon Ben Carson, Texas senator Ted Cruz, Ohio governor John Kasich, former Virginia governor Jim Gilmore, Florida senator Marco Rubio, real estate entrepreneur Donald Trump, former Texas governor Rick Perry, Wisconsin governor Scott Walker, Louisiana governor Bobby Jindal, South Carolina senator Lindsey Graham, former New York governor George Pataki, former Arkansas governor Mike Huckabee, former Pennsylvania senator Rick Santorum, Kentucky senator Rand Paul, former Hewlett Packard CEO Carly Fiorina, and New Jersey governor Chris Christie.

11.   Quoted in Heilemann and Halperin, *Game Change*, p. 63.

12.   Ibid., p. 108.

13.   Alexander Hamilton, "Federalist 68," in Edward Meade Earle, ed., *The Federalist* (New York: Modern Library, 1937), p. 50.

14.   Gallup Organization, poll, January 8–9, 2013. Text of question: "Would you vote for or against a law that would do away with the Electoral College and base the election of the president on the total vote cast throughout the nation?" For, 63 percent; against, 29 percent; no opinion, 8 percent.

15.   In 2008, Barack Obama won the congressional district in Nebraska that included Omaha, and therefore received one electoral vote from the state that John McCain carried.

16.   For more on some of these proposals, see Paul Schumaker, "Analyzing the Electoral College and Its Alternatives," in Paul D. Schumaker and Burdett A. Loomis, *Choosing a President: The Electoral College and Beyond* (New York: Chatham House Publishers, 2002), especially pp. 10–30.

17.   John F. Kennedy, Announcement Speech, Washington, DC, January 14, 1960.

18.   OpenSecrets.org, www.opensecrets.org/pres16/. Accessed May 20, 2017.

19.   Associated Press-National Opinion Research Center, Money in Politics Survey, November 2015. Text of question one: "Here are some possible ways to change the current system of financing political campaigns in the United States. How effective do you think each of the following would be in reducing the influence of money in politics? Extremely effective, very effective, somewhat effective, not very effective, not effective at all? Limits on how much an outside group can spend on a candidate's campaign." Extremely effective, 25 percent; very effective, 29 percent; somewhat effective, 33 percent; not very effective, 8 percent; not effective at all, 5 percent. Text of question two: "Here are some possible ways to change the current system of financing political campaigns in the United States. How effective do you think each of the following would be in reducing the influence of money

in politics? Extremely effective, very effective, somewhat effective, not very effective, not effective at all? Limits on how much a political party can spend on a candidate's campaign." Extremely effective, 23 percent; very effective, 29 percent; somewhat effective, 35 percent; not very effective, 8 percent; not effective at all, 5 percent. Text of question three: "Here are some possible ways to change the current system of financing political campaigns in the United States. How effective do you think each of the following would be in reducing the influence of money in politics? Extremely effective, very effective, somewhat effective, not very effective, not effective at all? Limits on how much a candidate can spend on his or her campaign, regardless of the source of the money." Extremely effective, 25 percent; very effective, 26 percent; somewhat effective, 33 percent; not very effective, 9 percent; not effective at all, 6 percent.

20.    *Citizens United v. Federal Election Commission,* 558 U.S. 50 (2010).

21.    OpenSecrets.org, www.opensecrets.org/pres16/raised-summ. Accessed May 20, 2017.

22.    Bernie Sanders, Announcement Speech, Burlington, Vermont, May 26, 2015.

23.    Donald J. Trump, *Crippled America: How to Make America Great Again* (New York: Threshold Editions, Simon and Schuster, 2015), p. 98.

24.    Quoted in James MacGregor Burns, *The Power to Lead* (New York: Simon and Schuster, 1984), p. 220.

25.    Quoted in James W. Ceaser, *Presidential Selection: Theory and Development* (Princeton, NJ: Princeton University Press, 1979), p. 147.

26.    Quoted in A. James Reichley, *The Life of the Parties: A History of American Political Parties* (New York: Free Press, 1992), p. 92.

27.    Ibid., pp. 133–134.

28.    Ibid., p. 134.

29.    Quoted in E. E. Schattschneider, *The Semi-Sovereign People: A Realist's View of Democracy in America* (Hinsdale, IL: Dryden Press, 1975 reprint), p. 84.

30.    Quoted in "Democrats End Two-Thirds Rule," *New York Times,* June 25, 1936, p. 1. It is interesting to note that Daniels equates the convention with the nation.

31.    Lyndon B. Johnson, Address to the Nation, Washington, DC, March 31, 1968.

32.    Theodore H. White, *The Making of the President, 1968* (New York: Atheneum, 1969), p. 376.

33.    George McGovern, *Grassroots: The Autobiography of George McGovern* (New York: Random House, 1977), p. 130. Eugene McCarthy became a candidate in November 1967; Robert Kennedy entered in mid-March, 1968; Lyndon Johnson withdrew from the race on March 31; Hubert Humphrey became an official candidate in late April (after most of the primary deadlines had passed). The charge that Humphrey was an unrepresentative candidate of the Democratic Party rank and file remains a contested one. Humphrey easily led McCarthy in the Gallup polls as the party's choice for the presidential nomination and was competitive in a three-way contest involving Eugene McCarthy, Robert Kennedy, and Humphrey. For more information, see Richard Scammon and Ben J. Wattenberg, *The Real Majority* (New York: Coward-McCann, 1970).

34.    *Mandate for Reform: A Report of the Commission on Party Structure and Delegate Selection to the Democratic National Committee* (Washington, DC, Democratic National Committee, April 1970).

35.    McGovern, *Grassroots,* p. 137.

36.    *Cousins v. Wigoda,* 419, U.S. (1975).

37.    McGovern, *Grassroots,* p. 48.

38.   Republicans have also been spared major changes in their delegate selection process because, unlike the Democrats, they avoided squabbles among presidential contenders involving party rules. This was possible because Republicans won most White House contests held between 1968 and 1988. Only once in this period did the rules figure in a GOP contest. In 1976, Ronald Reagan promulgated Rule 14C, which would have required prospective candidates to name their vice-presidential candidates in advance of their own selection by the convention. Reagan lost this battle and the nomination to Gerald Ford, and Rule 14C was relegated to the cobwebs of history.

39.   In addition, Democrats held closed primaries in Guam, Kentucky, and the District of Columbia. Republicans held closed primaries in Washington State.

40.   Clinton won caucuses held in Iowa, Nevada, American Samoa, the Northern Mariana Islands, and the Virgin Islands. Sanders won caucuses in Colorado, Minnesota, Kansas, Nebraska, Maine, Idaho, Alaska, Hawaii, Washington State, Wyoming, and North Dakota.

41.   Ted Cruz won caucuses in Iowa, Alaska, Kansas, Maine, and Wyoming. Donald Trump won caucuses in Nevada, North Dakota, Kentucky, Hawaii, the Virgin Islands, and the Northern Mariana Islands. Marco Rubio won caucuses in Minnesota and the District of Columbia.

42.   McGovern, *Grassroots*, p. 153.

43.   Cited in Nelson W. Polsby, *Consequences of Party Reform* (New York: Oxford University Press, 1983), p. 114.

44.   Tom Wicker, "A Party of Access?" *New York Times*, November 25, 1984, p. E17.

45.   NBC News/ *Wall Street Journal*, poll, April 25–28, 2008. Text of question: "In addition to primaries and caucuses, the Democratic selection rules for the presidential nominee include the votes of elected officeholders or party officials who are often called superdelegates. If one of the candidates loses among delegates selected by voters but still wins the nomination by winning among superdelegates, would you consider that nominee legitimate, would you consider that nominee not legitimate, or do you not have an opinion either way?" Would consider nominee legitimate, 31 percent; would consider nominee not legitimate, 37 percent; no opinion either way, 27 percent; not sure, 5 percent.

46.   See "Who's Winning the Presidential Delegate Count?" found in www.bloomberg.com/politics/graphics/2016-delegate-tracker/. Accessed September 21, 2016.

47.   David Weigel, "Democrats Vote to Bind Most Superdelegates to State Primary Results," *Washington Post*, July 23, 2016. See www.washingtonpost.com/news/post-politics/wp/2016/07/23/democrats-vote-to-bind-most-superdelegates-to-state-primary-results/. Accessed September 21, 2016.

48.   Richard Reeves, *President Kennedy: Profile of Power* (New York: Simon and Schuster, 1993), p. 14.

49.   Walter F. Morse, "Political Convention," *World Book Encyclopedia*, vol. 15 (Chicago: Field Enterprises Educational Corporation, 1964), pp. 553–554.

# 5

## Party Brand Loyalty and the American Voter

At the start of the night, a sense of excitement filled the convention-sized room where supporters of the Democratic presidential nominee prepared for what they thought would be a celebration of historic proportions. With virtually every pre-election opinion poll showing Hillary Clinton with a durable lead over Donald Trump, most political commentators and prognosticators considered it close to a sure thing that on November 8, 2016, America would elect its first female president. States with early poll closing times came in on cue: conservative Kentucky went for Trump, liberal Vermont supported Clinton. Florida was taking a bit longer to decide than expected, although Clinton held an early lead in a state where victory would all but make it mathematically impossible for her to lose. But as the rural vote came in, Clinton's margin narrowed, then disappeared. The same thing happened in North Carolina, another swing state where her campaign had been confident of victory. Then Virginia, home to Clinton's running mate Tim Kaine and where Clinton had consistently maintained comfortable leads in opinion polls, was reclassified by the major television networks from the relatively suspense-free designation "too early to call" to the nail-biting category "too close to call."

Clinton would hold on to win Virginia, but the evening was not unfolding as expected. She was narrowly winning states where polling suggested she would win comfortably and she was losing close states she had expected to win. If this pattern continued as the results came in from the Midwest, Donald Trump had a chance to score one of the biggest upsets in American political history. A jolt of electricity coursed through Trump's New York headquarters as his supporters reacted to the surprising results. Several blocks away, once celebratory Clinton enthusiasts responded to the same news with muted worry, then shock and bewilderment when the scope of what was happening settled in.

Every four years on election night, Americans gather to find out who will be elected president. Many of these evenings are routine, with the identity of the winner known long before the votes are counted. Others, like Election Night 2016, have become legendary for their suspense and high drama. For example, running for an unprecedented third term in 1940, Franklin D. Roosevelt saw trouble in the early returns. Breaking into a cold, heavy sweat, the president abruptly ordered everyone to leave the family dining room at his Hyde Park, New York, estate. Seated in his wheelchair, Roosevelt calculated whether he had enough votes to win as news tickers clattered away with the latest results. After a few suspense-filled hours, the numbers turned in Roosevelt's favor, whereupon family and friends rejoined him as he became his familiar, cheery self.[1]

Twenty years later, another Election Night was immortalized by journalist Theodore H. White. Spending the evening with John F. Kennedy at his Hyannisport, Massachusetts, compound, White described how the early figures were going Kennedy's way. At one point early in the evening, Kennedy's wife, Jacqueline, exclaimed, "Oh, Bunny [her pet name for her husband], you're going to be president now!"[2] But as midnight approached, Kennedy's Republican opponent, Richard M. Nixon, cut dramatically into Kennedy's lead, leaving the Democrat a few electoral votes shy of a majority. As night turned to day, no one knew who had won. Only when Chicago mayor Richard J. Daley found enough votes to put Illinois into the Democratic column was Kennedy declared the winner. Final figures showed Kennedy beat Nixon by just 112,881 popular votes out of nearly 70 million cast—a margin of just one-tenth of 1 percent.

Eight years later, Richard M. Nixon returned as a central character in another Election Night melodrama—this time defeating Hubert H. Humphrey by half a percentage point out of nearly 73 million popular votes cast. As in 1960, the lead seesawed between the two candidates throughout the night and into the next day. At midnight, Humphrey was ahead. By 6 a.m. the next morning, Nixon had taken a slim lead, but most television commentators were speculating that Mayor Daley was holding back Democratic votes in key Chicago precincts. Two hours later, Daley recognized that he could not stop Nixon and released his votes. Illinois and the presidency went to Nixon.

Perhaps the most exciting Election Night in modern times occurred in 2000. Early in the evening, the television networks projected the state of Florida for Al Gore, only to recant a few hours later. At 2:17 a.m. Fox News, in a rush to judgment, awarded Florida and the presidency to George W. Bush. Not wanting to be left behind, the other networks concurred. But Bush's victory was premature because the votes for one Florida county showed Gore at *minus* 16,000 votes.[3] At 2:40 a.m., Gore telephoned Bush to concede, only to call back a short while later to say that his earlier concession had been based on Florida's faulty election returns. Another 36 days would pass before the U.S. Supreme Court settled the matter in the infamous case of *Bush v. Gore.*

In today's charged partisan atmosphere, watching election results is a bit like cheering for your favorite football team along with everyone else who identifies with "team red" or "team blue." With partisan loyalties hardening during the past decade, fewer Democrats and Republicans are defecting from their party moorings to support the opposition. In 2008, for example, only 9 percent of Republicans supported Democrat Barack Obama, while just 10 percent of Democrats backed Republican John McCain.[4] Four years later, only 8 percent of Democrats cast a ballot for Mitt Romney, while just 7 percent of Republicans voted for Barack Obama.[5]

In 2016, partisan loyalties were just as strong as in the previous two presidential contests: 88 percent of Republicans cast ballots for Donald Trump and 89 percent of Democrats voted for Hillary Clinton.[6] This time, because Trump so dominated in white, non-college rural areas in key states—including Pennsylvania, Wisconsin, and Michigan—Trump was declared the winner in the wee morning hours the day after the election. But unlike most previous contests, the result triggered protests in cities around the U.S., as Democrats worried about the prospect of a Trump presidency, and the #NotMyPresident hashtag trended on Twitter.

In many ways, today's fierce partisan rivalries are nothing new. In 1884, the *Philadelphia Inquirer* observed that "party lines were as strictly drawn as were the lines of religious sects."[7] Southerners coined the nickname "yellow dog Democrat," meaning they would vote for a yellow dog instead of a dreaded Republican. Northerners, meanwhile, were mostly rock-ribbed Yankees and firmly committed Republicans. For much of the nineteenth century, voting was not a soul-searching exercise because most Americans were creatures of political habit. The excitement on Election Night came not because there was much doubt about what individual voters might do—they were loyal partisans—rather, it was because the parties were so evenly matched.

This chapter examines how political consumers—i.e., the voters—relate to the parties. First, we review how party brand loyalty develops and examine ways scholars have sought to measure it. Second, we examine what political scientists call partisan realignment and how it affects the way electoral politics is studied. Third, we describe the electoral coalitions that have emerged to shape today's politics.

# THE IMPORTANCE OF PARTY IDENTIFICATION

Few topics have received more scholarly attention over the last seven decades than political behavior, an area of research that focuses on the political attitudes, beliefs, and actions of individuals. Among the first to study how individual voters behave in the voting booths were Bernard R. Berelson and Paul F. Lazarsfeld, who contributed to *The People's Choice* (1940)[8] and *Voting* (1948).[9] Berelson and Lazarsfeld developed a sociological model in which socioeconomic standing (education, income, and class); religion (Catholic, Protestant, or Jewish); and place of residence (rural or urban) formed an "index of political predisposition" that often determined party identification, which, in turn, strongly influenced choices made at the ballot box. Thus, a well-educated, white, upper-class Protestant from upstate New York would most likely be a Republican, whereas a black, blue-collar worker from Detroit would most likely be a Democrat. Using this index of political predisposition, demography mattered most and political campaigns counted for little. Joining a political party was, in essence, a declaration about who you were and where you were born. During the campaign season, Republicans shouted at other like-minded Republicans to vote for their candidates, and Democrats did much the same—with few minds changed in the process.

The sociological model was best suited to explain the strong party era that existed from the post–Civil War period until the New Deal. And it may experience a resurgence amidst today's partisanship. But a weakening of party loyalties that began during the 1950s, and accelerated in the 1960s and 1970s, challenged the model. In 1952, millions of Democrats voted for Republican and World War II hero, Dwight D. Eisenhower, giving him a comfortable ten-point victory over Democrat Adlai Stevenson. What influenced many people (including Democrats and independents) to back Eisenhower were *issues*—especially the Korean War. Gallup polls found 65 percent chose Eisenhower as the best person able to break the stalemate in Korea.[10] Four years later, Eisenhower defied the existing Democratic majority to beat Stevenson again—this time with 57 percent of the vote to Stevenson's 43 percent. As in 1952, Eisenhower's advantage on cold war-related foreign policy issues proved decisive.

Eisenhower's landslide victories illustrated certain deficiencies associated with the sociological model. While race, ethnicity, and location mattered in helping to form partisan identifications, it was also true that voter attitudes about particular candidates and issues were important factors in determining who won or lost on Election Night. Two questions remained: What individual political attitudes were important, and how could they be measured?

Some answers were contained in *The American Voter*, published in 1960.[11] Authors Angus Campbell, Philip Converse, Warren Miller, and Donald Stokes created a sociological-psychological model of voting behavior. They agreed with Berenson and Lazarsfeld that demographics still mattered, but the authors also believed that partisanship had a strong psychological dimension. Thus, most Americans identified with their parents' party, whereas the children of parents without a clear partisan preference were ambivalent about politics. Once established, party identification frequently persisted throughout a person's adult life. Using data gathered in the 1950s, Campbell and his colleagues found that nearly 85 percent of respondents stuck with the same party throughout their adult lives, and a majority had never voted for a candidate of the other party.[12] It is in this vein that many political analysts consider the 2008 election to be historically important, since Barack Obama won 66 percent of the votes from those aged 18 to 29.[13] Likewise in 2012, Obama won 60 percent of votes cast by those aged 18 to 29,[14] and in 2016, Hillary Clinton won 55 percent of younger voters.[15] The fact that Obama and Clinton won majorities of young people in three consecutive presidential elections (albeit with reduced numbers) suggests that Democrats can win majority support from Millennials in future contests.

*The American Voter* is considered a seminal work because it introduced a new way of understanding how people vote. Ethnicity, race, region, religion, different economic structures (including education, occupation, and class), and historical patterns (including parental partisanship and social class) converge into a single act of voting. Together they create a person's party identification, which is usually long-lasting. Once partisanship is formed, voters selectively screen information using the lenses of their preferred party. For example, following passage of a sweeping healthcare reform bill proposed by President Obama and congressional Democrats, support for the new measure depended on which political party a survey respondent identified with. According to one poll, 71 percent of Democrats backed the new law; 82 percent of Republicans were opposed.[16] This enormous partisan divide on Obamacare continued throughout Obama's two terms, and was replicated on several other important issues confronting the Obama administration. The failure of Barack Obama (and of George W. Bush before him) to unite the country and transcend the widening partisan divisions remains a singular disappointment.

From its inception, *The American Voter* provided a baseline to measure how a person's party identification influenced individual voting choices. This is not to say that refinements were impossible and challenges were not forthcoming. In 1971, Gerald Pomper found a significant increase in the correlation between policy and party from the results reported in *The American Voter*. Using seven issues—(1) federal aid to education, (2) government provision of medical care, (3) government guarantees of full employment, (4) federal enforcement of fair employment, (5) housing, (6) school integration, and (7) foreign aid—Pomper found that a linear relation between issue and party identification existed in 1956 only for medical care. By 1968, there were correlations on all of the aforementioned issues except foreign aid. In addition, the proportion viewing the Democrats as the more liberal party had risen on every question. Pomper concluded that between 1956 and 1968, "considerable political learning" had taken place.[17]

Building on Pomper's work, Norman Nie, Sidney Verba, and John Petrocik argued in *The Changing American Voter* (1976) that issues were important influences on voting behavior.[18] This approach, called the cognitive voter model, assumed that citizens supported a particular candidate based on issue positions. For example, as the Vietnam War and civil rights debates of the 1960s and 1970s were given increased public prominence, and the two political parties nominated conservative Republican Barry Goldwater and liberal Democrat George McGovern who had strong positions on these issues, voters began to use candidate and party stances on key issues as their voting guides. Candidate-centered politics, with its focus on issues, replaced party-centered politics. This did not mean that party identification no longer mattered; rather, voters paid attention to issues when candidates took clear, unequivocal stands on them. But if candidates adopted similar positions, then party identification reemerged as the primary determinant of vote choice. It was a two-step process: issues first, party second.

Since the 1950s, several scholars have approached the study of parties and party identification using the rational choice model, which postulates that voters establish goals and achieve them using cost-benefit calculations. For example, someone might aspire to become rich, but finds that working 18-hour days to acquire wealth is not worth it. Applying the same rationale to party identification, Anthony Downs, in his 1957 book titled *An Economic Theory of Democracy*, argued that the benefits of arriving at a "correct" voting decision may not be worth the costs of compiling extensive information on the candidates.[19] Most voters want to cast an informed vote, but often lack the time and energy to sift through the complex details of each candidate's policy stands and personal character. Party identification gives the busy voter a quick and easy solution. Voters can take an information short-cut by understanding the basic contours of what each party stands for, matching that information with their own values (thereby developing a party identification), and then associate particular candidates with their party labels. Thus, an Election Day decision can be made in a few quick seconds, because the voter need only know each candidate's party in order to cast an "informed" vote.

## MEASURING PARTY IDENTIFICATION

If the scholarly quarrel over how party identification is acquired and how it influences vote choice has dominated the study of political behavior, a close second has been the controversy over how to measure party identification. The most commonly used technique employs a seven-point ordinal scale developed by public opinion pollsters. Voters are classified by their answers to two questions. First, respondents are asked if they consider themselves Republicans, Democrats, or independents. Those who answer that they are either Republican or Democrat are asked a follow-up question about how strongly they identify with their chosen party. Those who classify themselves as "independent" are subsequently asked whether they are closer to the Republican Party or the Democratic Party. Respondents are then grouped into one of seven categories: (1) strong Democrat, (2) weak Democrat, (3) independent-leaning-Democrat, (4) true independent, (5) independent-leaning-Republican, (6) weak Republican, and (7) strong Republican. The advantage of this approach is that it suggests degrees of partisanship. It is reasonable to assume that some Democrats and Republicans are more closely connected to their parties than others, and that many so-called independents lean more toward one of the parties. According to one poll taken during the 2016 presidential campaign, 19 percent of all adult respondents said they were strong Republicans; 8 percent identified themselves as a not very strong Republican; 9 percent said they were independents who leaned Republican; 25 percent said they were strong Democrats; 8 percent said they were not a very strong Democrat; 11 percent were independents who leaned Democratic; and just 13 percent were truly independent.[20]

But party identification is more complex and depends on a variety of other factors beyond whether a respondent is a Democrat, Republican, or independent. Herbert Weisberg offers three variables: (1) attitudes toward the Republican Party, (2) attitudes toward the Democratic Party, and (3) attitudes toward political independence.[21] Another approach to measure the strength of party identifiers is to have survey respondents rank each party on a "thermometer," with zero degrees representing very negative feelings and 100 degrees signifying very positive feelings. Scores for each party are compared, and a partisan preference is determined.[22] Others believe it is possible to gauge citizens' dispositions toward the parties by asking how they vote on Election Day.

The debate surrounding the validity of (and ways to measure) party identification is likely to continue, given the new technologies and modes of communication associated with today's networked age. Whereas voters once got most of their political information through interpersonal communications or daily newspapers, today's plugged-in electorate has vastly more options for obtaining election information through the media and on the Internet. CNN, for example, has a politics tab on its website that the online browser can summon at a moment's notice. The other major networks—CBS, ABC, NBC, MSNBC, and Fox News—also have sophisticated websites that contain vast amounts of political information. Each evening, MSNBC viewers can watch Chris Matthews, Chris Hayes, and Rachel Maddow querying an array of political guests. For a more conservative view, Fox News Channel viewers can tune in to Tucker Carlson and Sean Hannity for their takes on politics on their daily shows. The *Washington Post, New York Times, Huff Post, Political Wire*, and *Politico* also provide websites for interested voters. In addition, there are dozens of websites for individual newsletters and candidate organizations that voters can access (see Table 5.1).

## Table 5.1 Political Websites, 2016

| Website/Address | Description |
| --- | --- |
| Political Wire: www.politicalwire.com | Provides a running account of the latest political headlines. |
| Politico: www.politico.com | Offers analysis of contemporary politics by Washington, DC insiders. |
| Real Clear Politics: www.realclearpolitics.com | A nonpartisan website offering the latest political news and analysis. |
| CNN Politics: www.cnn.com/politics | Supplies web users with a supplement to CNN television reports, with analyses provided by CNN correspondents and a look at public opinion polls. |
| NBC Politics: www.nbcpolitics.com | The latest political headlines and polling information from NBC News with analysis. |

*(continued)*

**Table 5.1** *(continued)*

| Website/Address | Description |
|---|---|
| ABC News: www.abcnews. go.com/politics/election | The latest political news and polling from ABC News. |
| Huffington Post: www. huffingtonpost.com | Analyzes politics from a liberal perspective. |
| Daily Kos: www.dailykos. com | The largest online political community site that serves as a virtual home for progressive activists. |
| Townhall: www.townhall. com | Analyzes politics from a conservative perspective. |
| Drudge Report: www. drudgereport.com | A portal for political news and information with a conservative bent. |
| Daily Beast: www. dailybeast.com | A website that provides distinctive commentary on political news from different perspectives. |
| 270 to Win: www.270towin.com | An interesting electoral vote map that allows the user to make his/her own electoral vote calculations. |

# THE MAKING OF AN IDEA: PARTY REALIGNMENT

So far, we have discussed how individuals form partisan attachments, but what of the electorate as a whole? Taken together, the party affiliations of the entire body politic form an underlying structure of voting behavior. Thus, for political scientists, Election Nights in today's networked age still retain an aura of their former excitement. Besides knowing who the next president is going to be, the next most important question to be answered is what the election means. Surely, there must be something more behind the collective Xs placed next to a candidate's name. Thus, after Franklin D. Roosevelt's 1936 landslide victory, one analyst declared that he could "see no interpretation of the returns which does not suggest that the people of America want the president to proceed along progressive or liberal lines."[23] Similarly, after Ronald Reagan's stunning 1980 victory, many agreed with Republican pollster Richard Wirthlin when he interpreted the result as "a mandate for change ... [that meant] ... a rejection of the New Deal agenda that had dominated American politics since the 1930s."[24] In both cases, political scientists argued that the structure of the U.S. party system had undergone a significant transformation. In 1936 and 1980, Americans came to very different conclusions about the role of government in our society. These contests gave way to historic changes in overall partisan identification and the coalitions that comprised the Democratic and Republican parties. Realigning elections (like those of 1936 and 1980) provide important clues to a simple question: What does party change look like?

# V. O. KEY AND PARTY REALIGNMENT

Behind the speculation about what votes in any given election mean and which political party is favored, it is clear that some elections have far-reaching consequences. Political scientist V. O. Key Jr. was the first to argue that some elections were more important than others. Who remembers, for example, whether Franklin Pierce won the presidency in 1852, or James Buchanan in 1856, or James Garfield in 1880? Although the results of these contests might provide interesting material for a game of Trivial Pursuit, from Key's perspective, realigning elections are those in which catastrophe plays a significant role. For example, in 1860 the impending Civil War consumed everything in its wake. Lincoln's successful prosecution of that war, along with his proclamation of a "new birth of freedom" in the Gettysburg Address, convinced most voters that the Republican Party could be trusted to steer the ship of state.

Likewise, in the next century, the Great Depression, and Franklin Roosevelt's collection of New Deal programs to combat it, convinced most voters that the Democratic Party could best handle the nation's economy and look after the interests of the average American. When asked in 1951 what they would tell young people about whom the parties stood for, most said that the Democrats represented the "working man" whereas the Republicans promoted the "privileged few."[25]

Building on this idea, in 1955 Key developed a category of elections he described as "critical elections"—that is, contests characterized by sharp reorganizations of party loyalties over short periods of time. In these contests, voter turnout is quite high, and new, long-lasting party coalitions are formed. Studying the election outcomes of several New England towns from 1916 to 1952, Key found that when the Democrats nominated Catholic New York governor Alfred E. Smith in 1928, party support in urban areas increased significantly and remained high, whereas Democratic backing in rural, Protestant-dominated enclaves fell to record lows, where it remained in the years that followed.[26]

Shortly after Key introduced the concept of critical elections, he published a major modification of his original idea. In 1959, he wrote that changes in partisanship are sometimes not as dramatic as those that occurred in 1928. Instead, he noted, party loyalties can erode among some groups and regions over many years. Key termed these changes *secular realignments*, defining them as "a movement of the members of a population category from party to party that extends over several presidential elections and appears to be independent of the peculiar factors influencing the vote at individual elections."[27] Key placed no time limit on the pace of this change, noting that it could take as long as 50 years. But the premise was clear: gradual alterations in voting behavior, not a sharp reorganization of party loyalties, characterized secular realignments. Again, using election returns from some New England towns, Key found instances where the shift from Republican dominance to sustained Democratic victories during the New Deal era was slow, but steady. Key attributed the snail-like pace of change to the increased industrialization and urbanization of the region, as well as to the last wave of European immigrants who became acclimated to their new country, and over time came to the polls in support of the Democrats.

Key's ideas about critical elections and secular realignments gained widespread popularity in the political science community. Enhancing its appeal was the pro-party argument that underpinned realignment theory. Instead of resorting to arms or tearing up the U.S. Constitution when catastrophe struck, political scientists believed that voters used political parties to engineer significant policy changes. Parties were often credited with being important agents in maintaining the stability of the constitutional order. The U.S. Constitution works because political parties work, or so went the argument. Given this line of reasoning, political scientists had much at stake in making the case for party realignment.

As analysis of electoral change expanded to include polling data that could pinpoint changes within narrowly defined population groups (e.g., white male Catholics between the ages of 18 and 24), party realignment took on added significance. Walter Dean Burnham, a major proponent of the realignment concept, published *Critical Elections and the Mainsprings of American Politics* (1970), in which he transformed Key's simple idea of critical elections into a generalized theory of party realignment. Burnham outlined five conditions that characterized the "ideal-typical" partisan realignment:

♦ There are short, sharp reorganizations of the major-party voter coalitions that occur at periodic intervals.
♦ Third-party revolts often precede party realignments and reveal the incapacity of "politics-as-usual."
♦ There is abnormal stress in the socioeconomic system that is closely associated with fundamental partisan change.
♦ Ideological polarizations and issue distances between the major parties become exceptionally large by normal standards.
♦ Realignments have durable consequences and determine the general outlines of important public policies in the decades that follow.[28]

Using this classification scheme, Burnham cited the elections of Andrew Jackson in 1828, Abraham Lincoln in 1860, William McKinley in 1896, and Franklin D. Roosevelt in 1932 as having met the conditions of party realignment. In each case, voter interest and turnout was high; there were significant third-party revolts, either in the actual election (or in the contests leading up to it); and the differences between the parties were exceptionally large by U.S. standards. In making his calculations, Burnham discovered a rhythm to U.S. politics—namely, that realigning elections occur once every 28 to 36 years. Thus, if a realigning election happened in 1932 (as Burnham suggests) or in 1928 (as Key found in New England), one could expect another realignment to occur circa 1968.

Indeed, many believe that Republican Richard M. Nixon's close victory over Democrat Hubert H. Humphrey in 1968 met the conditions of a classic party realignment. The issue differences between the two parties on civil rights, the Vietnam War, and what became known as the "social issues" (crime, abortion, pornography, etc.)

were significant. Moreover, there was a major third-party revolt in the person of Alabama governor George C. Wallace, whose presidential candidacy garnered 14 percent of the popular vote—a feat not surpassed until 1992, when Ross Perot captured 19 percent of the ballots cast. Kevin Phillips, an astute Republican political analyst, wrote in his 1969 book *The Emerging Republican Majority*:

> Far from being the tenuous and unmeaningful victory suggested by critical observers, the election of Richard M. Nixon as president of the United States in November 1968 bespoke the end of the New Deal Democratic hegemony and the beginning of a new era in American politics.[29]

The Election Nights that followed Nixon's 1968 win gave credence to Phillips's vision of a Republican realignment. From 1968 to 1988, Republicans won five of the six presidential contests (Nixon in 1968 and 1972, Reagan in 1980 and 1984, and George H. W. Bush in 1988). Only Nixon's misadventures in the Watergate scandal permitted a Democratic victory—Jimmy Carter in 1976—and that was for only one term. The Republican hold on the presidency was so great that some analysts thought the GOP had an impenetrable lock on the Electoral College that would prevent any future Democratic victories.

But this Republican realignment had a very different feel from those that preceded it. Far from being vanquished, Democrats retained comfortable majorities in both houses of Congress for most of this period. Democrats controlled the Senate from 1968 to 1980—narrowly losing control in the 1980 Reagan landslide, but reclaiming majority status in 1986. The House showed an even greater Democratic advantage. After Ronald Reagan won reelection in 1984, Democrats held a 71-seat margin in the House—the largest edge given to a party that did not control the White House since 1895. Thus, while the party system created by Franklin D. Roosevelt had died, the "ideal-type" of partisan realignment forecast by Burnham failed to take its place. Many wondered what happened. Some attributed the Republican failure to produce a classic realignment to the aftereffects of Watergate. In 1974, Democrats added 49 seats in the House—enough to ensure control until Newt Gingrich and his Republican allies took over 20 years later. Others attributed the failure of either party to achieve a classic realignment to presidents who were all too willing to eschew their party affiliations in order to win more votes. Some believe that a realignment is already in the making. As Burnham noted in his review of history, realignments occur once every 28 to 36 years. If Nixon's 1968 election marked the beginning of a realignment, then we might have expected another realigning election to have occurred by 2004 (the outside limit of the 36-year period). Karl Rove, a key advisor to George W. Bush, maintained that Bush's 2000 and 2004 victories resembled those of Republican William McKinley, whose election in 1896 strengthened what had been a tenuous Republican majority, although that perspective is contradicted by Democratic victories in 2008 and again in 2012.[30] In 2016, Donald Trump prevailed in the Electoral College, but lost the popular vote by 2.9 million—a margin almost six times greater than George W. Bush's popular vote loss to Al Gore.

An opposing view was articulated in 2002, when John B. Judis and Ruy Teix-eira published an influential book titled *The Emerging Democratic Majority*. Judis and Teixeira asserted that the rise of Hispanic and Asian immigrants, the continued support of Democrats by African Americans, the emergence of a well-educated professional class, and the support given to Democrats by women created a new demography that would ensure future Democratic victories.[31] One of the authors of this book, John Kenneth White, argued that Barack Obama's victories highlight the new demographic terrain outlined by Judis and Teixeira. In 2008 and again in 2012, Obama won overwhelming support from nonwhites, who will comprise the majority of the U.S. population by 2050. Moreover, Obama received strong support from so-called "nontraditional" families (i.e., families comprised of single parents, co-habitating adults, and blended families), as well as religious seculars and single women. These demographic entities are on the rise, and their strong support for Obama suggested that the makings of a new Democratic era could be underway.[32] While these same groups supported Hillary Clinton in 2016, and whites comprised the smallest share of the vote since exit polls began (70 percent white versus 30 percent nonwhite), Donald Trump amassed large margins in rural white communities whose economies had long been in trouble and whose voters had little exposure to college. This gave Trump small, but important, margins of victory in the upper Midwest that allowed him to prevail in the Electoral College, even as Clinton won a large popular vote margin as compared to others who had previously won the popular vote but lost in the Electoral College.

While the debate continues over whether demography is destiny in politics following the 2016 results, the argument that a realignment in favor of the Dem-ocratic Party has been tempered by the results of the 2010 and 2014 midterm elections, in which Republicans won control of the House in 2010 and a Senate majority in 2014. Following the 2014 midterm elections, the Republican con-gressional majorities were the largest since 1928; and the GOP controlled 31 governor's mansions (the most since 1998), and they added an additional 320 state legislators to their ranks—an important number since these state officeholders form a talent bank that both parties draw upon to recruit candidates for higher office.[33] (In 2004, for example, Barack Obama was a member of the Illinois State Senate.) Today, Republicans have majorities in 67 state legislatures, while Dem-ocrats have majorities in just 31.[34] Moreover, in 2016, Republicans won new majorities in the Minnesota and Iowa legislatures, while in Kentucky, Republicans will have a majority for the first time in a century.[35] In 24 states, Republicans control both the state legislatures *and* the governorships, while Democrats have complete control in just six states.[36] David Avella, head of GOPAC, a group that grooms young, legislative candidates, says: "Republicans have been working for this moment for years, to have a federal government with Republican majorities and now at the state level."[37]

These Republican gains suggest that, as with the 1968 realignment, there are limits to any success the Democratic Party enjoyed with the elections of Barack Obama. The future of American politics is unclear at the moment, but what is clear is that the sort of realignment envisioned by Key, Burnham, and others does not appear to be in the offing.

# PARTY REALIGNMENT: THE DEATH OF A CONCEPT?

Despite the attempts of V. O. Key Jr. and Walter Dean Burnham to develop a theory of party realignment (and predict when it would occur), one problem persisted: voters refused to cooperate. During the 1970s and early 1980s, new terms to describe how the electorate was behaving came into vogue. The most common of these was *dealignment*—a term meaning that voters were moving away from both political parties. The widespread belief that parties did not count for much was reflected in public opinion surveys. One 1983 poll found most respondents said there was "no difference" between Democrats and Republicans when it came to reducing crime, stopping the spread of communism, dealing effectively with the Soviet Union, providing quality education, reducing the risk of nuclear war, providing healthcare, reducing waste and inefficiency in government, or protecting the environment.[38] Instead of rooting for their "home team" Democrats or Republicans, voters adopted neutral attitudes toward them. No wonder that more than one quarter of the electorate at the time classified itself as being "independent."

The failure of party realignment to live up to expectations during the Nixon and Reagan eras caused many political scientists to question the concept. In a major critique of party realignment theory entitled "Like Waiting for Godot," Everett C. Ladd maintained that Key and Burnham's emphasis on a party realignment modeled after the New Deal had been "mostly unfortunate."[39] In Ladd's view, the New Deal was a unique period when parties mattered and Franklin D. Roosevelt loomed over the political horizon. Key, Burnham, and other adherents to the party realignment idea grew up during the New Deal era and were shaped by it. Thus, said Ladd, by focusing on whether a party realignment happened in such interesting contests as 1968, 1980, 1992, or 1994, political scientists had been asking the wrong question. Rather than wonder whether each of these elections constituted a party realignment, Ladd suggested that it would be better to ask the following:

♦ What are the major issues and policy differences between the two major parties, and how do these separate political elites and the voting public?
♦ What is the social and ideological makeup of each major party at both the mass and elite levels?
♦ What are the principal features of party organization, nomination procedures, and campaign structure?
♦ In each of the previous three areas, are major shifts currently taking place? What kind? What are their sources?
♦ Overall, how well is the party system performing?[40]

Political scientist David R. Mayhew echoed Ladd's criticism of party realignment theory. In a powerful book titled *Electoral Realignments: A Critique of an American Genre* (2002), Mayhew argued that the application of

realignment theory missed the important context found in many other elections—
including the midterm elections of 1874, which resulted in a Democratic takeover of the House of Representatives; the surprising victory of Harry S. Truman
in 1948 (thanks to a shift within the Democratic Party in favor of civil rights);
and many others. Mayhew tested the assumptions made by realignment advocates
and concluded that they hardly measure up to close scrutiny. Only the New Deal
realignment of the 1930s came close, and that, Mayhew argued, was a unique
moment in U.S. political history.[41]

Ladd and Mayhew's critiques notwithstanding, political scientists still persist
in seeking elections that conform to their understandings of a traditional partisan
realignment. They have done so despite Key's 1955 admonition that "the actual
election rarely presents in pure form a case fitting completely any particular concept."[42] Instead of abandoning realignment, political scientists are busily refur-
bishing the idea. During the Reagan era, John Kenneth White and Richard B.
Wirthlin coined the phrase "rolling realignment" to describe the electoral changes
that were taking place.[43] Building on Key's concept of secular realignment, they
described party realignment as a process involving four distinct stages:

♦ A change in the political agenda. During the 1930s, Americans had a simple
  political agenda: big government works. By 1981, most Americans agreed
  with Ronald Reagan when he declared in his inaugural address, "In this
  present crisis, government is not the solution to our problem. Government is the problem."[44] The Reagan revolution consisted of limiting the
  expansion of federal responsibilities and returning power to state and local
  governments and to the individual.

♦ A change in partisan self-identification as expressed in public opinion polls.
  How one answers the question, "In politics, do you think of yourself as a
  Democrat, Republican, independent, or something else?" is a subjective
  query. When the political agenda changes, one's partisan identification will
  inevitably change as one party or another becomes identified with the new
  political thinking.

♦ Changes in party registration. All states regulate party membership. In some
  places, people must visit a local town hall and formally declare to which
  political party they belong. In other states, voting in a primary is a form of
  party registration. Either way, the commitment to a party involves an overt
  act. Frequently, alterations in party registration are lagging indicators of partisan change. For example, although Ronald Reagan had been campaigning
  for Republicans since 1952, it took him ten years to formally switch his
  California party registration from Democrat to Republican. As the Reagan
  illustration indicates, formal party registration is an imperfect barometer of
  how the electorate thinks about politics at any given moment.

♦ Changes at the bottom of the ballot. Every state ballot lists offices that are
  usually invisible. New Yorkers, for example, elect their local county coro-
  ners; Texans vote for railroad commissioners and judges; in Illinois, state
  university trustees are elected posts. In such races, party identification

means everything, whereas the campaigns of individuals who seek these posts count for little. Thus, when voters place an X next to the names of these obscure candidates, they are expressing a partisan preference. Alterations in the outcomes of these races are suggestive that a party realignment has at last taken place.

The stages White and Wirthlin described were not linear—voters could move back and forth from step to step. But the final result was an inevitable realignment—however slowly and imperfectly that process rolled along. Yet the rolling realignment they envisioned that would help the Republicans failed to materialize. By the time Reagan left office in 1989, Republicans held fewer seats in the House and Senate than they did after Reagan won the presidency in 1980. Moreover, George H. W. Bush suffered a massive rejection at the polls in 1992, winning just 38 percent of the ballots cast. Even after Republicans seized Congress in 1994, GOP identifiers in the public opinion polls failed to increase measurably. In 2000, George W. Bush *lost* the popular vote to Al Gore. And in 2004, Bush was able to muster a bare majority of the popular vote (51 percent) and only 286 electoral votes—this despite the overwhelming public support Bush received following the September 11, 2001, terrorist attacks. Republicans won the presidency once more without the benefit of the popular vote in 2016— meaning Democrats have won the popular vote in every presidential election but one dating back to 1992. Although White and Wirthlin were right to suggest that successive realignments to the New Deal were not going to be the short, sharp reorganizations of party loyalties akin to those of the 1930s, something went awry in the inevitable steps toward a Republican realignment that, however slowly, they believed would follow in Reagan's wake.

The 1994 midterm election gave party realignment theorists new ammunition with its apparent reorganization of voter loyalties—and right on schedule, 26 years after Richard Nixon's 1968 victory. For the first time in 40 years, Republicans won majorities in both houses of Congress, gaining 52 seats in the House and 8 seats in the Senate. Newt Gingrich and his fellow Republicans campaigned on a simple theme—the Contract with America, a document signed by all but four Republican House contenders in a flashy Capitol Hill ceremony. The contract promised that if Republicans won, party leaders would schedule votes during the first 100 days of the new Congress on such issues as term limits, a line-item veto for the president, and a balanced budget amendment (see Chapter 8). Walter Dean Burnham claimed that the 1994 results closely resembled an old-fashioned party realignment, and he challenged his critics to disagree:

Those who have stressed partisan dealignment will now have to consider how this abrupt emergence of something remarkably like an old-fashioned partisan election fits their models. And those who have placed their bets on the argument that critical-realignment analysis is irrelevant to this modern candidate-driven electoral universe will have to reconsider their position.[45]

Still, the debates about party realignment persist. Is realignment, as conceived by Burnham and Key, still possible? Do the Democratic victories in the presidential contests of 2008 and 2012, and their sizable popular vote victory in 2016, herald a long-term change in electoral preferences? Or are they particular to the candidates rather than a reflection of the standing of the parties? And does any of this mean that a new realignment is imminent?

## WHERE ARE THE VOTERS GOING?

Today, the decision as to which political party a voter belongs to is as much about which lifestyle and values they prefer as it is about the particular candidates and issues that surround a given campaign. This has given rise to a "values divide" that became evident in the dramatic 2000 Bush-Gore race and has persisted in every presidential contest held since.[46] In 2000, Democrat Al Gore won strong backing from Democrats, women, African Americans, Latinos, unmarried voters, those who did not attend church services, working women, union members, liberals, gays, those who did not own guns, voters who preferred that abortion be legal in all situations, and those who resided in big cities. George W. Bush got strong support from Republicans, men, whites, voters who were married and had children, those who attended religious services more than once a week, stay-at-home moms, nonunion members, conservatives, heterosexuals, gun owners, those who say abortion should be illegal in all cases, and rural voters. The same patterns have persisted in subsequent presidential elections—despite the fact that the Democrats had different nominees in the personas of John F. Kerry, Barack Obama, and Hillary Clinton—and Republicans had different candidates in the personas of John McCain, Mitt Romney, and Donald Trump.

## THE RISE OF HAMILTONIAN NATIONALISM

Barack Obama entered the presidency in 2009 determined to rise above the partisanship of the George W. Bush years. But his call for an end to excessive partisanship fell on deaf ears. Democrats strongly supported Obama (including the rank and file and members of Congress), while Republicans unified in their opposition to Obama (both inside Washington and in the country at large). Journalist Robert Draper writes that on Inauguration Night 2009, Republican leaders gathered for a dinner on Capitol Hill. Lamenting their fate, these party leaders—including Newt Gingrich and Paul Ryan, and then-Senators Jon Kyl, Jim DeMint, Tom Coburn, John Ensign, and Bob Corker—agreed that Republicans would stick together to unanimously oppose Obama on any policies he proffered. As future House Speaker Paul Ryan put it:"The only way we'll succeed is if we're united. If we tear ourselves apart, we're finished."[47]

The result is not only a more polarized electorate, but stronger national parties. The twenty-first century has given rise to an enhanced Hamiltonian-like party system wherein partisan activities are directed from the top down. Organizational competence—such as the ability to raise money and aid candidates with high-technology services—has become an indicator of party accomplishment. The partisanship exhibited by these organizations is synonymous with the partisanship held by voters. In short, the national parties excel at mobilizing their respective bases and motivating them to vote.

At the same time, this resurgence of a Hamiltonian-like party system has an interesting Jeffersonian twist to it. The Internet has become a partisan device, but unlike the parties whose strong organizations dwarf their state and local counterparts, voters can visit a variety of partisan websites where they can offer their own thoughts and analyses. Moreover, they can even "tweet" their own critiques and analyses on Twitter or post a more detailed analysis on Facebook to anyone and everyone who shares their interests. Thus, the nationalization of party politics from the top down has been accompanied by a strong bottom-up component.

If politics is about "who gets what, when, where, and how," to use political scientist Harold Lasswell's famous phrase, we know what candidates want: votes at election time.[48] With the assistance of new technologies, candidates have found new ways to target and reach out to voters. But these same technologies have also served to strengthen partisan attachments, as evidenced by the natural division of cyberspace into left and right blogospheres. While the debates about party realignment theory (and its various iterations) continue, the fact is that the U.S. electorate is over-caffeinated. Partisanship matters, and the parties' abilities to use the tools of the Internet and mobilize supporters (both inside and outside of Washington, DC), are the subjects of the next three chapters.

# NOTES

1. See James MacGregor Burns, *Roosevelt: The Lion and the Fox* (New York: Harcourt, Brace, 1956), pp. 452–454.

2. Theodore H. White, *The Making of the President, 1960* (New York: Signet Books, 1961), p. 30.

3. Quoted in Jake Tapper, *Down and Dirty: The Plot to Steal the Presidency* (Boston: Little, Brown, 2001), p. 41.

4. Edison Media and Mitofsky International, exit poll, November 8, 2008.

5. Edison Media Research, exit poll, November 6, 2012.

6. Edison Research, exit poll, November 8, 2016.

7. Quoted in Michael E. McGerr, *The Decline of Popular Politics: The American North, 1865–1928* (New York: Oxford University Press, 1986), p. 13.

8. Paul F. Lazarsfeld, Bernard R. Berelson, and Hazel Gaudet, *The People's Choice* (New York: Columbia University Press, 1940).

9. Bernard R. Berelson, Paul F. Lazarsfeld, and William N. McPhee, *Voting* (Chicago: University of Chicago Press, 1948).

10.   Gallup poll, October 9–14, 1952. Text of question: "Which presidential candidate—Stevenson or Eisenhower—do you think could handle the Korean situation best?" Eisenhower, 65 percent; Stevenson, 19 percent; no difference (volunteered), 8 percent; no opinion, 8 percent.

11.   Angus Campbell, Philip E. Converse, Warren E. Miller, and Donald E. Stokes, *The American Voter* (New York: Wiley, 1960).

12.   Ibid., p. 148.

13.   Edison Media Research and Mitofsky International, exit poll, November 4, 2008.

14.   Edison Media Research, exit poll, November 6, 2012.

15.   Edison Research, exit poll, November 8, 2016.

16.   Quinnipiac University Poll, March 22–23, 2010. Text of question: "From what you've heard or read, do you mostly approve or mostly disapprove of the changes to the health care system just passed by Congress?" Mostly approve, 40 percent; mostly disapprove, 49 percent; unsure, 11 percent. Republicans: approve, 9 percent; disapprove, 82 percent; unsure, 9 percent. Democrats: approve, 71 percent; disapprove, 18 percent; unsure, 11 percent. Independents: approve, 36 percent; disapprove, 53 percent; unsure, 11 percent.

17.   Gerald M. Pomper, "Toward a More Responsible Two-Party System? What, Again?" *Journal of Politics* 33 (1971), p. 936.

18.   Norman H. Nie, Sidney Verba, and John R. Petrocik, *The Changing American Voter* (Cambridge, MA: Harvard University Press, 1976).

19.   Anthony Downs, *An Economic Theory of Democracy* (New York: Harper, 1957).

20.   NBC News/*Wall Street Journal*, survey, July 31–August 3, 2016. Text of question: "Generally speaking, do you think of yourself as a Democrat, a Republican, an independent, or something else? (If Democrat or Republican ask:) Would you call yourself a strong (Democrat/Republican) or not a very strong (Democrat/Republican)? (If not sure, ask:) Do you think of yourself as closer to the Republican party, closer to the Democratic party, or do you think of yourself as strictly independent?" Strong Democrat, 25 percent; not very strong Democrat, 8 percent; independent/lean Democrat, 11 percent; strictly independent, 13 percent; independent/lean Republican, 9 percent; not very strong Republican, 8 percent; strong Republican, 19 percent.

21.   Herbert F. Weisberg, "A Multidimensional Conceptualization of Party Identification," in Richard G. Niemi and Herbert F. Weisberg, eds., *Controversies in Voting Behavior*, 2nd ed. (Washington, DC: Congressional Quarterly Press, 1984).

22.   According to the 2016 feeling thermometers, the parties rated as follows: Democrats: very cold, 0–24 degrees, 22 percent; somewhat cold, 25–49 degrees, 12 percent; neutral, 50 degrees, 26 percent; somewhat warm 51–75 degrees, 15 percent; very warm, 76–100 degrees, 23 percent; no answer, 2 percent. Republicans: very cold, 0–24 degrees, 25 percent; somewhat cold, 25–49 degrees, 15 percent; neutral, 50 degrees, 29 percent; somewhat warm, 51–75 degrees, 13 percent; very warm, 76–100 degrees, 16 percent; no answer, 2 percent. Source: Pew Research Center, American Trends Panel poll, March 2–May 9, 2016.

23.   Quoted in Alan Brinkley, *The End of Reform: New Deal Liberalism and War* (New York: Knopf, 1995), p. 16.

24.   "Moving Right Along? Campaign '84's Lessons for 1988: An Interview With Peter Hart and Richard Wirthlin," *Public Opinion* (December/January 1985): p. 8.

25.   Gallup poll, August 3–8, 1951. Text of question: "Suppose a young person just turned 21, asked you what the Republican party (Democratic party) stands for today—what would you tell them?" The number one Republican response, 16 percent, was "for

the privileged few, moneyed interests." The number one Democratic response, 19 percent, was "for the working man, for the public benefit, for the common man."

26. V. O. Key Jr., "A Theory of Critical Elections," *Journal of Politics* 17 (February 1955): pp. 3–18.

27. V. O. Key Jr., "Secular Realignment and the Party System," *Journal of Politics* 21 (May 1959): p. 199.

28. Walter Dean Burnham, *Critical Elections and the Mainsprings of American Politics* (New York: Norton, 1970), p. 10.

29. Kevin P. Phillips, *The Emerging Republican Majority* (New Rochelle, New York: Arlington House, 1969), p. 25.

30. See Karl Rove, *The Triumph of William McKinley: Why the Election of 1896 Still Matters* (New York: Simon and Schuster, 2015).

31. John B. Judis and Ruy Teixeira, *The Emerging Democratic Majority* (New York: Scribner, 2002).

32. See John Kenneth White, *Barack Obama's America: How New Conceptions of Race, Family, and Religion Ended the Reagan Era* (Ann Arbor: University of Michigan Press, 2009); and John Kenneth White, *What Happened to the Republican Party? (And What It Means for Presidential Politics)* (New York: Routledge, 2016). See also Stanley B. Greenberg, *America Ascendant* (New York: Thomas Dunne Books, 2015).

33. Cited in White, *What Happened to the Republican Party?*, p. 118.

34. See John Podhoretz and Noah Rothman, "How Obama Wrecked the Democratic Party," *Commentary Magazine*, November 17, 2016; and Barbara Hollingsworth, "Republicans Now Control Record Number of State Legislative Chambers," CNSNews.com, November 16, 2016.

35. See Podhoretz and Rothman, "How Obama Wrecked the Democratic Party."

36. See Reid Wilson, "Democrats Hit New Low in State Legislatures," *The Hill*, November 18, 2016.

37. Ibid.

38. Yankelovich, Skelly, and White, survey, September 20–22, 1983. Text of question: "Do you feel that the Democratic party or the Republican party can do a better job of handling. . . or don't you think there is any real difference between them?" The "no difference" results were as follows: reducing crime, 58 percent; stopping the spread of communism, 52 percent; dealing effectively with the U.S.S.R., 48 percent; providing quality education, 47 percent; reducing the risk of nuclear war, 46 percent; providing health care, 46 percent; reducing waste and inefficiency in government, 45 percent; protecting the environment, 45 percent.

39. Everett C. Ladd, "Like Waiting for Godot: The Uselessness of Realignment for Understanding Change in Contemporary American Politics," *Polity* XXII, no. 3 (Spring 1990): p. 512.

40. Ibid., p. 518.

41. See David R. Mayhew, *Electoral Realignments: A Critique of an American Genre* (New Haven, CT: Yale University Press, 2002), passim.

42. Key, "A Theory of Critical Elections," pp. 16–17.

43. See John Kenneth White, "Partisanship in the 1984 Presidential Election: The Rolling Republican Realignment," paper prepared for the 1985 Annual Meeting of the Southwestern Political Science Association, March 20–23, 1985, Houston, Texas.

44.  Ronald Reagan, Inaugural Address, Washington, DC, January 20, 1981.

45.  Walter Dean Burnham, "Realignment Lives: The 1994 Earthquake and Its Implications," in Colin Campbell and Bert A. Rockman, eds., *The Clinton Presidency: First Appraisals* (Chatham, NJ: Chatham House, 1996), p. 370.

46.  For more on this, see John Kenneth White, *The Values Divide: American Politics and Culture in Transition* (Washington, DC: Congressional Quarterly Press, 2003).

47.  Quoted in Robert Draper, *Do Not Ask What Good We Do* (New York: Free Press, 2012), p. xviii.

48.  Harold D. Lasswell, *Politics: Who Gets What, When, How* (New York: Meridian Books, 1958).

# 6

## Parties and Social Media

Had Donald Trump run for president in 2004, he would have been without his most potent media weapon. Throughout the 2016 campaign, Trump masterfully drew attention to himself through the use of Twitter, sending his unfiltered thoughts to followers and driving the traditional news agenda with the help of reporters who couldn't resist discussing the latest outrageous thing he said. Sometimes his tweeting got him in genuine trouble, as when he responded to Hillary Clinton's allegation that he had mistreated former Miss Universe Alicia Machado with an overnight Twitter explosion, where he ranted about Machado's appearance and incorrectly asserted that she had made a "sex tape."[1] In the final days of the campaign, Trump's advisors kept the candidate off Twitter to avoid unwelcome surprises.[2] But for his ability to make others respond to him on his terms, Trump's use of social media was as brilliant as it was unprecedented. The reality television host understood how to leverage millions of followers and the unparalleled visibility of a presidential race to maximum advantage.

In keeping with the candidate-centered nature of contemporary campaigns, Trump's use of social media was entirely personal. Twitter gave Trump freedom from the institutional constraints sometimes exercised by parties or the media by making him a free agent with respect to the Republican Party and a gatekeeper with equal power to journalists. If his campaign had a messaging strategy, it was executed by the candidate at the rate of 140 characters at a time, not by political professionals. He understood that social media rewards outrageous claims, and he had no problem playing to the norms of Twitter in defiance of long-established norms of what presidential candidates would say. Although this often brought him condemnation from his opponent, it enabled him to set the terms of the election whenever Hillary Clinton found herself reacting to the latest Trump tweet rather than advancing a vision for her presidency. Journalists found these Twitter eruptions and their fallout irresistible, knowing their viewers and readers would follow them like the latest installment of a reality TV show.

Donald Trump's Twitter campaign was the latest in a rapidly changing media environment that has left candidates and parties struggling to figure out how to maximize the political potential of the Internet and keep up with its changing scope and shape. His social media efforts represent the opportunities afforded by the Internet to candidates interested in running without the backing of traditional parties. At the other end of the Internet spectrum is a highly developed set of online institutions created by parties and social action groups, which have worked largely to the benefit of the political left. Together, they define the parameters of new media and politics. Notwithstanding President Trump's proficiency with social media, the left has built an impressive online organizational presence that it has mobilized to push the Democratic Party in a progressive direction and, in the Trump era, serves as a basis for political resistance.

## DEAN UNLOCKS THE GENIE

Just as Republicans proved adept at harnessing the power of television advertising in the 1950s and direct mail and cable technology in the 1980s, they took an early lead over Democrats in the use of the Internet in the 1990s. By the end of the first decade of the twenty-first century, however, Democrats and their allies on the left had emerged as more skillful practitioners of Internet politics.

During the 1996 election season, the RNC home page received 75,000 hits a day—a meager number by contemporary standards but a huge figure back then. Republicans used the Internet to broadcast immediate responses to Bill Clinton's State of the Union address in 1997, and the RNC chair held regular online chats. By 2000, the GOP site boasted numerous links to facilitate making financial contributions, fact finding on policy topics, buying GOP-related products, and—significantly—enabling rudimentary grassroots email efforts by ordinary users. The site was regarded as so substantive that it was dubbed "Best Party Site" by *Campaign and Elections* magazine. That publication noted:

> The RNC gave its all into an "e-campaign" this year, not only creating a meaty, updated home page for interested Republicans but by an effective use of banner advertisements on outside sites. The RNC also led a successful grassroots email campaign, collecting around 935,000 addresses. Larry

Purpuro, the RNC's deputy chief of staff who led the "e-GOP" efforts, likes to point out that the RNC had 32,000 "email activists" in Florida, where Texas Gov. George W. Bush won the election with little to spare.[3]

By 2002, the RNC had spent some $60,000 to create gopteamleader.com, designed to give nearly 100,000 activists information on how to contact radio stations and newspapers to disseminate Republican views on a range of issues. The site also offered incentives, such as mouse pads and fleece pullovers, for users who completed "action items" listed on the site. Points were awarded, for example, for recruiting GOP activists or for emailing members of Congress to support Republican initiatives.[4]

Once again, Democrats found themselves playing catchup. In 1996, the DNC's website received only 50,000 hits per day. One year later, the DNC updated its home page to include a user survey, volunteer sign-up sheet, and a help page that downloaded voter registration forms from the Federal Election Commission. By 2002, visitors could access daily news briefings and links to other state and local Democratic Party organizations, and even take a chance at winning $1,000 for the most creative flash animation. Taking a cue from Republicans, they turned to the Internet to organize rudimentary grassroots efforts on their website, democrats.org.[5] But the Internet didn't emerge as a contemporary political force or reveal its potential for grassroots mobilization until an obscure former Vermont governor named Howard Dean came out of nowhere on the strength of an Internet campaign to become the frontrunner for the 2004 Democratic presidential nomination.

Howard Dean did not set out to run the first national Internet campaign. In fact, he wasn't particularly proficient with computers when he and a small group of supporters set up a small office in Burlington, Vermont, for what would have to be considered the longest of long-shot presidential campaigns. It would be more accurate to say that Dean's Internet supporters found the candidate rather than the other way around.

Dean was an opinionated politician who was not afraid to challenge his party's orthodoxy, and his outspokenness contributed significantly to his online appeal. At the Democratic National Committee's Winter Meeting in February 2003, Dean appeared with other Democrats vying to challenge President George W. Bush the following year. Where the others made safe political speeches, Dean used the opportunity to appear before party activists to give voice to what many in the room were likely thinking or saying privately to one another about how Democrats had been approaching the Bush administration and its economic and military policies. "What I want to know," a full-throated Dean told his audience, "is why in the world the Democratic Party is supporting the president's unilateral attack on Iraq." He continued:

> What I want to know is why are Democratic Party leaders supporting tax cuts. . . . What I want to know is why we're fighting in Congress about the Patient's Bill of Rights when the Democratic Party ought to be standing

up for health care for every single American man, woman, and child in this country. What I want to know is why our folks are voting for the president's No Child Left Behind bill that leaves every child behind, every teacher behind, every school board behind, and every property tax payer behind. I'm Howard Dean, and I'm here to represent the Democratic wing of the Democratic Party.[6]

Dean's remarks struck a nerve with the audience and reverberated beyond the party gathering. For disenchanted liberals, Dean offered something new: a Democrat not afraid to take on his party in full view of key party figures. All they needed was a way to find each other and express their support, and the Internet provided them with a vehicle. The venue was as unlikely as the candidate himself: Meetup.com, a non-political site designed to unite people with common interests. The concept was simple: type in the activity you're interested in and your zip code, and the website returned a date and time for like-minded others to meet in the real world and discuss their common interest. By making it possible for disparate people with the same concerns to find each other and facilitate in-person meetings, Meetup.com coincidentally addressed the initial organizational problem faced by supporters of an obscure candidate, and soon after Dean's DNC address, "Howard Dean" rapidly became a prominent meet-up category (Dean would eventually become the most requested meet-up topic, surpassing the previous record holder, witches).[7]

The Dean meet-up effort expanded exponentially in the spring and summer of 2003, and the candidate's small staff struggled to remain one step ahead of what their supporters were building. Working around the clock, they launched the weblog "Blog for America" in March to serve as a nerve center for the blossoming online campaign.[8] The blog provided a way for the Burlington staff to keep supporters apprised about what they were doing, but more importantly, it gave supporters a way to connect with each other and self-organize. Blog for America hosted diary and comment features, permitting supporters to initiate their own topics and respond to what others were writing. And respond they did—to everything ranging from policy ideas to the candidate's polling numbers to how the mainstream media was covering their candidate to ideas for political action they could take on behalf of the campaign.[9] At its peak, hundreds of thousands of ordinary supporters had taken it upon themselves to engage in Internet-based campaigning on behalf of Dean, creating a citizen army that multiplied the efforts of the candidate's staff and propelled the Vermont governor to frontrunner status weeks before the 2004 Iowa caucus.[10]

They also raised money in unprecedented amounts and in an entirely new way—through small-dollar contributions made by ordinary citizens who responded to the candidate's online pitch for cash. As a sign of their level of investment in the candidate and in what would have to be considered a campaign manager's dream, Dean's online activist core asked and at times *begged* the campaign to ask *them* to contribute money. The campaign had developed a convention whereby they would post a baseball bat icon on the blog whenever they wanted to raise funds, and fill the bat in with red ink proportional to the percentage of the goal they had achieved. After a while, some blog readers began asking the campaign to "put up a bat" to raise money off an achievement like strong polling numbers or a particularly impressive public performance by their candidate. When blog readers believed they were being invaded by a "troll"—someone supporting an opposing campaign who masquerades as an online community member in order to stir up trouble in comment threads— supporters would respond by trying to raise money for the campaign in the troll's name (they called it a "troll goal"), thereby undermining the troll's subversive purpose.[11]

Despite these virtues, Internet activism came with risks to the campaign's leadership. Giving supporters the means to mobilize on behalf of Howard Dean also meant relinquishing control over their actions while having to take responsibility for anything done or said in the candidate's name. If a supporter said something off-message or did something embarrassing that was caught on video, the campaign organization would have to address it. Furthermore, the rapid acceleration of Dean's online movement outpaced the campaign's ability to hire and train full-time staff, leaving Dean's staff exhausted and always trying to keep pace with its Internet growth.[12] These factors combined to make Dean's Internet supporters both a necessary blessing and a source of constant strain as they powered his drive toward the nomination, even as they unintentionally threatened to swallow it.

For much of 2003, the Dean campaign was a phenomenon and the talk of the political world. Few could remember the last time a candidate had bolted from obscurity to the doorstep of a major-party presidential nomination. High-profile competitors like John Kerry and Joe Lieberman and their seasoned Washington advisors watched the Dean juggernaut with a mixture of envy, anger, and dread, trying to understand what Dean was doing and figure out how to stop it. Because no one had ever succeeded at this level on the strength of new media, many conventional political advisors were baffled. "Other than raising money, the [other] campaigns generally continued to treat the Internet like a TV with keys," wrote Dean campaign manager Joe Trippi, "and ignored the ways that this technology actually invites people to be involved, rather than just throwing pictures and slogans at them in the hope they donate money."[13]

Ultimately, Dean's opponents resorted to traditional political methods—a withering television advertising attack on the frontrunner—to undermine his campaign. Dean experienced the limitations of Internet politics as well. As the primary season approached, the once-exponential growth in his supporters flattened considerably, in part a reflection of the limited reach of high-speed Internet access in 2003. For all its novelty, the Dean campaign still had to reach voters through traditional means, and the candidate who was a folk hero online had difficulty communicating on television. As a result, Dean was unable to withstand the assault waged by his opponents, and finished a distant third in Iowa when just weeks before he was favored to win. His fate was sealed when he addressed his supporters with a loud yelp of support designed to lift their spirits that made the candidate appear unhinged on camera. Video of the moment went viral on the

Internet overnight; in an ironic twist, the medium that made the Dean campaign possible had helped bury it.

Although Dean had failed, something new had happened that turned traditional campaigning on its head. Ever since party reforms turned presidential campaigns into candidate-centered affairs with the rise of primaries and concomitant decline in the influence of party elites, ingenious long-shot candidates like Jimmy Carter had occasionally succeeded in upending more seasoned opponents. But no one had ever done it like Howard Dean, on the strength of bottom-up political fund-raising and citizen-initiated organizing channeled through the Internet. It set the stage four years later for a more advanced Internet effort by another long-shot candidate, Barack Obama. And it heralded the rise of the political influence of online blogs and organizations, which would self-organize in a manner similar to the Dean campaign and challenge the autonomy of the two parties from without.

## OBAMA SETS THE STANDARD

During the 2008 presidential campaign, Republican vice presidential nominee Sarah Palin mocked Barack Obama for having been a community organizer. It turned out that Obama's knowledge of bottom-up organizing meshed perfectly with the advantages of Internet politics, enabling him to leverage the medium to identify and mobilize millions of new voters en route to the first successful Internet-fueled presidential victory.

Like Dean, Obama was a relative newcomer to national politics, having emerged from obscurity in 2004 when he gave the keynote address at the Democratic National Convention while still an Illinois state senator. That speech showcased Obama's oratorical abilities and thrust him into the national spotlight, where he continued to shine after he was elected to the U.S. Senate in November 2004. Although this gave Obama a larger platform than serving as the governor of a small, obscure state, he was hardly in a commanding position to challenge his party's presidential frontrunner for the 2008 nomination—especially when that frontrunner was senator and former first lady Hillary Rodham Clinton.

Obama entered the campaign with a host of disadvantages that in an earlier time would have been fatal to his hopes. He had neither the money nor the likelihood of raising the sums of money that Clinton could command by virtue of a network built over decades in politics. Similarly, he lacked the extensive number of political IOUs amassed by his opponent, who built an impressive list of early endorsements from Democratic officials who were either loyal or obligated to her or her husband from their days in the Clinton White House. Where Hillary Clinton enjoyed universal name recognition and a double-digit lead in early national polls, Obama struggled to establish sufficient public support to be taken seriously by reporters as a credible challenger. And, while Clinton battled monumental barriers in her quest to be elected the first female president, Obama confronted long-standing racial prejudices compounded by a thin national resume. He had to convince voters that an African American candidate could be elected president while fending off charges from his critics that he was too inexperienced to serve in the office.

Obama's shrewd understanding and skillful manipulation of the Internet served as a critical counterweight to these disadvantages, generating unprecedented amounts of money while identifying and mobilizing millions of voters. Like Dean before him, Obama excelled at building an online presence that encouraged his partisans to form an army of supporters to campaign in his name. But, unlike Dean, the Obama online effort struck an effective balance between centralized control and decentralized activism, making it more manageable and ultimately more successful. Benefitting from a more advanced Internet that reached more people and a campaign team that had learned from Dean's successes and failures, Obama blended traditional candidate-centered, television-based campaigning with a powerful Internet operation that proved effective enough to topple the Democratic Party's biggest name and go on to capture the presidency.

Obama sought to avoid the pitfalls that dogged the Dean campaign without extinguishing his supporters' enthusiasm and initiative. The effort required finding the right combination of empowerment and control, balancing a campaign's need for top-down coordination with the decentralization necessary to take advantage of the Internet's social networking capabilities. The engine running this effort was Obama for America (OFA), a state-of-the-art website offering a host of online tools through which supporters could customize their contribution to the campaign without the risk that their actions would run the campaign off the rails.

Where the Dean campaign outsourced its networking through Meetup.com, Obama's website integrated social networking tools. An icon labeled "Make a Difference" directed users to a campaign event finder and a tool for making calls to voters in competitive states. A "Take Action Now" icon served the interests of supporters who wanted to email friends or strangers to share positive impressions of the candidate. Through MyBO (pronounced "my boh" and standing for "my Barack Obama"), supporters could customize their web presence and participate in the campaign's version of Facebook—or link directly to Obama's actual Facebook page. On MyBO, users could establish a profile, write their own campaign blog, comment on the blog posts of others, find other Obama supporters in their zip code, and identify and join local Obama groups with people who had similar interests, ranging from Veterans for Obama to Environmentalists for Obama.[14] As the *Washington Post* noted, the Obama campaign made sure it had a presence anywhere you could find possible supporters:

> Obama was the first candidate to have profiles on AsianAve. com, MiGente. com and BlackPlanet.com, social networking sites (a.k.a. socnets) targeting the Asian, Latino and black communities. His presence on BlackPlanet,

which ranks behind MySpace and Facebook in terms of traffic, is so deep that he maintains 50 profiles, one for each state. On ALforObama, his Alabama page on BlackPlanet, for example, supporters can read an updated blog, watch YouTube videos and learn more about his text program. It's difficult to measure the value of these socnets in persuading voters to choose Obama. What's clear, however, is that online networking—how supporters communicate with one another within their online communities—has its advantages. A Facebook group called Students for Barack Obama, started in July 2006 by Bowdoin College student Meredith Segal, was so successful that it became an official part of the campaign.[15]

This organizational structure liberated Obama from relying on local party operatives to perform the fieldwork for primary and caucus challenges, enabling him to build his own organizational structure from the ground up with the help of volunteers who came to the campaign through the Internet. The same held true for the campaign's sophisticated turnout operation, which funneled responsibility for identifying and mobilizing voters to low-level volunteers operating within a highly differentiated organizational structure, balancing the freedom of supporters to self-motivate with traditional elements of campaign command-and-control. The Obama campaign made the unprecedented decision to share its turnout goals—considered confidential by campaigns worried about underperforming—with volunteers, who in turn felt empowered by the campaign's decision to entrust them with getting voters to the polls. "If we tell a team leader that the vote goal for this neighborhood is 100 votes," said one of the campaign's state directors, "and we give them a list with 300 names of supporters and persuadable voters on it, they respond with, 'Wow, I can make this happen.'"[16]

After he was elected president and became de facto head of the national Democratic Party, Obama retooled his website and folded it into the everyday operation of the DNC, as we mentioned in Chapter 3. This signaled his intention to keep a social networking presence alive during his presidency while remaking the party in the image of his successful Internet model. Rechristened Organizing for America, OFA worked alongside the administration from its new home inside Democratic National Committee headquarters in Washington to build support for key Obama initiatives, notably the healthcare reform effort that dominated politics in 2009. As the 2010 congressional midterm elections drew near, OFA went to work on behalf of congressional Democrats, applying social networking tools to mobilize first-time voters who were inspired by Obama in 2008, gambling that Obama's bottom-up mobilization approach would work without the president's presence on the ballot. The results were not good. Facing a strong headwind in the form of a poor economy and widespread anger from swing voters who felt the administration had over-reached and overspent, OFA was unable to mobilize the 2008 electorate that put Obama in office, and Democrats suffered historic losses in congressional and state contests.

# THE NETROOTS CHALLENGE DEMOCRATS

Advances in the availability of high-speed Internet access during the first decade of the twenty-first century facilitated the growth of a virtual space where ordinary people could engage in political discourse, venting about things they did not like and planning to take action to change them. As like-minded individuals on the left and right began publishing political blogs, and as a few of these blogs developed into sizable virtual communities, a political blogosphere took shape. Reflecting deeply held partisan feelings on both sides, bloggers on the left would link to each other with abandon while generally refusing to link to bloggers on the right in order to avoid giving them additional traffic that would inflate the size of their community. Bloggers on the right reciprocated, generally refusing to link to liberal blogs. As a result, two distinct hemispheres evolved in political cyberspace: a conservative or "right blogosphere" and a progressive or "left blogosphere."

Although they emerged simultaneously, they differed in size and structure. Like the Republican Party, conservatives were first to establish a notable presence in cyberspace; in the years immediately following the turn of the century, the largest and most active blog communities were on the right[17]; as with previous technological innovations, the left found itself playing catchup. However, animated by opposition to the Iraq War in particular and the Bush Administration in general, a vital left blogosphere took shape by 2005, and between 2003 and 2005, a period when overall political blog traffic increased sixfold, progressive online sites increased their traffic at a much sharper rate than comparable conservative sites.[18]

Moreover, the left blogosphere was developing in a horizontal fashion suitable to taking advantage of the social networking capabilities of the Internet. Toward the end of the first decade of the century, the top blogs of the left were all community blogs, meaning they permitted ordinary users to post original ideas in diaries rather than restricting that function to "front page" bloggers formally affiliated with the sites, and allowed people to post comments about blog posts, diaries, and even the comments of other users.[19] This facilitated virtual discussions in "comment threads" where people could respond to the ideas of others. On the left blog with the largest readership, Daily Kos, it is commonplace to find threads with hundreds of comments, reflecting the size and level of engagement of that online community.

Over time, this structure birthed a movement, which self-consciously modeled itself on the twentieth-century reform-minded Progressives we discussed in Chapter 3. Emerging online from the grassroots, the progressive "netroots" (or "Internet grassroots") movement came to life via the left (or progressive) blogosphere. Structurally, the netroots encompass a web of national, state, local, and issue-oriented blogs, along with like-minded progressive organizations with a strong web presence, like MoveOn.org (which formed to oppose Republican efforts to impeach Bill Clinton during the modern Internet's infancy in the late 1990s), Act Blue (a website for directing small-dollar campaign contributions to progressive candidates), and Democracy for America (an online organization devoted to identifying, recruiting, and funding progressive candidates that grew out of the Dean campaign). In keeping with the horizontal structure of the netroots, they developed as the organic product of many people using the Internet to work toward a shared set of goals,[20] and by linking to each other, these sites enhanced each other's visibility and effectiveness. In recent years, the progressive netroots have become more centralized and coordinated, as first-generation organizations matured into professionalized institutions with paid staff and consultants working on behalf of online progressive advocacy groups.[21] But they originated with the uncoordinated efforts of people with an activist bent at a time when it was easy for them to establish their presence on the Internet.

The right blogosphere emerged differently, owing in part to the existence of a long-standing conservative movement operating within and outside the Republican Party. From elected Republicans to conservative think tanks, talk radio, and other media outlets, conservatives had fashioned over time an idea and messaging apparatus that operated with great efficiency and effectiveness. The right blogosphere developed within this vertically organized structure, offering conservatives a new outlet for messaging and maintaining interest among the faithful. However, the hierarchical structure of the existing conservative movement had the effect of limiting the development of community blogs on the right, restricting the emergence of new voices, and limiting the number of venues where many voices would gather to argue and debate as in a virtual town hall.[22] Consequently, the preeminent ideas expressed in the right blogosphere typically mirrored those expressed by Republican politicians.

Not so for the netroots. As a movement that developed online without mainstream party support, netroots progressives often find themselves at odds with elected Democrats. Animated by challenges to corporate influences they feel tip the political balance of power away from ordinary citizens, netroots activists have shown themselves willing to take on the Democratic Party whenever they feel it tilts too heavily toward the interests of the privileged, to the point of recruiting and raising funds for primary challenges to Democrats who otherwise would not feel the heat of accountability to progressive interests. During the 2006 election cycle, the netroots channeled their organizing and fund-raising toward winning a Democratic majority in the House and Senate, but once that objective was realized, their attention shifted to pushing Congress in a progressive direction by supporting "better Democrats" over incumbents, who in their view worry more about what others in Washington think about them than the concerns of progressive voters. Daily Kos founder Markos Moulitsas put it this way in a blog post in 2007:

> Too many bad Democrats in DC don't feel they need to fulfill campaign promises on Iraq and other national priorities. They don't care about you or their constituents. They are more concerned about what [*Time* magazine columnist] Joe Klein and George Bush think. They are afraid of Republicans, but figure they can take you for granted. What are you going to do, vote

for Republicans? They know we don't have that option. Are we going to withhold our money? The lobbyists will be more than happy to pick up the slack. We're going to call them, or email them, or write them? Their staff can deal with those inconveniences.

What we CAN do is to threaten their jobs. And you do that with primary challenges. We've seen how good [Democratic representative] Jane Harman became after hers, and how merely a threat of a primary challenge to [Representative] Ellen Tauscher whipped her into proper shape. That's the *only* tool we have to keep our caucus accountable. So it's important we win these races, to send a message that we don't just threaten, but can actually deliver real pain. And the more successful we are, the more challengers we'll have to bad Democrats in 2010, and we can continue on this long and arduous path toward a more responsive and accountable Democratic Party.[23]

In recent years, the netroots have proved to be a factor in Democratic primary contests, occasionally inflicting the "pain" Moulitsas addressed. In 2009, they emerged on the victorious side of a challenge to Senator Arlen Specter of Pennsylvania by a netroots favorite, Representative Joseph Sestak (whose election to the House in 2006 was supported by netroots efforts, and who went on to lose a close general election contest to Republican Pat Toomey). Specter, a former moderate Republican who had switched parties the previous year to avoid a difficult primary challenge from his right by Toomey, enjoyed widespread institutional support, including the DNC and the Obama administration.

That same year, the netroots failed to unseat their number one target, Arkansas senator Blanche Lincoln, although their candidate, Arkansas Lieutenant Governor Bill Halter, kept the incumbent below 50 percent of the primary vote, forcing a runoff that he narrowly lost. Lincoln provoked the ire of progressives by opposing a public healthcare option and for opposing strong climate change and financial reform legislation because, in the view of the netroots, she was beholden to large corporate interests for her campaign funds. These positions had done nothing to improve her position with general election voters, and she fared poorly in polling match-ups with all Republican comers. Netroots activists felt she would make a good test case for their opposition to "corporate Democrats" in that they felt if she lost the primary, the Democratic Party would be in *better* shape to hold the Arkansas seat.

In their efforts to unseat Lincoln, they were opposed by an array of powerful forces, including the U.S. Chamber of Commerce, the White House, and Arkansas' favorite son, Bill Clinton. Even though these forces proved too strong to get Halter over the finish line, the netroots, in defeat, realized an important policy achievement. Joan McCarter, writing at Daily Kos, explained that

The repercussions of Blanche Lincoln's hotly contested primary are playing out in the Wall Street reform effort in a complex and potentially massive way. Because of Bill Halter's challenge, Lincoln proposed—and passed in her Ag[riculture] committee—a very tough derivatives reform package. So tough, in fact, that it has strong opposition from the White House and from key Senate Dems. But, they can't strip it now, because it's too important for Lincoln to use in her primary.[24]

Throughout the progressive blogosphere, the stronger Wall Street reform package—one of the netroots' key legislative objectives—was a sign of vindication for their strategy of running Halter against Lincoln, coming as it did at the hands of one of their most disliked Democrats. "It's very possible," blogged McCarter, "that we'll have Bill Halter to thank for a tough Wall Street reform bill."[25]

One of the ironies of these efforts is how they came at the expense of a Democratic president who owed his election victory to a sophisticated understanding of Internet politics. In Pennsylvania and Arkansas, President Obama was on the other side of the fight, supporting the incumbent against a netroots-endorsed challenger. This rift owes more to the inside-outside dynamic separating the Washington political establishment from the netroots than to an appreciation of how to use the Internet as a political tool.

As party leader, it was Obama's responsibility to protect the Democratic congressional majorities he inherited when he was elected in 2008. Given the high rate of incumbent reelection over time, the path of least resistance to maintaining that majority would ordinarily be to discourage primaries that, if successful, create open seats that the party would have to defend without the advantages of incumbency. From the president's perspective, stumping for Democratic incumbents was in the best interest of the party. It is also a given in Washington that members of the same party will work for mutual political self-preservation. When Arlen Specter switched sides, he temporarily gave Democrats a 60-seat Senate supermajority, enough to block Republican filibusters should Democrats vote in concert. It was not surprising that Obama would want to reward that effort with his political support.

However, bloggers and activists on the political left do not see things this way. Instead, they believe that a candidate who is not hamstrung by corporate obligations and who is therefore free to campaign on behalf of middle-and working-class interests will always do better on Election Day, even if that candidate lacks the track record, name recognition, and fund-raising capability of an incumbent. They regard blind support for incumbents as counterproductive to maintaining congressional majorities, believing that select open-seat challenges can have a better chance of success, despite the aggregate odds favoring incumbents. And they believe that having more such candidates in Congress would work to strengthen the long-term political prospects of the Democratic Party. These strategic differences put them at odds with many party regulars, including, at times, President Obama.

Differences between mainstream Democrats and netroots activists extended beyond campaigning to legislating. Nowhere was this more evident than during the long campaign to enact healthcare reform in 2009 and 2010, when an online push for reform often clashed with administration efforts, and bloggers who had supported Barack Obama's election found themselves deeply at odds with his governing approach.

Netroots engagement in the healthcare policy debate was impressive and demonstrated that Internet-based organizing could be applied to policymaking. Their objective was to secure passage of healthcare reform with a strong public component—initially a single-payer plan, then, when the administration took this option off the table, a plan with a strong government component, like a public insurance option or wider accessibility to Medicare. As progressives, they believed that private, for-profit insurance operated to the benefit of insurance companies first, the public second, and they felt that government was the only institution that could effectively address these perceived inequities.

A sophisticated inside-outside strategy developed online through the network of progressive sites that had previously engaged in political action. Working on the inside, the netroots partnered with the congressional progressive caucus, a large but—in the view of netroots activists—generally ineffectual group that tended to give in to more conservative Democrats. Led by several bloggers who rose to the forefront, but supported by a large network of less-visible individuals connected online, they coordinated strategy with congressional progressives while simultaneously pressuring them to hold the line on progressive objectives. This included cajoling progressive Democrats to publicly pledge to reject legislation that did not include a public healthcare plan, and keeping a "whip count" of who was on board and who was not, akin to how the House or Senate Democratic whip would keep track of his caucus. Simultaneously operating from the outside, they used their online resources to raise money for Democrats who supported a public option while organizing against sending progressive dollars to those who did not, utilized online social networking tools to keep the pressure on wavering Democrats, and even threatened progressive primary opponents to wavering Democrats in safe districts who might be successfully opposed from the left.[26]

Their chief opposition came from the White House, where President Obama was fixed on getting Congress to pass healthcare legislation, whether or not it met progressive goals. To this end, the White House launched its own Internet campaign, engaging Organizing for America through its perch at the Democratic National Committee to stimulate some of the people who had participated in Obama's online campaign to work for passage of healthcare legislation. Unlike the campaign, however, and in sharp contrast to the horizontally organized netroots, the White House effort was top-down, with the administration asking people to go to the OFA website and lobby Congress to pass healthcare legislation. By the numbers, the results of their efforts were impressive: mobilizing volunteers in every congressional district, with 2.2 million supporters working for passage; over 1.5 million testimonials of support for Obama's priorities; over 230,000 letters submitted to newspaper editors; over 238,000 personal healthcare stories shared online.[27] The dilemma, as netroots activists were quick to point out, is that the president was intentionally vague on exactly what his priorities were.

While never closing the door to a public option, Obama also never pushed for one. Working on a highly complex piece of legislation in a difficult political climate—the longer congressional debate dragged on, the less popular healthcare reform became—required maximum flexibility. The lack of responsible parties and the sometimes divergent political interests between the president and some members of his own congressional caucus made it difficult for the president to shepherd the legislation through the political process without making compromises and adjustments. Billions of dollars were at stake, and those who stood to lose money lobbied strongly to members of the president's party to have their interests represented. Against this backdrop, Obama's Internet effort amounted to an additional source of pressure to keep the reform process moving forward and counterbalance those forces that might pull it apart, but—unlike the netroots' efforts and in contrast to Obama's Internet election campaign—it was not a grassroots movement designed to accomplish an objective any more specific than passage of some form of healthcare legislation. That meant it was not specifically a progressive effort, differentiating and putting it at odds with netroots goals.[28]

Ironically, the netroots at times were one of the forces threatening to undermine the process, particularly when an eleventh-hour Senate deal to expand Medicare eligibility fell apart. For a brief moment, the netroots were divided between those who wanted to scrap healthcare policy and start from scratch, and those who wanted to take what they could get, even though it fell short of what they wanted. Ultimately, most netroots voices expressed support for the bill that eventually passed, with the caveat that it was simply a first step as they continued to push the Democratic Party and a Democratic president in a progressive direction.

# THE "TEA PARTY" CHALLENGES REPUBLICANS

Although sometimes equated in the press with netroots progressives for their mirror-image political objectives, "Tea Party" conservatives—who emerged as a visible force during the healthcare debate—are not exclusively an online movement. Several websites lay claim to a version of the Tea Party name and claim to be home to the movement, including Tea Party Patriots (teapartypatriots.com) and Tea Party Nation (teapartynation.com). These sites, like their counterparts on the left, include discussion forums, provide action alerts and information on movement activities, and house blogs with discussion threads. Unlike the netroots, however, some groups flying the Tea Party banner have Washington connections, like FreedomWorks, a group run by former Republican House majority leader Dick Armey, which funded and organized a Tea Party march on Washington in 2009.[29]

Where netroots activists work to reduce corporate influences in the Democratic Party as they pursue progressive legislation, Tea Party activists have emerged as an ideologically conservative influence on mainstream Republicans. In a brief time, they have made their mark on electoral politics, advancing a brand of libertarian conservatism that challenges the constitutionality of all but the most essential activities of the federal government, condemns deficit spending and high taxes, and rejected Obama administration efforts to expand the government's role in healthcare and energy policy.

Like the progressive netroots, Tea Party candidates have targeted wayward incumbents for defeat, and with visible success. Notable among these is Senator Bob Bennett of Utah, a reliably conservative Republican who was defeated in his bid for renomination to a fourth term at the 2010 Utah Republican Party Convention because of Tea Party opposition and a $200,000 advertising and mail campaign directed against him by the Club for Growth, a conservative Washington-based organization. Bennett's adversaries accused him of being insufficiently conservative; for his part, the senator expressed the sentiment that his problem was less about ideology and more about his willingness to strike a conciliatory tone with his colleagues across the aisle.[30]

In Florida, Republican Governor Charlie Crist was the de facto incumbent for an open Senate seat in that state in early 2010. Popular with Democrats and sporting high overall approval ratings, Crist looked ready to sail to victory in the Republican primary against Marco Rubio, a former Florida House Speaker who had enthusiastic Tea Party backing. As Rubio hammered away at Crist for being too moderate, his standing among Republican voters shot up at the expense of his better-known opponent. Crist had welcomed President Obama to Florida with a hug in early 2009, and the gesture—caught on video that circulated on the Internet—served as a symbolic reminder to conservative voters of the governor's larger transgressions, such as his support for the $787 billion federal stimulus package that helped ignite Tea Party anger.[31] By the spring of 2010, Crist's once commanding lead in the Republican primary had collapsed, and he chose to withdraw from the race, leave his party, and run (unsuccessfully) as an independent candidate in a three-way race against the eventual victor Rubio and Democrat Kendrick Meek.[32] Doing so meant foregoing all party support, a huge challenge for a statewide candidate. But it also liberated Crist to move leftward to appeal to moderate voters and Democrats who gave him high job-approval ratings as governor, raising the possibility that Crist would have caucused with Senate Democrats had he been elected.

In other high-profile primary contests, Tea Party–backed candidates upset candidates who normally had the decisive backing of national Republican Party officials. In Kentucky, Senator Mitch McConnell, the powerful Senate Republican leader, was backing Secretary of State Trey Grayson in the race for his party's nomination for an open U.S. Senate seat in McConnell's home state. Ordinarily, having the support of a powerful party figure like McConnell would be sufficient to make Grayson the prohibitive favorite in his party's primary. But Grayson was opposed by Tea Party favorite Rand Paul, son of libertarian Republican representative Ron Paul, who generated a small but intense online following during his 2008 quest for the Republican presidential nomination. The primary results were stunning: Paul, an ophthalmologist with no previous political experience, handily defeated McConnell's hand-picked candidate by a wide margin.[33]

In Nevada, former state assemblywoman Sharron Angle, a long shot who had previously run unsuccessfully for Congress, was trailing badly to Sue Lowden, languishing in single digits two months before the primary. Lowden, a former chair of the Nevada Republican Party, was the preferred candidate of the Republican establishment to run against incumbent Democratic senator Harry Reid, the Senate majority leader. Then Angle was endorsed by the Tea Party Express and rapidly won the backing of Tea Party enthusiasts for her deeply conservative views. When Lowden's campaign stumbled, Angle capitalized on her Tea Party support and shot into the lead, eventually winning the Republican nomination over her more established opponent.

Given Kentucky's right-leaning tendencies, and with Reid deeply unpopular among his constituents, both Paul and Angle emerged from their nomination battles as viable general election candidates. Paul would go on to win his contest; Angle would lose hers. However, both general election races started out close, owing in part to the limited reach of Tea Party ideology among nonlibertarian independent voters and making the Tea Party movement simultaneously a boon to the Republican Party and a potential electoral problem. Energized and mobilized, Tea Party supporters were reliable general election voters, eager to turn out during a normally low-turnout off-year election. However, as they picked off more mainstream Republican candidates in primaries, they made it harder for Republicans to win over voters in the political middle who are decisive in close contests, while forcing the Republican Party to expend resources contesting elections that might not be close with more conventional nominees. Primary victories by Tea Party–backed candidates over mainstream Republicans in Delaware and Colorado may have prevented Republicans from taking control of the Senate in an otherwise strong Republican year when they lost to Democrats in the general election.

Another cautionary tale of the relationship between the Republican Party and the Tea Party movement may be found in a remote congressional district in upstate New York, where in a special election held in late 2009, a Tea Party uprising cost the Republican Party a House seat it had held since Reconstruction. The local Republican Party nominated State Assemblywoman Dede Scozzafava to run against Democrat Bill Owens in what normally would have been the end of the story: no Democrat had been elected from New York's 23rd congressional district since Ulysses S. Grant was president. However, there was a third candidate in the race. Accountant Doug Hoffman, who had been passed over for the Republican nomination by local party officials, accepted the nomination of the Conservative Party, which has a dedicated ballot line in New York State, insuring Hoffman a place on the ballot without having to perform the cumbersome tasks of circulating and filing petitions for ballot access.

Hoffman attacked Scozzafava from the right, painting her as too moderate for the district. Accordingly, Tea Party support rapidly coalesced behind Hoffman, who was promoted by Dick Armey's FreedomWorks group. The results were similar to what would happen the following year in Florida, Nevada, and Kentucky: the establishment Republican's support cratered, making Hoffman the de facto Republican candidate in the race. The weekend before the election, Scozzafava dropped out of the race and endorsed her *Democratic* rival. However, her name remained on the ballot, and she ended up siphoning off 6 percent of the vote, enough to put Democrat Bill Owens in Congress with a plurality of the vote, despite the feverish efforts of Hoffman's Tea Party supporters, who had flooded the district in an effort to mobilize conservative voters.[34] Some Tea Party activists saw Scozzafava's loss as a victory for ideology over party loyalty,[35] not exactly music to the ears of Republican leaders. And Owens was seated in time to vote in favor of a bill that was a premier target of Tea Party anger, the healthcare reform measure.

# INTERNET POLITICS: JEFFERSONIAN POLITICS ON A HAMILTONIAN SCALE

For Tea Party activists and netroots progressives, the image of an ideal America could not be more different. The Tea Party would move America in the direction of a rugged individualism without much taxation or the social safety net it supports, where states would be free to make decisions without the interference of the national government, businesses would be less burdened by regulatory control, and individual and corporate tax burdens would be reduced. Netroots progressives envision an America based on community, where taxes and regulation are necessary to support a commons that would be destroyed if government were downsized, and where government would serve popular rather than corporate interests. It is a vision rooted more directly in Hamiltonian nationalism, where the nation is a family presided over by a strong central government, than in Jeffersonian localism, which in turn is closer to the libertarian bent of the Tea Party. In this regard, the two groups line up with the long-standing alignment of Hamiltonian-minded Democrats and Jeffersonian Republicans. Beyond these generalizations, however, distinctions between the two groups are less clear. Tea Party activists are far more comfortable with the unfettered capitalism promoted by Hamilton, while netroots activists share with Jefferson an abiding faith in the goodness of ordinary citizens. And each group poses a bigger threat to the party to which it is closest than to the other side.

As for their means, Internet politics—regardless of the ends to which they are applied—enable people to come together in virtual gatherings for the purpose of taking collective social action. It is in this respect a sort of twenty-first century town meeting—the Jeffersonian commons in cyberspace—where anyone of like mind with Internet access can read a blog, post a diary, engage in spirited exchanges on comment threads, plot strategy, give money, and mobilize and motivate friends, relatives, and strangers. By virtue of its scale, however, it is something more than a town hall; rather, it is a national forum independent of location, an organic meeting that people enter and exit at will, unbounded by the limitations of space or time. It is something neither Jefferson nor Hamilton could have imagined: a town meeting with national reach, Jeffersonian localism on a Hamiltonian scale.

As Internet-based activists on the left and to some degree on the right engage the new media to push the parties to move in new directions, the parties have no choice but to respond. Even Barack Obama, an Internet-savvy president, found that he could not ignore the efforts of an animated netroots as they attempted to move him in directions he felt his fellow partisans in Congress were not willing to go. As progressive activists made their voices heard, party regulars took note and made adjustments, as evidenced by a number of progressive planks in the 2016 Democratic Party platform. Republicans also made adjustments to avoid being victims of Tea Party anger, refusing to reach across the aisle and make themselves targets. In the short term, the distinctions symbolized by the two separate blogospheres that do not link to each other have been manifested in greater party polarization in government.

In the long term, it is possible that both parties will turn more and more to networked politics to air and iron out differences. However, as the results of the 2016 election illustrate, online politics is not a one-size-fits-all proposition, and there are limits to what parties and candidates can achieve because the bottom-up structure of the Internet permits supporters to determine the final word on the effectiveness of a campaign or candidacy. Hillary Clinton employed some of the same media strategies as Barack Obama but never ignited the spark among her followers that propelled the 2008 Obama Internet campaign. Arguably, Bernie Sanders found that spark—the loyalty of some of his supporters was legendary—but an organically developed online presence that generated a fortune in small-dollar contributions was not enough to propel him to the nomination. Donald Trump's use of Twitter as an attention-getting device will not work as effectively for a traditional candidate operating within the norms of conventional political discourse. Dull tweets, like candidates who fail to strike a nerve with the public, are not the stuff of successful Internet politics.

However, the Internet does hold great promise for ordinary citizens. If, as we said in Chapter 1, many people do not like to choose between Jeffersonian localism and Hamiltonian nationalism, politics on the Internet offers a new set of possibilities through the creation of a virtual national commons. As a matter of means rather than ends, both parties are struggling to understand the new technology and make it work for them. Recall that we also said that parties have evolved before, sometimes dramatically, in the wake of social changes and technological advances. As they feel continued heat from Internet communities that have already realized a fair degree of political success, it is hard to imagine they will not evolve again.

# NOTES

1. Louis Nelson, "Trump Assails Former Miss Universe and Clinton in Early Morning Tweet Blitz," *Politico*, September 30, 2016. www.politico.com/story/2016/09/trump-alicia-machado-clinton-tweet-attack-228940.

2. Maggie Haberman, Ashley Parker, Jeremy W. Peters, and Michael Barbaro, "Inside Donald Trump's Last Stand: An Anxious Nominee Seeks Assurance," *New*

*York Times*, November 6, 2016. www.nytimes.com/2016/11/07/us/politics/donald-trump-presidential-race.html?_r=0.

3.   Mary Clare Jalonick, "The Best Sites of the 2000 Campaign," *Campaigns and Elections* (January 2001): pp. 70–74.

4.   Chuck Raasch, "Political Parties Deploy Web Erratically, Study Says," Gannett News Service, April 11, 2002.

5.   Ibid.

6.   Remarks by Governor Howard Dean to the Democratic National Committee Winter Meeting, Washington, DC, February 21, 2003.

7.   Joe Trippi, *The Revolution Will Not Be Televised: Democracy, the Internet, and the Overthrow of Everything* (New York: Harper Paperbacks, revised 2008).

8.   Ibid.

9.   Matthew R. Kerbel and Joel David Bloom, "Blog for America and Civic Involvement," *Harvard International Journal of Press/Politics* 10, no. 4 (2005): pp. 3–27.

10.   Trippi, *The Revolution*.

11.   Matthew R. Kerbel, *Netroots: Online Progressives and the Transformation of American Politics* (Boulder, CO: Paradigm Publishers, 2009), p. 135.

12.   Trippi, *The Revolution*.

13.   Ibid., p. 100.

14.   Kerbel, *Netroots,* pp. 138–139.

15.   Joe Antonio Vargas, "Obama's Wide Web," Washingtonpost.com, August 20, 2008.

16.   Cited in Sean Quinn, "On the Road: Toledo, OH," Fivethirtyeight.com, October 14, 2008.

17.   Chris Bowers and Matthew Stoller, "Emergence of the Progressive Blogosphere: A New Force in American Politics," Newpolitics.net, August 10, 2005.

18.   Ibid.

19.   Ibid.

20.   Jessica Clark and Tracy Van Slyke, *Beyond the Echo Chamber: Reshaping Politics Through Networked Progressive Media* (New York: The New Press, 2010).

21.   Matthew R. Kerbel and Christopher J. Bowers, *Next Generation Netroots: Realignment and the Rise of the Internet Left* (New York: Routledge, 2016).

22.   Ibid.

23.   Markos Moulitsas, "Better Democrats," Daily Kos, December 14, 2007, emphasis in original.

24.   Joan McCarter, "AR-Sen and Wall Street Reform: The Value of a Good Primary Challenge," Daily Kos, May 13, 2010.

25.   Ibid.

26.   Matthew R. Kerbel, "The Dog That Didn't Bark: Obama, Netroots Progressives, and Healthcare Reform." Presented at the 2010 Dilemmas of Democracy Conference, Loyola Marymount University, Los Angeles, March 2010.

27.   Christina Bellantoni, "OFA Metrics Nine Months In." Talking Points Memo, November 11, 2009.

28.   Ibid.

29.   Christopher Snow Hopkins, Siddhartha Mahanta, and Theresa Poulson, "Twelve Tea Party Players to Watch," NationalJournal.com, February 4, 2010.

30.   Chris Cillizza, "Utah Senator Bob Bennett Loses Convention Fight," Washingtonpost.com, May 8, 2010.

31.   Brendan Farrington, "Crist, Obama Hug Haunting Florida Governor in Senate Primary," *Huffington Post*, www.huffingtonpost.com/2009/10/25/crist-obama-hug-haunting-_n_332963.html, October 25, 2009.

32.   Tom Brown, "Florida's Crist Launches Independent Senate Bid," Reuters, April 29, 2010.

33.   Steve Kornacki, "Rand Paul Wins Kentucky Senate Primary," Salon.com, May 18, 2010.

34.   David Weigel, "Conservatives Rework Rhetoric After High-Profile New York Loss," *The Colorado Independent*, November 4, 2009.

35.   John Tomasic, "Musgrave to GOP: 'Don't Just Assume We're Yours.'" *The Colorado Independent*, November 4, 2009.

# 7

# Campaign Finance and Transitional Political Parties

As parties are buffeted by a changing media environment, so are they shaped by a gusher of money that has been flooding the political system at an increasingly rapid pace. In late January 2010, Barack Obama stepped forward to the rostrum in the U.S. House of Representatives to give his official State of the Union address. Before him were assembled members of Congress, the Cabinet, and the justices of the U.S. Supreme Court. As expected, Obama spoke of the economic and foreign policy challenges facing the country. But in an unusual move, the president directly attacked the Supreme Court. Only days before, the Court had rendered a five-to-four opinion in a case entitled *Citizens United v. Federal Election Commission*. This decision eliminated much of the campaign finance regulatory system assembled by previous congresses and presidents following the Watergate scandal in the 1970s. Staring directly at the Court justices, Obama took aim at the Republican-appointed jurists who wrote the opinion, saying, "With all due deference to separation of powers, last week the Supreme Court reversed a century of law that I believe will open the floodgates for special interests—including foreign corporations—to spend without limit in our elections."[1] Immediately, the television cameras zoomed in on Justice Samuel Alito, who could be seen mouthing the words, "Not true."

The debate concerning the ability of the federal government to regulate the flow of money in politics is a long-standing one. For nearly two centuries, the

## Table 7.1 Issues Raised by Federal Campaign Finance Laws

**Monetary Issues**

1. How much money given to a political candidate is too much?
2. Are corporate donations inherently corrupt?
3. What limits, if any, should be placed on corporate and/or individual donations to political candidates?
4. Should federal campaigns rely mostly on local contributions?
5. Should the national parties have greater involvement and help candidates with out-of-state monies?

**Constitutional Issues**

1. Is money truly a form of speech that deserves protection under the First Amendment to the U.S. Constitution?*
2. Do corporations fall under the protection of the First Amendment as conceived by the Framers?

*The First Amendment to the U.S. Constitution states, "Congress shall make no law respecting an establishment of religion, or prohibiting the free exercise thereof; or abridging the freedom of speech, or of the press; or of the right of the people peaceably to assemble, and to petition the Government for a redress of grievances."

tension between the rights of individuals, corporations, and labor unions to participate in the political process, and the interest of the federal government in making sure that candidates and campaigns participate on a level playing field, is one that has been the subject of much debate in the U.S. Congress and ongoing litigation in the courts (see Table 7.1). Today, 63 percent say "elected officials enacting policies and spending taxpayer money that benefit the special interests they favor" is a problem,[2] and 76 percent "agree strongly" that "there is too much money spent on political campaigns and elections today, and limits should be placed on campaign spending."[3]

This chapter traces the history of money in political campaigns in the United States. Over the past two centuries, there has been a torrent of dollars funneled into partisan campaigns and numerous efforts by Congress to regulate and stem the flow of dollars. At the same time, these laws have raised profound constitutional questions that have been repeatedly addressed by the Supreme Court. Throughout the twentieth century and now extending into the twenty-first, a familiar pattern has emerged: as the major parties become stronger nationally, more dollars from outside any given state have flowed into political campaigns. It is, therefore, not surprising that the outsized role of money in party politics is an increasingly powerful force, pushing the system toward the Hamiltonian pole. It is, we argue, the fulcrum of a new, professionalized, and centralized party system.

# A BRIEF HISTORY OF MONEY AND POLITICAL CAMPAIGNS

The dominant means of reaching voters during the early days of campaigning was the print media—namely, newspapers. As discussed in Chapter 1, the surest way to win favorable attention for candidates was either to own a newspaper or sponsor the editor. Thus, in 1791, Thomas Jefferson gave Philip Freneau a part-time clerkship in the State Department so that he would move to Philadelphia to become editor of the *National Gazette*, the paper that became the mouthpiece for Jefferson's Democratic-Republican Party. Alexander Hamilton, meanwhile, was a major financial backer of the competing *Gazette of the United States*. As late as the mid-nineteenth century, newspapers were a major source of campaign expenditures. For example, when a wealthy backer wanted to aid the presidential candidacy of James Buchanan in 1856, he contributed $10,000 to start a sympathetic newspaper. Likewise, Abraham Lincoln secretly purchased a small Illinois newspaper to advance his presidential ambitions in 1860.[4]

"Treating" was another common form of electioneering during the early days of the republic. Candidates would sponsor events at which voters would be treated to lavish feasts.[5] Thus, when George Washington ran for the Virginia House of Burgesses in 1751, he reportedly purchased a quart of rum, wine, beer, and hard cider for every voter in the district (there were only 391 voters).[6] In 1835, Ferdinand Bayard, a Frenchman traveling in the United States, commented that "candidates offer drunkenness openly to anyone who is willing to give them his vote."[7] Besides owning newspapers and treating potential supporters, candidates also sent mailings to voters, printed pamphlets for distribution, and organized rallies and parades. By the 1840s, pictures, buttons, banners, and novelty items were widely distributed.

Although controlling newspapers and treating and distributing campaign paraphernalia were costly endeavors, collecting massive sums of money was unnecessary. Prior to 1828, only white males could vote, there were property qualifications in some states, and voting was even restricted in some places to those belonging to a particular religious denomination.[8] Fewer voters meant fewer expenditures. Modes of communication were limited to word of mouth and the print media. After the formation of the spoils system in the 1830s (whereby party workers were rewarded with government jobs), volunteers were called upon to organize parades and get voters to the polls. Finally, because party loyalty was extremely pronounced for much of the nineteenth century, there was very little movement from one election to the next, and straight-ticket voting was the norm. At the same time, party politics was truly local politics. Jeffersonian localism provided the means by which candidates sought federal offices: control of local newspapers, local party jobs, and local volunteers. It was amateur-based, but also very effective.

# MARK HANNA, THE CAMPAIGN OF 1896, AND THE RISE OF HAMILTONIAN NATIONALISM POLITICS

Mark Hanna is often credited with being the first campaign consultant in U.S. history, having orchestrated William McKinley's 1896 presidential victory.[9] He also helped transform the role of money in politics, once famously saying, "There are two things that are important in politics—the first is money, and I can't remember what the second one is."[10] This was an astonishing statement, given the secondary role of money in elections during the first century of our nation's history. Why did things change so quickly?

The reasons for the tremendous surge in campaign funds were linked to the vast transformation of the U.S. economy following the Civil War. By the 1870s, the Industrial Revolution was in full swing. The nation's industrial infrastructure was booming, and Americans were migrating to the nation's largest cities. Relationships were forged between party machines and captains of industry, in which the latter pumped money into party coffers in exchange for preventing elected officials from interfering with the so-called free market. The election of 1896 marked a turning point in the tale of money and politics. William McKinley pledged to continue the GOP's laissez-faire economic policies, whereas William Jennings Bryan, McKinley's Democratic opponent, wanted more government regulation of business.

Fearing a Democratic Party groundswell and the ruin of the free-market economic system should Bryan become president, Republicans mounted the best-bankrolled campaign ever. For the first time, corporations made political contributions directly from their company treasuries. Mark Hanna met with financiers in New York and Boston, including the legendary J. P. Morgan and John D. Rockefeller, to successfully solicit funds.[11] These included $250,000 from Rockefeller's Standard Oil Company; $174,000 from western railroads; and even $50,000 in cash from one railroad executive.[12] The Republicans' massive war chest, estimated at $3.5 million, allowed Hanna and the Republicans to sponsor hundreds of speakers for small gatherings and debates; produce more than 200 million pamphlets (the GOP headquarters employed over 100 full-time mail clerks) as well as hundreds of thousands of posters, buttons, and billboards; invest heavily in newspaper advertising; and hire legions of workers to register new Republicans and get them to the polls.[13] McKinley simply stayed at home in Canton, Ohio, where trainloads of supporters numbering 750,000 in all (or one out of every 20 voters), many of them carrying envelopes of cash, were brought to his front porch.[14] In September alone, McKinley and the Republicans had raised $570,000, while the Democrats raised a mere $650,000 for their entire campaign.[15] Democratic nominee William Jennings Bryan charged that McKinley was trying to buy the presidency.[16] Not surprisingly, McKinley won with 51.7 percent of the vote, the highest Republican percentage since the reelection of Ulysses S. Grant in 1872.[17]

Mark Hanna's efforts were significant in two ways. First, the 1896 election was the first time that systematic fund-raising techniques were used in a presidential campaign. No longer would party operatives wait for the money to come in; instead, they would go out and get it. Second, Hanna demonstrated that political advertising could rule the day. Word-of-mouth campaigning, relying on volunteers, and placing newspaper ads were becoming passé. Press releases, direct mail, billboards, and soon radio (and later television and the Internet) would transform electioneering by creating national messages that were developed by strategists at the highest levels and could be disseminated to voters using new messaging tools.

In addition to a shift in campaign tactics, the U.S. was experiencing a rapid expansion of the electorate thanks to immigration and women's suffrage. With more voters to reach, political parties needed more resources, and so an age of aggressive fund-raising began. It was once reported that when a union leader came to a U.S. senator to urge support for protections against child labor at the turn of the century, the senator supposedly replied,

> But, Sam, you know damn well as I do that I can't stand for a bill like that. Why those fellows this bill is aimed at—those mill owners—are good for $200,000 a year to the party. You can't afford to monkey with a business that friendly.[18]

In short, Hanna and the Republican Party created a new type of Hamiltonian nationalism in politics. By centralizing power at the top of a federal campaign, and using new, top-down techniques to communicate with a mass electorate, Hanna and his colleagues began a movement away from locally based politics—a movement that grew with the passage of time and vastly transformed U.S. politics. In this new era, political parties became more professionally based and were a central point for gathering large sums of money. Elections were conducted by party professionals, and the party machines exerted considerable control over policymaking. Party bosses expected those in government to ante up, and anyone interested in shaping public policy was expected to woo them. Party coffers were filled through small numbers of huge contributions from the so-called fat cats. During the presidential race of 1928, for example, over half of both the Democratic and Republican treasuries came from contributions of $5,000 or more—a sum that could buy ten family cars at that time.[19] In sum, the cornerstone of Hamiltonian parties is money—lots of it.

## TELEVISION MARKETING AND THE SKYROCKETING COSTS OF CAMPAIGNS

If the cost of elections rose during the Industrial Revolution, it skyrocketed during the technological revolution that was well underway by the 1960s. By 2016, the major-party presidential candidates raised *$2 billion*, with Hillary Clinton accumulating $1.2 billion and Donald Trump raising $600 million.[20] It is estimated that the total costs for *all* candidates in 2016 will total more than *$7 billion*, with future years likely to see even greater expenditures.[21] Indeed, the cost of running for any political office has grown at a staggering rate. Today, the average House race costs more than $1.6 million (a 344 percent increase since 1988), while the average Senate seat costs more than $10.4 million (a 62 percent increase since 1988).[22]

The single greatest force behind this change has been the way candidates communicate with voters. Today, most voters hear from politicians through the electronic media—television, radio, and, especially, the Internet, which allows for the acquisition of digital information about individual voters. The first television advertisements for presidential candidates appeared in 1952. By the 1980s, nearly all candidates for public office relied on television advertisements to spread their messages. But television advertising is extraordinarily expensive: in 1860, Abraham Lincoln's campaign cost just over $100,000; a century later, that amount bought only 30 minutes of television air time.[23] Today, national commercials produced by an advertising agency have an average cost of $342,000 (or more) for a 30-second spot.[24]

Another reason for the growing cost of elections is the emergence of professional campaign consultants. Prior to the 1950s, most campaigns were headed by candidates, their spouses, or party activists—usually the most seasoned "hacks" in the party organizations. With the advent of television advertising, product marketing experts became useful. By the 1960s, a new profession blossomed—campaign consulting. Over time came a greater specialization within the consulting profession that included media gurus, pollsters, fund-raising professionals, and direct-mail experts. As the professionals took over the mechanics of campaigning, the cost of elections further escalated. In 2016, Donald Trump charged his companies more than $8.2 million for campaign-related expenses, and the Republican nominee paid more than 350 employees for their professional services.[25] For her part, Hillary Clinton employed more than 800 people in her unsuccessful campaign, costing approximately $5.5 million per month as Election Day neared.[26]

# THE RISE OF POLITICAL ACTION COMMITTEES

Interest groups have played an important role in funding elections for over a century. During the Industrial Revolution, businesses, trade associations, and labor unions channeled large donations to parties and their candidates. Even though reform measures limited direct contributions from corporations, banks, and labor unions, many loopholes existed. In 1943, the Congress of Industrial Organizations (CIO) circumvented contribution restrictions by creating a separate fund to receive and spend voluntary contributions—a new organizational unit it called the political action committee (PAC). It was legal, the CIO argued, because none of the monies used to support the group or given to candidates came directly from the labor union itself.

By the late 1950s, scores of business and professional associations began to develop their own PACs.[27] But the real growth period began in the 1970s. In 1974, there were roughly 600 PACs; by 2009, there were 4,611 PACs registered with the Federal Election Commission.[28] During the same period, PAC expenditures grew from $12.5 million to $600 million.[29] And most PACs gave to incumbents. During the past decade, PACs gave a minimum of 70 percent of their contributions to incumbents; less than 15 percent went to challengers.[30] Today, political action committees are a major source of funding for presidential campaigns. These so-called Super PACs spent heavily in 2016: Hillary Clinton received $97.5 million in support from her Super PAC; Donald Trump got $23.9 million.[31] Table 7.2 shows the top PACs giving to candidates in 2015–2016 as compiled by OpenSecrets.org. The list includes well-known companies such as AT&T, Honeywell, Lockheed Martin, and Blue Cross/Blue Shield, as well as organizations such as the National Association of Realtors and the National Beer Wholesalers Association. (Followthemoney.org also compiles excellent data on individual contributions and party expenditures.)

**Table 7.2 Top PACs Giving to Candidates, 2015–2016**

| Political Action Committee | Total Amount |
| --- | --- |
| National Association of Realtors | $3,912,200 |
| National Beer Wholesalers Association | $3,515,700 |
| AT&T Inc. | $3,100,750 |
| Honeywell International | $2,785,864 |
| National Auto Dealers Association | $2,747,250 |
| Lockheed Martin | $2,600,750 |
| Blue Cross/Blue Shield | $2,585,898 |
| American Bankers Association | $2,524,507 |
| Credit Union National Association | $2,462,350 |
| International Brotherhood of Electrical Workers | $2,413,200 |
| National Association of Insurance and Financial Advisors | $2,312,400 |

*Source:* See www.opensecrets.org/pacs/. Accessed December 19, 2016.

# CONGRESS, THE SUPREME COURT, AND CAMPAIGN FINANCE

What difference does it make that some groups and individuals give money during elections while others do not? One could argue that contributing money is one way citizens participate in the democratic process. This argument is often heard from opponents of campaign finance reform, who claim that the more money there is in electoral politics, the better off the system is. After all, they reason, is not the act of contributing money an exercise of freedom of speech guaranteed by the First Amendment? Viewed from this perspective, the massive influx of money into campaigns is nothing more than democracy churning along on all cylinders.

Most Americans do not share this upbeat view. In 2016, 57 percent of Americans agreed with the statement "Politics and elections are controlled by people with money and by big corporations so it doesn't matter if I vote."[32] Not surprisingly, 67 percent believe it is a "good idea" that Congress should restrict the amount of money that corporations and labor unions are allowed to give to political parties and individual campaigns.[33] These results are not surprising, as there is a long-standing belief that money plays a corrupting role in the development of public policy and should be subject to government regulation. Americans are suspicious of the role of money in politics, as the vast majority never send a check either to a candidate or to a political party. According to a 2015 study, only 23 percent have ever contributed to a political candidate; 15 percent have donated to a political party; and just 5 percent have donated to a political action committee.[34]

Prior to the Progressive Era, there were few efforts to curb the flow of money in elections. In 1867, Congress passed legislation prohibiting assessments on navy yard workers. Nine years later, the ban was extended to all federal employees.[35] The most prominent of these reforms occurred in 1883 when Congress, prompted by the 1881 assassination of President James A. Garfield by a disappointed office seeker, passed the Civil Service Reform Act. Besides creating the civil service, the law continued the ban on assessing federal government employees for political contributions.[36]

In 1907, Congress passed the Tillman Act, which made it a crime for any corporation or national bank to contribute to either congressional or presidential candidates. A Senate report concluded that

> [t]he evils of the use of [corporate] money in connection with political elec-
> tions are so generally recognized that the committee deems it unnecessary
> to make any argument in favor of the general purpose of this measure. It is
> in the interest of good government and calculated to promote purity in the
> selection of public officials.[37]

Three years later, Congress required House candidates to disclose the source of their party committee contributions if they operated in two or more states—but only after the elections. The law, passed by a Republican-controlled Congress, was strength-ened in 1911 when the Democrats came to power. The new law established spending limits and required pre-election disclosure of finances in House and Senate races.[38]

The Teapot Dome scandal that gripped the Warren Harding Administration led to additional cries for reform. In 1925, Calvin Coolidge signed the Federal Corrupt Practices Act into law. This legislation required quarterly reports (even in non-election years) of contributions to federal candidates and to multi-state political committees. The law reaffirmed the spending limits, but it was easily circumvented as candidates established a multitude of supporting committees, thus making it hard to determine the total amount of receipts and expenditures in any given campaign.[39]

Another flurry of reform measures occurred during the late 1930s and early 1940s—most notably the Hatch Act of 1939, officially called the Clean Politics Act. This measure made it a crime for any federal employee to become an active political participant, and for anyone to solicit funds from people receiving federal relief. Within a year, several amendments were added—including the first federal limit on contributions from individuals (they could give no more than $5,000 to a candidate for federal office), and a prohibition against contributions to federal-level candidates from any business doing work for the U.S. government. By 1943, Congress extended the prohibition on contributions from banks and corporations to include labor unions as part of the Taft-Hartley Act. In enacting the measure, Congress overrode the veto of President Harry S. Truman, who warned that the expenditure ban was a "dangerous intrusion on free speech."[40]

But these reform efforts proved to be meaningless. The flow of large sums of money into campaigns did not slow down; it was simply channeled along different paths.[41] Although these statutes sounded impressive, they failed to create public authorities responsible for collecting the disclosure reports and prosecuting any illegal activity. In addition, the laws were fraught with loopholes. For example, reporting requirements were limited to "campaign periods." Thus, contributors evaded the law by donating to candidates prior to the start of any designated period. Moreover, expenditure limits applied only to a particular candidate, not to the separate committees that sprang up on a candidate's behalf (e.g., "Friends to Elect Mary Smith to Congress"). In addition, corporations evaded contribution prohibitions by reimbursing corporate executives who sent money to candidates. Under-the-table gifts were also commonplace. Finally, there was a lack of will among elected officials to enforce the existing regulations. It is no wonder that from the passage of the Corrupt Practices Act of 1925 until the 1970s, there is no record of a single prosecution for campaign contributions and violations.

# WATERGATE AND CAMPAIGN FINANCE REFORM

By the 1970s, reform was back on Congress's agenda. First, the cost of elections was rising owing to the growing use of television. Second, incumbents from both parties were worried that well-financed challengers could connect with voters through the mass media and toss them out. Finally, there were shocking disclosures of fat-cat contributions, including businessman Clement Stone's $3 million gift to Richard M. Nixon's 1968 presidential campaign.

Two significant measures became law in 1971. First, the Revenue Act created a fund for presidential campaigns and allowed voters to check off a one-dollar donation on their tax forms to help support the fund, later increased in 2001 to three dollars. (To get around a veto threat posed by President Nixon, the act did not go into effect until the 1976 election.) Second, the Federal Election Campaign Act (FECA) was an ambitious attempt to tighten reporting requirements and limit media expenditures. Unlike prior disclosure laws, FECA mandated that all expenditures and contributions over $100 be disclosed, regardless of when they were given. Moreover, reports would be filed with the General Accounting Office and made public within 48 hours. Media expenditures—including television, radio, billboards, and newsprint—would be limited to $50,000, or 10 cents per voting-age resident (whichever amount was larger).[42]

The FECA did increase disclosure levels, but the law had little impact on the 1972 elections. As before, candidates found different channels through which to spend their funds. But the story of finance reform was about to take a dramatic turn. During the course of investigating Richard M. Nixon's involvement in the cover-up of the break-in of the Democratic National Committee headquarters located at the Watergate Hotel, it was discovered that the Committee to Reelect the President (CREEP) had established its own secret fund-raising program. Many of the donations to Nixon's 1972 reelection campaign war chest were illegal—ranging from the $200,000 delivered in an attache case, to nearly $1 million in illegal corporate donations. Of the $63 million collected by Nixon, $20 million came from 153 donors who gave $50,000 or more. Commenting on the breadth of the Watergate scandal, John Gardner, head of Common Cause, said in April 1973:

> Watergate is not primarily a story of political espionage, nor even of White House intrigue. It is a particularly malodorous chapter in the annals of campaign financing. The money paid to the Watergate conspirators before the break-in—and the money passed to them later [to keep quiet]—was money from campaign gifts.[43]

## Table 7.3 Highlights of the 1974 Campaign Finance Reforms

1.  Created a Federal Election Commission consisting of six members (three Democrats and three Republicans) and charged them with enforcing federal election statutes.

2.  Set an individual contribution limit of $1,000 per primary, runoff, and general election not to exceed $25,000 to all federal candidates annually.

3.  Set a contribution limit of $5,000 per political action committee (PAC) to federal candidates with no aggregate limit.

4.  Set a $1,000 independent expenditure limit on behalf of a federal candidate.

5.  Banned any contributions to federal candidates from foreign sources.

6.  Set a $10 million spending limit per presidential candidate for all presidential primaries.

7.  Set a $20 million limit per presidential candidate for the general election.

8.  Set a $100,000 limit for U.S. Senate primary candidates.

9.  Set a $150,000 limit for U.S. Senate general election races.

10.  Set a $70,000 limit for U.S. House primary races.

11.  Set a $70,000 limit for U.S. House general elections.

12.  Limited party spending to $10,000 per candidate in U.S. House elections.

13.  Limited party spending to $20,000 per candidate in U.S. Senate elections.

14.  Limited party spending to 2 cents per voter in presidential general elections.

15.  Expanded public funding of presidential elections (both primary and general). Primary elections would allow private funds to be matched with public funds to a certain level.

16.  Created an extensive list of disclosure and reporting requirements. Each campaign must have one central committee through which all contributions and expenditures on behalf of a candidate must be reported to the Federal Election Commission.

*Source:* Cited in Mary W. Cohn, ed., *Congressional Campaign Finances: History, Facts, and Controversy* (Washington, DC: Congressional Quarterly, 1992), pp. 44–46. These were amendments to the 1971 FECA law.

A shocked public, together with a Democratic-controlled Congress, led a reform effort and passed legislation that established contribution limits and created a regulatory system for enforcement (see Table 7.3). Despite his reservations, President Gerald R. Ford signed it into law, noting that "the times demand this legislation."[44]

# A CHALLENGE IN THE SUPREME COURT: *BUCKLEY V. VALEO*

The jubilation over enacting the new reform laws did not last long. As soon as FECA took effect in 1976, it was challenged in the courts. The case comprised a diverse set of plaintiffs, including U.S. senator James Buckley, a conservative Republican from New York; U.S. senator Eugene McCarthy, a liberal Democrat from Minnesota; the

New York Civil Liberties Union; and *Human Events*, a conservative publication. In *Buckley v. Valeo* (Francis R. Valeo was the secretary of the Senate),[45] the core arguments were rather simple. Buckley and his allies maintained that campaign spending was a form of speech protected by the First Amendment. The government argued that the democratic process compelled a level playing field, and this meant limits must be placed on both campaign contributions and expenditures.

On January 30, 1976, the Supreme Court rendered its decision. The Court found that some, but not all, of the FECA restrictions were constitutional. They let stand limits on how much money individuals and political committees could contribute; they allowed public financing of presidential elections, so long as it was voluntary (meaning that candidates could refuse public monies and spend their own money instead); and they required disclosure of campaign contributions and expenditures of more than $100. But the Supreme Court also struck down several features of the new law, including the overall spending caps; limits on what candidates and their spouses could contribute to their own campaigns; and limits on individual expenditures.[46] Concerning its rejection of overall spending limits, the Court noted,

A restriction on the amount of money a person or group can spend on political communication during a campaign necessarily reduces the quantity of expression by restricting the number of issues discussed, the depth of their exploration and the size of the audience reached.[47]

# REFORMING THE REFORMS: THE BIPARTISAN CAMPAIGN REFORM ACT OF 2001

Public opposition to the increased amounts of money given to candidates and campaigns during the 1980s and 1990s gave rise to new reforms. Several novel types of campaign contributions found their way around existing laws. One of these was "soft money," which was money not regulated by the Federal Election Commission. Rather, it was money collected by the national parties—including the Democratic National Committee, the Republican National Committee, and their corresponding House and Senate committees—and used for party-building activities ranging from public education to voter mobilization. "Hard money" refers to contributions made by individuals to federal candidates that are subject to the caps imposed by FECA and are monitored by the Federal Election Commission.

From 1994 to 2000, the total amount of soft money raised by the Democratic and Republican parties rose more than fourfold, from $102 million to $495 million.[48] Disgusted by the bipartisan evasions of FECA, consumer activist Ralph Nader ran for president in 2000, contending that the campaign finance system was broken and had corrupted the system of checks and balances created by the Framers of the U.S. Constitution. Said Nader:

If we don't have a more equitable distribution of power, there is no equitable distribution of wealth or income. And people who work hard will not get their just rewards. And the main way to shift power, if you had to have one reform, is public financing of public elections.[49]

Nader was not alone in his assessment. Elected officials from both parties agreed that the system was broken and in need of reform. Former senator Paul Simon (D–Illinois) noted:

> While I was in Congress, the Democratic Congressional Campaign Committee (DCCC) and the Democratic Senatorial Campaign Committee (DSCC) would ask Members to make phone calls seeking contributions to the party. They would assign me a list of names, people I had not known previously, and I would just go down the list. I am certain they did this because they found it more effective to have Members make calls.[50]

Former senator David Boren (D–Oklahoma) argued that "a busy Senator with ten minutes to spare will spend those minutes returning the call of a large soft money donor rather than the call of any other constituent."[51] Republicans, too, admitted the obvious. According to former senator Alan Simpson (R–Wyoming):

> Large donors of both hard and soft money receive special treatment. No matter how busy a politician may be during the day, he or she will always make time to see donors who gave large amounts of money. Staffers who work for members know who the big donors are, and those people always get their phone calls returned first and are allowed to see the Member when others are not.[52]

Former senator Warren Rudman (R–New Hampshire) stated it best: "You can't swim in the ocean without getting wet; you can't be part of this system without getting dirty."[53] Even donors acknowledged that money bought access. As one of them put it, "As a result of my $500,000 soft money donation to the Democratic National Committee (DNC), I was offered the chance to attend events with [President Clinton], including events at the White House a number of times."[54]

Prior to the 2000 election, senators John McCain, a Republican from Arizona, and Russ Feingold, a Democrat from Wisconsin, led a bipartisan effort to change the campaign finance laws. The two senators were joined in the House by representatives Christopher Shays, a Republican from Connecticut, and Martin Meehan, a Democrat from Massachusetts. But their collaborative efforts, despite overwhelming public support, were to no avail. In the Republican-controlled House, parliamentary procedures were used to forestall debate. High-ranking Republicans in both the House and Senate offered countless amendments that either weakened the proposed bills or broke up the bipartisan coalition that supported stronger measures. Spearheading the opposition to any changes was Senator Mitch McConnell, a Republican from Kentucky. Clinging to the idea that donating and spending money to campaigns is a form of free speech, McConnell, along with a handful of Republicans, filibustered any reforms. Unless McCain and Feingold could somehow muster 60 votes needed to end a McConnell-led filibuster, campaign finance would go nowhere.

The election of 2000 was pivotal to the reformers. Democrats made gains in both houses, with many newcomers pledging to "clean things up." Moreover, after John McCain failed to secure the 2000 GOP presidential nomination against George W. Bush, he set his sights on campaign finance reform. McCain became the darling of the media during his presidential bid, and a growing number of citizens seemed ready to follow his lead. McCain used his newfound popularity to help dozens of Republican House candidates win election. In exchange, he received their pledge of support for his campaign reform efforts.

The debate was set for March 2001. After nearly two weeks of compromise, McCain and Feingold were able to break the filibuster—thereby bringing the bill to a vote, and winning over some moderate Republicans by increasing the cap on individual contributions from $1,000 to $2,000. But the battle was far from over. House Republicans offered an alternative to the Shays-Meehan plan that allowed for contributions to the party committees above the proposed $90,000 limit. This less sweeping measure was meant to appeal to black and Hispanic Democratic legislators, since the national party committees were instrumental in mobilizing minorities to vote. But Shays and Meehan knew that their bill would have to be identical to the one passed in the Senate in order to avoid a House-Senate conference committee that could potentially kill the measure. As 2001 turned into 2002, most congressional observers were pessimistic that the Shays-Meehan bill would ever come to a vote.

The break came with the Enron scandal in which monumental accounting fraud led to the energy company's bankruptcy. George W. Bush, whose campaign benefitted from Enron's generous contributions, stated he would support the bill if it passed Congress.[55] Armed with this presidential endorsement, Shays and Meehan were able to collect enough signatures to force a vote, and in February 2002, the House passed the bill by a 51-vote margin. One month later, the Senate approved the most sweeping campaign finance bill in more than 25 years. On March 27, 2002, the Bipartisan Campaign Reform Act (BCRA), more popularly known as the McCain–Feingold law, was approved by George W. Bush, who signed the bill into law despite his misgivings.

The final version of the law included a ban on contributions to any national political party. The bill also banned issue-advocacy ads 30 days before primary elections and 60 days prior to a general election. However, the ban on soft money did not apply to PACS, which were free to raise unlimited amounts of money. Even so, the passage of the McCain-Feingold law created its own set of controversies. The very day that the BCRA was signed into law, Kentucky senator Mitch McConnell and a host of other federal legislators, along with various interest groups and minor parties, challenged it in the federal courts. The core of their complaints was that McCain-Feingold represented an assault on free association and expression. This was based on the restrictions the new law placed on issue advocacy and expressed advocacy for a given candidate 60 days prior to an election.[56] Previously, the Supreme Court had ruled that political parties could spend unlimited amounts on issue-advocacy advertisements so long as they were not done in concert with any candidate's campaign.[57]

Constitutional arguments in support of the law stressed that limits on contributions may be imposed without being a burden on the First Amendment.

Supporters noted that Congress's interest in limiting corruption had been previously endorsed by the courts, including *Buckley v. Valeo*. As Trevor Potter, a former Federal Election Commissioner, observed:

> The Supreme Court has accepted that large contributions to political parties and candidates... is a serious national problem, contributing to both corruption and the appearance of corruption, and to diminished public faith in government. The Court has also consistently held that those concerns amply justify reasonable regulation.[58]

By the end of 2002, the complaints against McCain-Feingold were merged into one case, *McConnell v. Federal Election Commission*. On December 10, 2003, the Supreme Court ruled that McCain-Feingold's ban on soft-money contributions was constitutional. Writing for a five-to-four majority, Justices John Paul Stevens and Sandra Day O'Connor abhorred the use of soft money in political campaigns:

> Just as troubling to a functioning democracy as classic *quid pro quo* corruption is the danger that officeholders will decide issues not on the merits or the desires of their constituencies but according to the wishes of those who have made large financial contributions. . . . The best means of prevention is to identify and remove the temptation. The evidence set forth... convincingly demonstrates that soft-money contributions to political parties carry with them just such a temptation.[59]

But the final paragraph of the majority opinion contained a prescient prediction: "Money, like water, will always find an outlet."[60] The flow of money into campaigns would continue, and *McConnell v. FEC* would not be the last word from the Supreme Court on the issue of campaign finance.

## THE DEBATE BEGINS ANEW

Evidence that the Supreme Court decision in *McConnell v. FEC* was beginning to fray mounted during George W. Bush's second term. Justice Sandra Day O'Connor decided to retire to help her ailing husband, and President Bush initially asked John Roberts to succeed O'Connor. But in the interregnum, Chief Justice William Rehnquist died, and Bush elevated Roberts to that position while naming Samuel Alito to succeed O'Connor. This rapid turnover proved decisive. For 11 years, the composition of the Supreme Court had not changed. But with the additions of Roberts and Alito, the Court shifted further to the right.[61]

In 2007, the Roberts-led Court ruled that the McCain-Feingold ban on using a candidate's name in issue-advocacy advertisements 30 days before a primary and 60 days prior to a general election was unconstitutional. In a five-to-four decision, the Supreme Court declared: "Discussion of issues cannot be suppressed simply because the issues may also be pertinent in an election. Where the First Amendment is implicated, the tie goes to the speaker, not the censor."[62] Meanwhile, the flow of money into campaign coffers became a torrent. In 2000, George W. Bush became the first Republican presidential candidate to refuse federal financing for his primary campaign, a stance he repeated four years later.[63] In 2004, Democrat Howard Dean raised an astounding $45 million, becoming the first Democratic presidential primary candidate to forgo federal matching funds.[64] Four years later, no serious presidential contender accepted federal funding. In fact, both Barack Obama and Hillary Clinton raised more money in 2008 than all of their Democratic competitors *combined*. Obama garnered an astonishing $456.1 million; Clinton amassed a war chest totaling $216.6 million. For the entire presidential campaign, Obama raised $745 million.[65] On the Republican side, the two leading contenders, John McCain and Mitt Romney, were also numbers one and two, respectively, in fund-raising: McCain received $216.4 million in donations; Romney, $108.8 million. In the fall of 2008, Barack Obama became the first major-party nominee since 1976 to forgo federal financing of his general election campaign. Four years later, both major-party nominees, Barack Obama and Mitt Romney, eschewed federal funding of their campaigns. In 2016, Republican Donald Trump and Democrat Hillary Clinton did the same. Today, federal funding of presidential contenders—either in the primaries or in a general election—is no longer an option for a serious candidate. This portion of FECA has become a dead letter, since candidates are able to raise so much money from individual donors, either in large or small quantities. In 2016, for example, Bernie Sanders received an average contribution of $27 from individuals drawn to his anti–Wall Street message, raising a total slightly exceeding $228 million.[66] Because serious candidates are no longer accepting federal funds, there is currently a reserve of $315 million in the federal campaign treasury, along with a significant decline in the number of citizens checking off the $3 contribution on their tax returns—down from 29 percent in 1980 to less than 6 percent in 2015.[67] Individuals, if they desire to give political money, are far more inclined to donate to particular candidates, not to the U.S. Treasury.

Meanwhile, money continues to flow in other ways designed to evade federal laws. So-called 527 groups, a name that refers to a provision in the federal tax code, have proliferated. These tax-exempt organizations seek to affect election outcomes, and they are not subject to any limits in the amount of monies they receive or how they spend them. Citizens United, on the right, and MoveOn.org, on the left, are examples of such organizations. And the McCain-Feingold ban on soft money made these organizations even more attractive to political activists. In 2004, philanthropist George Soros gave $15 million to two liberal organizations— MoveOn.org and America Coming Together—hoping to defeat George W. Bush for reelection.[68] While these organizations could not expressly advocate for the Democratic nominee, John F. Kerry, they could point out why they believed Bush did not deserve another term. On the Republican side, a 527 group entitled "Swift Boat Veterans for Truth" ran advertisements raising questions about Kerry's service record during the Vietnam War. In 2008, 527 groups spent $258 million to influence the outcome of federal elections.[69] Eight years later, their spending grew to more than $951.2 million.[70]

In addition, campaign money found still another way to flow like water. So-called 501c groups (also named after a provision of the Internal Revenue Service code), labor unions, trade associations, or social welfare organizations can raise and spend virtually unlimited sums of money so long as it is not their "primary activity" or "major purpose."[71] In other words, electioneering is not the primary purpose of the organization. The principal difference between 527 groups and 501c groups is that 527s are required to disclose the identities of their donors; 501c's are not. Moreover, 501c's are not required to disclose their expenditures. This makes the 501c group preferable to a 527 group among contributors who wish to remain in the shadows. In 2016, 501c organizations spent more than $160 million on political activities.[72] This is now referred to as "dark money," since neither the contributors to nor the expenditures made by these organizations are subject to reporting requirements. Today, oil magnates Charles and David Koch are important figures in the shadowy dark money movement, raising and spending millions of dollars on behalf of Republican candidates and causes.[73]

# THE SUPREME COURT SPEAKS AGAIN: CITIZENS UNITED V. FEDERAL ELECTION COMMISSION

In 2010, the Supreme Court issued a landmark decision in *Citizens United v. Federal Election Commission*. The case arose in 2008 when Citizens United, a conservative group led by longtime Republican activist David Bossie, created a movie about then-presidential candidate Hillary Clinton. For much of 2007 leading into 2008, Clinton was a leading contender for the Democratic presidential nomination. Long a polarizing figure, Clinton evoked the ire of conservatives—even more so in 2008, as she seemed on the verge of becoming George W. Bush's successor. The film created by Bossie and his colleagues at Citizens United was entitled *Hillary: The Movie* and, not surprisingly, it depicted Clinton in the most negative light, claiming she was "driven by power," "steeped in sleaze," "deceitful," and "would lie about anything."[74]

In January 2008, Citizens United sought to broadcast its movie on the video-on-demand channels provided by cable service providers. To implement its plan to air the movie, Citizens United was prepared to pay for the video-on-demand channel, and it wanted to promote the film on the cable networks in two 10-second advertisements and one 30-second advertisement. The advertisements and movie were scheduled to air within 30 days of the first presidential primaries, violating the provision in the McCain-Feingold Act that prohibited third-party groups from broadcasting advertisements that advocated against a candidate immediately before an election. Although the words "vote against" were not found in *Hillary: The Movie*, the message contained in the film was that Clinton did not merit any votes in her quest to become president. The case quickly reached the Supreme Court.

At the Supreme Court, the outcome was not initially clear. In fact, *Citizens United v. Federal Election Commission* was argued twice before the Court, partly because President Obama appointed Justice Sonya Sotomayor to succeed Justice David Souter, who heard the initial argument. Expectations were that the Court would issue a narrow ruling. Citizens United had a $12 million budget that included corporate donations, and it was this money that was illegally used to finance and promote *Hillary: The Movie*. Citizens United also had its own political action committee, and if that entity had been employed to promote the film, it would not have violated the provisions of McCain-Feingold.[75]

But the Supreme Court decided to issue a much broader ruling. In its five-to-four decision, the Court sought to demonstrate that the First Amendment as conceived by the Founders included the right for corporations to engage in free, unregulated speech.[76] By making it a felony for corporations to expressly advocate either the election or defeat of candidates (either 30 days before a primary or 60 days prior to a general election), the Court determined that this portion of McCain-Feingold violated the First Amendment and was therefore unconstitutional.[77] Writing for the majority, Justice Anthony Kennedy declared:

No sufficient governmental issues justified limits on the political speech of non-profit corporations. . . . For these reasons, political speech must prevail against laws that would suppress it, whether by design or inadvertence. . . . There is simply no support for the view that the First Amendment, as originally understood, would permit the suppression of political speech by media corporations.[78]

Chief Justice Roberts agreed, saying, "The First Amendment protects more than just the individual on a soapbox and the lonely pamphleteer."[79]

The Court also rejected the argument that corporate political speech was inherently corrupt. Reversing the decision in *Buckley v. Valeo* that found otherwise, Justice Kennedy wrote, "[W]e now conclude that independent expenditures, including those made by corporations, do not give rise to corruption or the appearance of corruption."[80] Kennedy added:

Our Nation's speech dynamic is changing, and informative voices should not have to circumvent onerous restrictions to exercise their First Amendment rights. Speakers have become adept at presenting citizens with sound bites, talking points, and scripted messages that dominate the 24-hour news cycle. Corporations, like individuals, do not have monolithic views. On certain topics corporations may possess valuable expertise, leaving them the best equipped to point out errors or fallacies in speech of all sorts, including the speech of elected officials.[81]

Virtually the only portion of McCain-Feingold the Court majority left intact was its disclosure requirements. Justice Kennedy found that disclosure did not inhibit political speech, noting that "disclosure permits citizens and shareholders to react to the speech of corporate entities in a proper way. This transparency enables the electorate to make informed decisions and give proper weight to different speakers and messages."[82] This point was vigorously contested by Justice Clarence Thomas, who argued that disclosures of political contributions supporting California's Proposition 8, a 2008 law that overturned the California Supreme Court's decision legalizing gay marriage in that state, had resulted in intimidation and harassment. Said Thomas:

> I cannot endorse a view of the First Amendment that subjects citizens of this Nation to death threats, ruined careers, damaged or defaced property, or pre-emptive and threatening warning letters as the price for engaging in core political speech, the primary object of First Amendment protection.[83]

The majority view was countered by Justice John Paul Stevens. In his opinion, Stevens ridiculed the majority's view that corporations are akin to persons and are therefore subject to First Amendment protections, saying:

> Corporations have no consciences, no beliefs, no feelings, no thoughts, no desires. Corporations help structure and facilitate the activities of human beings, to be sure, and their "personhood" often serves as a useful legal fiction. But they are not themselves members of "We the People" by whom and for whom our Constitution was established.[84]

By treating them as such, Stevens maintained that

> corporations and unions will be free to spend as much general treasury money as they wish on ads that support or attack specific candidates, whereas national parties will not be able to spend a dime of soft money on ads of any kind.[85]

Stevens concluded that the ruling "enhances the role of corporations and unions—and the narrow interests they represent—vis a vis the role of political parties—and the broad coalitions they represent—in determining who will hold public office."[86] He maintained that Congress was entirely correct to view corporate money as a corrupting influence:

> [O]ver the course of the past century Congress has demonstrated a recurrent need to regulate corporate participation in candidate elections to "[p]reserv[e] the integrity of the electoral process, preven[t] corruption, . . . sustai[n] the active, alert responsibility of the individual citizen, protect the expressive interests of shareholders, and [p]reserv[e] . . . the individual citizen's confidence in government." . . . Time and again, we have recognized these realities in approving measures that Congress and the States have taken.[87]

Stevens further noted that corruption "can take many forms," adding:

Bribery may be the paradigm case. But the difference between selling a vote and selling access is a matter of degree, not kind. And selling access is not qualitatively different from giving special preference to those who spent money on one's behalf.[88]

Thus, Stevens argued that unrestricted use of corporate money in political campaigns would result in a loss of public confidence in government:

When citizens turn on their televisions and radios before an election and hear only corporate electioneering, they may lose faith in their capacity, as citizens, to influence public policy. A Government captured by corporate interests, they may come to believe, will be neither responsive to their needs nor willing to give their views a fair hearing. The predictable result is cynicism and disenchantment: an increased perception that large spenders "call the tune" and a reduced "willingness of voters to take part in democratic governance."[89]

Stevens issued this final broadside: "While American democracy is imperfect, few outside the majority of this Court would have thought its flaws included a dearth of corporate money in politics."[90]

Reaction to *Citizens United* was swift. As mentioned at the outset of this chapter, Barack Obama repudiated the Court, and he repeated his denunciations of the decision during the remainder of his presidency. Obama was hardly the lone critic. When asked about the case, former Justice Sandra Day O'Connor tartly responded, "If you want my legal opinion, you can go read *McConnell* [*v. Federal Election Commission*]."[91] Others, however, supported the Roberts Court. Republican senator Mitch McConnell was ecstatic, claiming that the outcome in *Citizens United* was "an important step in restoring the First Amendment rights," adding:

For too long, some in this country have been deprived of full participation in the political process. With today's monumental decision, the Supreme Court took an important step in the direction of restoring the First Amendment rights of these groups by ruling that the Constitution protects their right to express themselves about political candidates and issues up until Election Day.[92]

Republican National Chair Michael Steele added his party's backing: "Today's decision by the Supreme Court in *Citizens United v. FEC* serves as an affirmation of the constitutional rights provided to Americans under the first amendment. Free speech strengthens our democracy."[93] In 2014, Republican senators blocked Democratic attempts to reverse the *Citizens United* decision through passage of a constitutional amendment.[94] That same year, the Supreme Court issued another landmark decision that expanded upon its ruling in *Citizens United*.

# A FINAL DENOUEMENT? *MCCUTCHEON V. FEDERAL ELECTION COMMISSION*

In the wake of the controversial *Citizens United* ruling, Republican lawyer Jan Baran noted that any congressional attempt to regulate campaign finance "is going to hit a brick wall."[95] That wall became even higher after the Supreme Court announced its 2014 ruling in *McCutcheon v. Federal Election Commission*. Shaun McCutcheon was an Alabama resident who donated to various Republican Party committees, including the Republican National Committee and its congressional counterparts. In the 2011–2012 cycle, McCutcheon contributed $33,088 to 16 different federal candidates, and wanted to contribute to 12 more Republicans running for congressional office, seeking to give each of them a symbolic $1,776 contribution. The Alabama Republican also contributed $27,328 to several non-candidate committees, and $25,000 in total to the Republican National Committee, the National Republican Senate Committee, and the National Republican Congressional Committee. McCutcheon said his objective was to encourage the adoption of conservative principles by Republican candidates who would adhere to the doctrine of "smaller government and more freedom."[96]

But McCutcheon wanted to spend even more, and was forbidden from doing so by a portion of the McCain-Feingold law left intact by the Supreme Court in its *Citizens United* decision. That statute capped individual contributions to all federal candidates for office at $48,600, and also limited individual contributions to political parties at $74,600. Joined by the Republican National Committee, McCutcheon contended that these limits violated his First Amendment rights, since money is a form of speech and the limits placed on him by the McCain-Feingold law were unconstitutional, arguing that they did not serve a "cognizable government interest."[97] A federal district court ruled against McCutcheon, saying the limitations served the public interest by preventing actual corruption and even the appearance of corruption.

But the Supreme Court overruled the district court and sided with McCutcheon. In its five-to-four decision, the Court left intact limits on individual contributions to particular candidates for federal office, but lifted the $48,600 and $74,600 individual limits placed on total contributions to all candidates and to political parties, respectively. Chief Justice John Roberts spoke for the majority:

> To require one person to contribute at lower levels because he wants to support more candidates or causes is to penalize that individual for robustly exercising his First Amendment rights. In assessing the First Amendment interests at stake, the proper focus is on an individual's right to engage in political speech, not a collective conception of the public good. The whole point of the First Amendment is to protect individual speech that the majority might prefer to restrict, or that legislators or judges might not view as useful to the democratic process.[98]

Roberts added that the only congressional interest when it came to regulating campaign money is preventing *quid pro quo* corruption. Allowing individuals, including McCutcheon, to spend large sums of money does not fall within that purview: "No matter how desirable it may seem, it is not an acceptable governmental objective to 'level the playing field,' or to 'level electoral opportunities,' or to "equalize the financial resources of candidates.""[99] Justice Clarence Thomas wanted to go even further by abolishing all federal campaign finance regulation: "I am convinced that under traditional strict scrutiny, broad prophylactic caps on both spending and giving in the political process. . . are unconstitutional."[100]

Justice Stephen Breyer disagreed with the majority view. In his dissent, Breyer noted that the decision

> creates a loophole that will allow a single individual to contribute millions of dollars to a political party or to a candidate's campaign. Taken together with *Citizens United v. Federal Election Commission* . . ., today's decision eviscerates our Nation's campaign finance laws, leaving a remnant incapable of dealing with the grave problems of democratic legitimacy that those laws were intended to resolve.[101]

Forecasting the impact of the *McCutcheon* decision, Breyer wrote: "[W]here enough money calls the tune, the general public will not be heard," adding:

> The result. . . is a decision that substitutes judges' understandings of how the political process works for the understanding of Congress; that fails to recognize the difference between influence resting upon public opinion and influence brought by money alone; that overturns key precedent; that creates huge loopholes in the law; and that undermines, perhaps devastates, what remains of campaign finance reform.[102]

Any possibility that either *Citizens United* or *McCutcheon* would be overturned vanished with the outcome of the 2016 presidential election. Earlier that year, Supreme Court Justice Antonin Scalia died suddenly. Barack Obama's nominated replacement, Merrick Garland, was refused a hearing by the Republican-controlled Senate. Banking on a Republican presidential victory, majority leader Mitch McConnell argued that any Supreme Court replacement should be made by a new president, and his bet paid off with the election of Donald Trump. During the campaign, Trump issued a list of potential Supreme Court replacements (an unprecedented step), and promised to choose among them. Each candidate was a die-hard conservative, aligned with the majority decisions in *Citizens United* and *McCutcheon*. Trump delivered on his promise and elevated judge Neil Gorsuch to the Supreme Court. Thus, any immediate possibility of overturning either *Citizens United* or *McCutcheon* appears remote. For the time being, *McCutcheon v. Federal Election Commission* appears to be the final denouement in a string of Supreme Court decisions on campaign finance.

# WHERE WE STAND

In sum, we are at a point where any federal action on campaign finance reform is unlikely. Congress has refused to consider attempts to amend the Constitution by giving it the power to regulate federal campaign monies, even though 17 states have petitioned the Congress for such an amendment, and the Supreme Court as constituted is not likely to revisit its recent decisions.[103] Meanwhile, the role of so-called "dark money" has become ever more important, and the amount of dollars both raised and spent in all campaigns has risen to astronomical levels. Only the limited reporting requirements remain in place, and the Federal Election Commission is responsible for overseeing that function. In an op-ed for *The Washington Post*, Federal Election Commissioner Ellen Weintraub noted that the agency has become dysfunctional, as the three Democratic and three Republican commissioners have brought the agency to a standstill. From 2009 to 2013, penalties assessed by the Commission plummeted by 79 percent; and the number of investigations into violations of existing laws totaled just four.[104] In sum, political money continues to be akin to water, and its flow has become an unregulated deluge of funds to both candidates and parties.

# NOTES

1.  Barack Obama, State of the Union Address, Washington, DC, January 27, 2010.

2.  Princeton Survey Research Associated International, poll, March 26–30, 2014. Text of question: "Which of the following do you think is a more serious problem? Special interest groups spending private money on campaigns to elect the politicians they favor, elected officials enacting policies and spending taxpayer money that benefit the special interests they favor?" Special interest groups spending private money on campaigns they favor, 30 percent; elected officials enacting policies and spending taxpayer money that benefit special interests they favor, 63 percent; neither are a problem (volunteered), 1 percent; don't know, 5 percent; refused, 1 percent.

3.  Pew Research Center for the People and the Press, poll, March 11–21, 2010. Text of question: "As I read a few criticisms people have made of elected officials in Washington, please tell me if you think each is a major problem, a minor problem, or not a problem. . . . They are influenced by special interest money." Major problem, 82 percent; minor problem, 11 percent; not a problem, 2 percent; don't know/refused, 4 percent.

4.  Herbert E. Alexander, *Financing Politics: Money, Elections, and Political Reform*, 3rd ed. (Washington, DC: Congressional Quarterly Press, 1984), pp. 5–6.

5.  Robert J. Dinkin, *Campaigning in America: A History of Election Practices* (Westport, CT: Greenwood Press, 1989), p. 8.

6.  Center for Responsive Politics, *A Brief History of Money in Politics* (Washington, DC: Center for Responsive Politics, 1999), p. 3.

7.  As cited in Dinkin, *Campaigning in America*, p. 13.

8.  Center for Responsive Politics, *A Brief History of Money in Politics*, p. 3.

9.  For more on this, see Karl Rove, *The Triumph of William McKinley: Why the Election of 1896 Still Matters* (New York: Simon and Schuster, 2015).

10. As cited in Center for Responsive Politics, *A Brief History of Money in Politics* (Washington, DC: Center for Responsive Politics, 1999), p. 3.

11. See Rove, *The Triumph of William McKinley*, p. 333.

12. Cited in Paul W. Glad, *McKinley, Bryan, and the People* (Chicago: Ivan R. Dee Publisher, 1991), p. 168.

13. See Glad, *McKinley, Bryan, and the People*, p. 169; and Kenneth Jost, "Campaign Finance Debates," *CQ Researcher* 20: 457–480. CQ Researcher Online, http://library. cqpress.com.proxycu.wrlc.org/cqresearcher/cqresrre2010052800. Accessed July 7, 2010.

14. Rove, *The Triumph of William McKinley*, pp. 373–374.

15. Ibid., p. 333.

16. Ibid., p. 338.

17. Ibid., p. 262. For an interesting discussion of the role of money in the 1896 election, see Keith Ian Polakoff, *Political Parties in American History* (New York: Wiley, 1981), pp. 259–266.

18. The union leader mentioned here was Samuel Gompers, founder and first president of the American Federation of Labor; the senator was Boies Penrose. This quotation is cited in Center for Responsive Politics, *A Brief History of Money in Politics*, p. 5. See also George Thayer, *Who Shakes the Money Tree? American Campaign Practices From 1789 to the Present* (New York: Simon & Schuster, 1974).

19. The study was conducted by Louise Overacker. See Frank J. Sorauf, *Money in American Elections* (Scott, Foresman/Little, Brown College Division, 1988), pp. 16–25.

20. Issac Arnsdorf, "Trump Won With Half as Much Money as Clinton Raised," *Politico*, December 8, 2016.

21. See www.opensecrets.org/overview/cost.php. Accessed May 20, 2017.

22. See Paul Steinhauser and Robert Yoon, "Cost to Win Congressional Election Skyrockets," CNN.com, July 11, 2013.

23. Alexander, *Financing Politics*, p. 12.

24. See http://smallbusiness.chron.com/much-television-advertising-really-cost-58718.html

25. See Kenneth P. Vogel and Isaac Arnsdorf, "Trump's Campaign Paid His Businesses $8.2 Million," *Politico*, September 22, 2016; and Associated Press, "Donald Trump and Hillary Clinton Are Spending Like Crazy as Election Day Nears," October 21, 2016.

26. See Associated Press, "Donald Trump and Hillary Clinton Are Spending Like Crazy as Election Day Nears," October 21, 2016.

27. PACs are defined in the law as organizations that receive contributions from 50 or more individuals and contribute money to at least ten candidates for federal office.

28. "Number of Federal PACs Increases," Federal Election Commission, press release, March 9, 2009.

29. See Louis Sandy Maisel and Mark D. Brewer, *Parties and Elections in America* (Lanham, MD: Rowman & Littlefield, 2007), p. 178.

30. Ibid., p. 180.

31. See www.statista.com/statistics/516499/presidential-pac-spending-2016-us-election/

32. PRRI, poll, September 1–27, 2016. Text of question: "Please read the following statements and say if you agree or disagree with each one. . . . Politics and elections are controlled by people with money and by big corporations so it doesn't matter if I vote." Completely agree, 22 percent; mostly agree, 35 percent; mostly disagree, 28 percent; completely disagree, 14 percent; don't know/refused, 1 percent.

33.   Pew Research Center for the People and the Press, poll, January 6–10, 2010. Text of question: "A few years ago, a law was passed that put major restrictions on corporations and labor unions giving money to political parties and campaigns. Do you think these restrictions are a good idea or a bad idea?" Good idea, 67 percent; bad idea, 25 percent; don't know/refused, 8 percent.

34.   Associated Press–National Opinion Research Center, poll, November 12–17, 2015. Text of question: "There are many different ways to contribute to and participate in political campaigns. Have you ever done any of the following? Please select all that apply." Displayed a number sticker, wore a button, or placed a sign in your yard at home, 36 percent; signed a petition for a political candidate, 35 percent; donated money to a political candidate, 23 percent; attended a campaign rally or event, 25 percent; volunteered for the political campaign of a candidate, 15 percent; donated money to a political party, 15 percent; donated money to a PAC, or political action committee, 5 percent; none of the above, 29 percent; don't know/refused, 11 percent.

35.   See Jost, "Campaign Finance Debates."

36.   Under the spoils system, it was common for public employees to kick back a portion of their salary to the party machine. This practice remained commonplace at the local level.

37.   Cited in *Citizens United v. Federal Election Commission*, 558 U.S. 50, at p. 42 (2010).

38.   See Jost, "Campaign Finance Debates."

39.   Ibid. The Federal Corrupt Practices Act of 1925 applied only to congressional candidates. It said nothing about presidential campaigns.

40.   Cited in *Citizens United v. Federal Election Commission*, 558 U.S. 50, at p. 27 (2010).

41.   Sorauf, *Money in American Elections*, p. 36.

42.   Ibid.

43.   Cited in Mary W. Cohn, ed., *Congressional Campaign Finance: History, Facts, and Controversy* (Washington, DC: Congressional Quarterly, 1992), p. 42.

44.   As cited in Alexander, *Financing Politics*, p. 38.

45.   *Buckley v. Valeo*, 424 U.S. 1 (1976).

46.   The Supreme Court also ruled that only the president, not Congress, could appoint members of the Federal Election Commission.

47.   *Buckley v. Valeo*, 424 U.S. 1 (1976).

48.   Maisel and Brewer, *Parties and Elections in America*, p. 150.

49.   Ralph Nader, *Crashing the Party: Taking On the Corporate Government in an Age of Surrender* (New York: St. Martin's Press, 2002), p. 289.

50.   Quoted in *McCutcheon v. Federal Election Commission* (2014), 572 U.S., Appendix A.

51.   Ibid.

52.   Ibid.

53.   Ibid.

54.   Ibid.

55.   See David E. Rosenbaum, "Campaign Finance: Behind Debate, Jockeying for Advantage," *New York Times*, February 14, 2002, p. A-34.

56.   Issue-advocacy advertisements do not expressly tell voters to vote for or against a particular candidate. Rather, they imply such a position by featuring a candidate's position on an important issue. Thus, an issue-advocacy advertisement can say, "Candidate Jones

supports a balanced budget amendment" or "Candidate Smith opposes a balanced budget amendment."

57.   See *Colorado Republican Federal Campaign Committee v. FEC*, 518 U.S. 604 (1996). The Court ruled that as long as the issue-advocacy advertisement did not say the words "elect," "vote for," "defeat," or "vote against," they were permitted. Many believed that the Court's decision erased the wall between issue advocacy and expressed advocacy (i.e., vote for Candidate X) that had been constructed in several previous court cases (including *Buckley v. Valeo*).

58.   Trevor Potter, "New Law Follows Supreme Court Rulings," *BNA Money and Policy Report*, April 22, 2002.

59.   Quoted in Maisel and Brewer, *Parties and Elections in America*, p. 164.

60.   Ibid.

61.   See Adam Liptak, "Court Under Roberts Is Most Conservative in Decades," *New York Times*, July 24, 2010, p. 1.

62.   *Federal Election Commission v. Wisconsin Right to Life, Inc.*, 551 U.S. 449 (2007).

63.   Year 2000 Republican presidential candidate Steve Forbes also refused to accept federal matching funds.

64.   For more on this, see Joe Trippi, "Down from the Mountain," speech, February 9, 2004. See https://archive.org/details/digidemo2004-trippi. Accessed May 21, 2017.

65.   See www.opensecrets.org. Accessed March 18, 2010.

66.   See www.opensecrets.org/pres16/candidate.php?id=N00000528. Accessed December 19, 2016.

67.   See Marilyn W. Thompson, "Taxpayers Help Fund Stein Campaign," *Washington Post*, September 21, 2016, p. A-2.

68.   See Maisel and Brewer, *Parties and Elections in America*, p. 187.

69.   Ibid., p. 188.

70.   See www.opensecrets.org/527s/527cmtes.php?level=E. Accessed December 19, 2016.

71.   See Maisel and Brewer, *Parties and Elections in America*, p. 188.

72.   See www.opensecrets.org/outsidespending/nonprof_summ.php. Accessed December 19, 2016.

73.   See Jane Mayer, *Dark Money: The Hidden History of the Billionaires Behind the Rise of the Radical Right* (New York: Doubleday, 2016).

74.   See www.youtube.com/watch?v=BOYcM1z5fTs. Accessed December 22, 2016.

75.   See Justice Stevens's dissent in *Citizens United v. FEC*.

76.   The five justices in the majority were Anthony Kennedy, John Roberts, Clarence Thomas, Antonin Scalia, and Samuel Alito. The four dissenters were John Paul Stevens, Ruth Bader Ginsberg, Sonya Sotomayor, and Stephen Breyer.

77.   McCain-Feingold restricted television advertisements that were capable of reaching 50,000 persons in the 30- or 60-day period prior to a primary or a general election. These advertisements were banned if there was "no reasonable interpretation other than as an appeal to vote for or against a specific candidate."

78.   *Citizens United v. FEC*, 558 U.S. 50, at p. 37 (2010).

79.   Ibid., p. 1.

80.   Ibid., p. 57.

81.  Ibid., p. 49.

82.  Ibid., p. 55.

83.  Ibid., p. 6.

84.  Ibid., p. 76.

85.  Ibid., p. 21.

86.  Ibid.

87.  Ibid., p. 56.

88.  Ibid., p. 57.

89.  Ibid., p. 60.

90.  Ibid., p. 90.

91.  Quoted in Liptak, "Court Under Roberts is Most Conservative in Decades," p. A-1.

92.  Quoted in Jost, "Campaign Finance Debates," and Chris Good, "*Citizens United* Decision: Republicans Like It, Liberals Don't," *The Atlantic*, January 21, 2010.

93.  Ibid.

94.  See Ramsey Cox, "Senate GOP Blocks Constitutional Amendment on Campaign Spending," *The Hill*, September 11, 2014.

95.  Ibid.

96.  Adam Liptak, "Supreme Court Strikes Down Political Donation Cap," *New York Times*, April 2, 2014.

97.  *McCutcheon v. FEC*, 572 U.S. (2014).

98.  Ibid. The five justices in the majority were John Roberts, Antonin Scalia, Anthony Kennedy, Clarence Thomas, and Samuel Alito. The four justices in the minority were Ruth Bader Ginsberg, Stephen Breyer, Sonya Sotomayor, and Elena Kagan.

99.  Ibid.

100.  Ibid.

101.  Ibid.

102.  Ibid.

103.  Public Citizen, "New York Becomes the 17th State to Call for a Constitutional Amendment to Rein in Election Spending," June 15, 2016. See www.citizen.org/pressroom/pressroomredirect.cfm?ID=7923. Accessed December 22, 2016.

104.  Ellen Weintraub, "Trump's Pick for White House Counsel is Wrong for the Job," *Washington Post*, December 9, 2016.

# 8

# Elected Officials and the New Partisanship

On Thanksgiving eve 1994, a buoyant Newt Gingrich drove along the country roads of Georgia with his then-wife, Marianne. Only two weeks earlier, House Republicans added 52 representatives to their ranks—enough to form a congressional majority for the first time in 42 years. Not since 1946, the year John F. Kennedy and Richard M. Nixon both entered Congress, had there been this many new Republicans. As the car raced along the road, an excited Gingrich exclaimed, "This is really a big change!" At this, Marianne turned to her husband and gently reproved him, "You don't have any clue how big this change really is."[1]

Six months later, the change seemed very real as House Republicans strutted down the steps of the U.S. Capitol and a partisan crowd held small American flags and signs that read, "Contract with America—Promises Made—Promises Kept—Restoring the American Dream."[2] The occasion was to mark the 100th day since Gingrich put the U.S. House under new management. The rally's high point came when Speaker Gingrich strode to the podium and proudly declared, "Editorial writers and pundits scoffed. But we did mean it. We made promises and we kept promises."[3]

There is an old sports adage that says "Winning is not everything—it's the only thing." But what happens *after* the ballots are counted is often even more important than winning elections. In the United States, the victor wins an office, but elections alone do not confer power. Specifically, the Framers of the U.S. Constitution did not want political parties to become instruments of government, believing that parties corrupt and prevent leaders from doing the right thing. Instead, the Founders agreed with Alexander Hamilton that the best thing is to eschew parties and rely on the outstanding characters of distinguished citizens who would act in the public interest. Defending the Electoral College as a means for choosing a president, Hamilton wrote in *The Federalist* that "there would be a constant probability of seeing the station filled by characters pre-eminent for ability and virtue," adding that "the true test of a government is its aptitude and tendency to produce a good administration."[4] Hamilton's equation of character with effective administration still appeals to many Americans. Over the years, would-be presidents have promised to put the interests of their country ahead of their party. In 2008, for example, Republican John McCain's campaign slogan was "Country First," a reference to the many times he had previously bucked the GOP, and an indication that he would do so again should he be elected president. Announcing his presidential candidacy in 2015, Donald Trump excoriated politicians from both parties, including his fellow Republicans:

> I've watched the politicians. I've dealt with them all my life. If you can't make a good deal with a politician, then there's something wrong with you. You're certainly not very good. And that's what we have representing us. They will never make America great again. They don't even have a chance. They're controlled fully by the lobbyists, by the donors, and by the special interests, fully.[5]

Yet the pages of American history are suffused with examples demonstrating that character alone is an insufficient basis for good administration. During his single term as president, Jimmy Carter was extolled for his honesty and trustworthiness. But Carter's outstanding character did not translate into effective leadership.[6] Similarly, Donald Trump is admired for his business acumen, and became the first president in this century to be elected without any prior political experience. But this hardly guarantees that Trump will have a successful presidency. The separation of powers among the executive, legislative, and judicial branches; the "special interests" that populate Washington, DC; and getting a sufficient number of the 535 members of Congress to agree on anything are huge obstacles to making things happen—as presidents have learned to their regret.

## THE PRESIDENT AS PARTY LEADER

Historically, political parties have been viewed as necessary mechanisms that make government work. During the New Deal, Democrats led by Franklin D. Roosevelt were unified and passed a sweeping list of government-aid programs during a breathtaking 100 days in 1933. In his inaugural address, Roosevelt called for "action, and action now," noting that the Great Depression created conditions whereby he would "wage a war against the emergency, as great as the power that would be given to me if we were in fact invaded by a foreign foe."[7] When Roosevelt's bank reform bill was introduced shortly afterwards, a Democratic House member reportedly said, "Here's the bill. Let's pass it!"[8] And that's what happened, without a word of the new law being read by most legislators.

Another example of a political party uniting to change the course of government happened after Ronald Reagan assumed the presidency in 1981. This time, it was the Republicans who rallied to effect a conservative change. The "Reagan revolution" cut taxes, raised the federal deficit, and substantially increased defense spending. In 2001, George W. Bush took a page from Reagan and won quick congressional approval of tax cuts and education reforms during a brief five-month period when Republicans controlled both houses of Congress and were united in support of a new president.[9]

The Roosevelt-Reagan-Bush effect was so powerful that would-be presidents wanted to emulate it. In 2008, Democratic presidential candidate Barack Obama lauded Reagan, telling reporters, "I think Ronald Reagan changed the trajectory of America in a way that, you know, Richard Nixon did not, and in a way that Bill Clinton did not," adding that it was "fair to say the Republicans were the party of ideas for a pretty long chunk of time."[10] When Obama became president, he wanted to become a change agent and he beseeched a Democratic-controlled Congress to enact a healthcare reform bill—something that Democrats had advocated since 1948. In fact, when it came to passing a $787 billion stimulus package, healthcare reform, and financial reform, Obama received almost no Republican support and had to rely on a unified Democratic Party to make these changes happen. Former Democratic congressman turned White House chief of staff Rahm Emanuel summarized the administration's thinking when he declared that "no crisis should go to waste." According to Emanuel, "Things that we had postponed for too long, that were long-term, are now immediate and must be dealt with. This crisis provides the opportunity for us to do things that you could not do before."[11] In little more than two years, Obama and the Democrats enacted their $787 billion stimulus bill, passed healthcare reform, and overhauled the financial regulatory system. But once Obama and the Democrats lost control of Congress, almost nothing got done and gridlock ensued.

Franklin Roosevelt, Ronald Reagan, and Barack Obama form a trio of presidents who paid attention to their party. They are hardly alone in the pages of history. Back in 1912, Woodrow Wilson and his fellow Democrats promised to create a Federal Reserve Board to control the flow of the nation's money supply and a Federal Trade Commission that would rein in corporate interests. He promised to pass workmen's compensation for those injured on the job and ease the way for the abolition of child labor. Voters agreed with Wilson and the Democrats, giving Wilson a plurality of 42 percent and, more significantly, adding 73 more Democrats in the House and 6 Democrats in the Senate. Wilson made much of the Democratic victory in his 1913 inaugural address: "No one can mistake the purpose for which the Nation now seeks to use the Democratic Party. It seeks to use it to interpret a change in its own plans and point of view."[12] More than a decade later, a conservative Republican president, Herbert Hoover, also saw his party as an indispensable partner in governing:

> We maintain party government not to promote intolerant partisanship but because opportunity must be given for the expression of the popular will, and organization provided for the execution of its mandates. It follows that Government both in the executive and legislative branches must carry out in good faith the platform upon which the party was entrusted with power.[13]

But as the twentieth century progressed and television allowed presidents to become personalities, the effect was to liberate presidents from their party obligations. Nowhere is this more true than with Donald Trump, who emerged onto the national scene as an entrepreneur with the successful television programs *The Apprentice* and *Celebrity Apprentice*. These shows helped cement Trump's image as a "can-do" person, and propelled him onto our television screens and social media and into the White House. Like his predecessors, Trump was free to ignore the Republican Party in government (which had been cool to his candidacy) whenever it suited his interests. In doing so, Trump was not alone. Richard M. Nixon advocated a guaranteed annual income for the poor and national health insurance that were designed to mollify his Democratic opponents over the opposition of most Republicans.[14] Years later, Bill Clinton adopted a strategy of "triangulation" by setting himself above the partisan wrangling when Republicans assumed control of Congress in 1994—sometimes siding with the Democrats, other times with the Republicans, and at other moments with neither party. At the beginning of 2011, Barack Obama faced a similar quandary: Should he abandon the Democratic Party's base by seeking support from newly empowered congressional Republicans (as Clinton did in 1995–1996), or draw a proverbial line in the sand and do partisan battle as leader of the Democratic Party? Obama initially tried to negotiate a budget deal with John Boehner, but the Republican House Speaker could not carry the bulk of his party members with him, and the deal was abandoned. After winning reelection in 2012, Obama sought a deal with congressional Republicans on an immigration reform package. The bill won bipartisan support in the Senate, but in the House, Republicans never cast a vote as Speaker Boehner could not find 218 Republicans to support it and bring it to the floor. Unlike Clinton, Obama could not find an accommodation with a Republican-controlled Congress as partisanship had become so rigid—and Republican opposition was so intransigent—that Obama was left with a pen and a phone, able to issue executive orders and take unilateral action when available, but unable to secure the substantive legislative achievements that characterized his first two years in office.

## THE PARTY IN CONGRESS

Although presidents have attempted to use their party as a way of bringing the executive and legislative branches together, Congress has been historically incapable of achieving a similar result, as regional diversity and special interests have overwhelmed appeals for party loyalty. This has not stopped key legislators from trying to use parties as action-centered instruments of government. Helping them is the fact that parties are important organizing mechanisms. For example, the side of the aisle on which one sits in Congress is determined by party affiliation. Likewise, committee chairs are often reserved for the senior majority party member of a particular committee, and the ranking member is a senior member of the minority party. Ideological appeals also help bind Democrats and Republicans together. And both parties have established congressional campaign committees that have assumed a growing role in the recruitment and election of members of Congress.

From the outset, congressional parties were an important "extra-constitutional" device that were inserted into the Framers' handiwork. For example, the Federalists, led by Alexander Hamilton, were strong supporters of the Jay Treaty, whereas their Democratic-Republican rivals, led by Thomas Jefferson, were unified in their opposition. As their policy disagreements escalated, party voting became the norm. From the 3rd Congress (1793–1795) to the 7th Congress (1801–1803), Federalist Party unity scores increased from 83.3 percent to 89.9 percent. Likewise, the Democratic-Republicans saw their bloc voting rise from 73.5 percent to 79.6 percent. Looking at this period, political scientist John F. Hoadley writes that party development passed through four distinct stages: (1) factionalism, (2) polarization, (3) expansion, and (4) institutionalization. In the first stage, factions developed and were centered on a variety of disparate issues and charismatic personalities. But these divisions were rarely organized and lasted only a short while. In the second stage, the factions stabilized into permanent groups that opposed each other on a broad range of issues. During the expansion phase, the public was drawn into the partisan arguments. Finally, in the institutionalization phase, a permanent linkage was made among the party organizations, the party in the electorate, and the party in government.[15]

Formalized party structures have developed over the centuries in Congress, as well as in 49 state legislatures. (Nebraska has a nonpartisan unicameral legislature.) Both parties meet every two years at the beginning of each congressional session to select their leaders. There are two institutionalized leadership positions, one for each house of Congress. Article I of the Constitution states that the House "shall choose their Speaker."[16] The Speaker presides over that chamber, rules on points of order, announces results of votes, refers legislation to committees, names lawmakers to serve on the committees, and maintains order and decorum. In addition, the Speaker sets the House's agenda, controls the Rules Committee, chairs his or her party's committee assignment panel, and can bestow (or withhold) various tangible and intangible rewards to members of both parties. Both parties nominate candidates for the Speakership, but the majority party's candidate always prevails. It is extremely rare that a member will cross over and support the nominee of the other party. But in 2009, Alabama Democrat Parker Griffith became a Republican after telling a local newspaper that Democratic House Speaker Nancy Pelosi was "too divisive," and that if she did not like his opposition, he would "provide her with a gift certificate to a mental health center."[17] In 2015, an astounding 25 Republicans voted against John Boehner as Speaker in his reelection bid for that job, the largest number of defections in a century. Many were members of the party's Freedom Caucus, who found Boehner to be not conservative enough for their tastes.[18] Boehner resigned his Speakership in 2015 and was replaced by Paul Ryan, the Republican Party's former 2012 vice presidential candidate and a respected member of the House from Wisconsin who emerged as the GOP's consensus candidate. In 2016, House minority leader Nancy Pelosi faced a spirited challenge after a disappointing result in the House congressional races, where the Democrats added a mere six seats. Congressman Tim Ryan, an Ohio Democrat from the Midwest's Rust Belt where Donald Trump ran strongly, won an astounding 63 votes to Pelosi's 134—a warning to Pelosi that Democrats needed to improve their standing in Congress.[19]

There are other important party leaders in Congress. The majority leader is the second in command of the majority party and works closely with the Speaker. The minority leader serves as the head of his or her party in the House. Minority leaders are the "Speakers-in-Waiting" should their party become a majority. During the 115th Congress (January 2017–December 2018), House minority leader Nancy Pelosi was the "Speaker-in-Waiting." If Democrats regain a majority in the House, it is expected that Pelosi would become Speaker.

Following the Speaker are the majority and minority whips. Each party uses a variety of whips—ranging from head whip to deputy, at-large, regional, and assistant whips. The whips gather intelligence, encourage attendance at important votes and party events, count votes, persuade colleagues to support party measures, and forge lines of communication between the rank and file and party leaders. The foremost job of a whip is to encourage party discipline. Two other important party positions are (1) chair of the policy committees, and (2) head of the campaign committees. The former is responsible for developing a policy plan for the coming session, and the latter for fund-raising and distributing party funds during elections.

In the U.S. Senate, the Constitution stipulates that the vice president serve as the presiding officer and, in case of a tie, cast the deciding vote. Other than on ceremonial occasions and when votes are expected to be very close, the vice president hardly ever sits in a Senate session. In the vice president's absence, the Constitution stipulates that a "president pro tempore" preside. Recently, a custom has developed whereby this officer is a member of the majority party with the longest continuous service. Today, that person is Republican Orrin Hatch, a Utah Republican who was elected to the Senate in 1976. As in the House, both parties in the Senate separately choose their leaders: the majority leader is the head of the majority party in the Senate; the minority leader leads the loyal opposition. Both persons are elected biennially by secret ballot. The remaining leadership posts in the Senate are much the same as in the House. There are whip organizations and chairs of policy committees and campaign committees. Table 8.1 notes the leadership of both parties in the 115th Congress, which began in January 2017.

**Table 8.1 Party Leadership Positions in the House and
Senate, 115th Congress**

| House | Senate |
|---|---|
| Speaker: Paul Ryan (R-WI) | President pro-tempore: Orrin Hatch (R-UT) |
| Majority leader: Kevin McCarthy (R-CA) | Majority leader: Mitch McConnell (R-KY) |
| Majority whip: Steve Scalise (R-LA) | Majority whip: John Cornyn (R-TX) |
| Minority leader: Nancy Pelosi (D-CA) | Minority leader: Chuck Schumer (D-NY) |
| Minority whip: Steny Hoyer (D-MD) | Democratic whip: Dick Durbin (D-IL) |

# DIVIDED PARTIES IN CONGRESS, 1937–1994

For most of the twentieth century, it was not *inter-party* divisions but *intra-party* divisions that required members of Congress to seek allies in order to pass legislation. The Democratic Party was especially divided. From 1937 until 1994, Congress was controlled by the Dixiecrat coalition—an alliance of conservative Southern Democrats (called Dixiecrats) and old-guard Republicans who opposed extending Franklin Roosevelt's New Deal, especially when it came to civil rights legislation. Virginia Democrat Howard Smith was a potent symbol of the Dixiecrat coalition. As chairman of the powerful House Rules Committee, Smith vetoed proposed legislation presented by Democratic presidents and congressional leaders, and he even opposed the elections of John F. Kennedy in 1960 and Lyndon B. Johnson in 1964. With Smith and the Dixiecrat-Republicans in opposition, President Kennedy (who had previously served in both the House and Senate) lamented:

> The fact is that the Congress looks more powerful sitting here than it did when I was there in Congress. But that is because when you are in Congress you are one of 100 in the Senate or one of 435 in the House. So the power is divided. But from here I look at Congress, particularly the bloc action, and it is a substantial power.[20]

As Kennedy's frustrations with an intractable Congress demonstrate, only when there are grave national crises (such as both World Wars, the Great Depression, or the September 11 terrorist attacks), or when foreign policies require congressional approval (as was the case during the cold war), or when there are periods of political abnormality (such as Lyndon Johnson's 1964 landslide and Ronald Reagan's 1980 Republican sweep, or the economic calamity of 2008–2009) can party-oriented presidents overcome the congressional tendency to delay and not act.

# THE EMERGENCE OF RESPONSIBLE PARTY GOVERNMENT, 1994 TO THE PRESENT

By the mid-twentieth century, the inability of both parties to produce a truly party-oriented government frustrated political scientists and led them to search for ways to achieve greater party accountability. Those who believed parties should have the decisive role in making public policy advocated a doctrine commonly referred to as "responsible party government." Simply put, responsible party government occurs when the party in power manages the government and enacts the program spelled out in its platform. For its part, the opposition party develops alternative policies and makes its case to the voters. The public is asked to judge whether the party in power has done a good job and which party has the better program for the future.

The doctrine of responsible party government was best expressed in a 1950 report commissioned by the American Political Science Association (APSA) entitled *Toward a More Responsible Two-Party System*.[21] This book was the capstone of a multi-year effort by an APSA-sanctioned Committee on Political Parties consisting of the leading party scholars of that time. After four years of deliberations, *Toward a More Responsible Two-Party System* operated from the following premise: "Throughout this report political parties are treated as indispensable instruments of government."[22] Thus, it followed that if the parties were in trouble, so was the nation's system of government. This is exactly the conclusion the committee reached—noting the doubts that surrounded Democratic president Harry S. Truman's ability to lead following the death of Franklin D. Roosevelt, the division of power created by the 1946 elections when Republicans assumed control of Congress while Democrats held the presidency, and the inability of either branch to agree on much-needed civil rights legislation. By the time the report was published in 1950, the APSA committee concluded that both parties had disintegrated to the point where they could no longer effectively address the problems facing the country. The report warned that unless the party system was overhauled, three disastrous consequences would follow: (1) the delegation of "excessive responsibility to the president," who would have to generate support for new public initiatives through personal efforts without the benefit of party; (2) continued disintegration of both major parties caused by their relative ineffectiveness; and (3) a presidential-congressional logjam that "might set in motion more extreme tendencies to the political left and the political right."[23]

In the decades following its publication, *Toward a More Responsible Two-Party System* became required reading for party scholars. Most extolled the report for its analysis of the problems parties faced, and they saw the report's warning of a weaker party system fulfilled in a more powerful but party-less presidency. But in reality, the APSA committee actually stifled what was once a lively debate about the role parties should play in government that began at the turn of the twentieth century. Back then, scholars viewed the responsible party doctrine with considerable skepticism. As one wrote,

This theory [of responsible party government] appeared alluring enough to be adopted by some writers of prominence, and expanded in certain cases, with brilliancy of literary style. It has, however, one defect: it is not borne out by the facts.[24]

Another political scientist disagreed, saying: "The individual candidate must be sunk to a large extent in the party. Individual responsibility must give place to party responsibility."[25]

Perhaps no better scholar demonstrated the inexorable movement of political scientists toward accepting the doctrine of responsible party government during the twentieth century than Woodrow Wilson. A prominent political scientist who once served as APSA president, Wilson told the Virginia Bar Association in 1897:

I, for my part, when I vote at a critical election, should like to be able to vote for a definite line of policy with regard to the great questions of the day—not for platforms, which Heaven knows, mean little enough—but for men known and tried in public service; with records open to be scrutinized with reference to these very matters; and pledged to do this or that particular thing; to take a definite course of action. As it is, I vote for nobody I can depend upon to do anything—no, not even if I were to vote for myself.[26]

A decade later, Wilson saw party-centered government more favorably:

There is a sense in which our parties may be said to have been our real body politic. Not the authority of Congress, not the leadership of the President, but the discipline and zest of parties has held us together, has made it possible for us to form and to carry out national programs.[27]

# THE FRUSTRATION OF RESPONSIBLE PARTY GOVERNMENT, 1950–1994

The doctrine of responsible party government got a powerful grip on the academic community, even as events made the idea of a strong party in government less of a possibility at the time. During the 40-year Democratic reign in the House of Representatives (1954–1994), responsible party government had little meaning. Instead of relying on their party to win, Democrats used the tools of incumbency to preserve their offices. Congressional staffs became a new-style permanent campaign staff—answering mail, acting as ombudsmen, and serving as the "eyes and ears" of the legislator in the district. Money also helped Democrats win, as PAC directors steered their dollars to incumbents with a demonstrated ability to win.

But once in Congress, Democrats generally were free to ignore their party. Southerners had long abandoned appeals to party loyalty—as exemplified by the emergence of the Dixiecrat coalition. By the 1970s, Democrats began stripping their congressional leaders of what few remaining powers they had left. Following the Watergate-dominated elections of 1974, a crop of newly elected Democrats was determined to sacrifice party leadership for the purpose of more openness. In a surprising move, these so-called Watergate babies deposed three incumbent committee chairs—a repudiation of the once ironclad seniority rule. Moreover, they adopted a Subcommittee Bill of Rights that reduced the power of both the Speaker and the committee chairs. These changes allowed committee Democrats to pick their chairs; fixed the jurisdictions of subcommittees so that their ability to control certain subjects would not be given to another committee; gave each subcommittee a budget that it controlled; created more staff positions; and guaranteed that members of the full committee would have a right to at least one "choice" subcommittee assignment. These reforms stripped recalcitrant conservative Southern Dixiecrats, many of whom had accumulated enough seniority to become committee chairs, of their jealously guarded powers to frustrate the Democratic majority. But in so doing, they fragmented power among members who served on an ever-larger number of committees and spent their days literally running from one meeting to another.

By 1994, party leadership in Congress was at a low ebb. A series of relatively weak Democratic speakers were held hostage by stubborn committee chairs who were quite willing to resist demands for party loyalty. Bill Clinton, who had high hopes that unified Democratic Party control of the presidency and Congress would result in significant legislative accomplishments, found his hopes dashed when his healthcare initiative (led by First Lady Hillary Clinton) went down in flames. Even Clinton's much-touted economic recovery program—the basis for his 1992 election and his promise to focus on the economy "like a laser beam"—barely won House approval and was passed by the Senate only after Vice President Al Gore cast a decisive tie-breaking vote. Democrats limped into the 1994 midterm contests, hoping that history would prevail yet again and incumbents—meaning Democrats—would be reelected. It was not to be.

# THE REVIVAL OF RESPONSIBLE PARTY GOVERNMENT, 1994–PRESENT

The Republican takeover of Congress following the 1994 midterm elections was more than a mere shift from one party to another. The incoming 73 Republican freshmen differed significantly from their predecessors in both style and ideological persuasion. Stylistically, many saw themselves as "citizen politicians"—dispatched by their constituents to Washington, DC, for a brief period before coming home.

To further fortify themselves from becoming too comfortable in Washington, DC, many Republican newcomers chose to live in their congressional offices—sleeping on their couches by night and showering in the House gymnasium by day, a practice that House Speaker Paul Ryan continues to this day. This reluctance to relocate in the nation's capital differentiated the Republican freshmen from their GOP predecessors, whose families lived year-round in or near Washington, DC. During the 1960s, for example, House minority leader Gerald R. Ford had a home in Alexandria, Virginia, where he resided with his wife, Betty, and their four children. Once, President Lyndon B. Johnson called from the White House during a Thanksgiving recess and thought he had reached Ford in Michigan when, in fact, Ford was just a few miles away.[28]

But it was in their politics that the Republican freshmen were truly different. Motivated by conservative principles, the 1994 class was especially responsive to pleas to keep the faith when it came to implementing their Contract with America. As previously noted, the contract consisted of ten poll-tested items that included balancing the federal budget, tough anti-crime measures, a line-item veto for the president, welfare reform, and tax cuts targeted at families. Of 33 House roll calls taken in 1995 on contract-related items, House GOP members were *unanimous* on 16. For the entire series of roll calls, the median number of Republican dissents was *one*.[29] On average, 97 percent of the Republican freshmen voted in lockstep with their party, and no one fell below 90 percent.[30]

The contract gave Speaker Newt Gingrich an opportunity to assume powers that none of his Democratic predecessors dared imagine. He twice passed over the ranking Republican on the Judiciary and Commerce committees and installed his own loyalists as those committee chairs.[31] On the all-important Appropriations Committee, Gingrich let his colleagues know that he was in charge by promoting a Republican who was *fifth* in seniority on that committee.[32] Just to make sure that everyone knew who controlled this all-important committee, Gingrich required each Republican member to sign a "letter of fidelity" that gave the Speaker the final say over how much of the federal budget would be cut. In addition, Gingrich abolished three committees that had been liberal Democratic bastions: District of Columbia, Merchant Marine and Fisheries, and Post Office and Civil Service. Others were renamed to fit the new GOP-led conservative agenda. The Education and Labor Committee became Economic and Educational Opportunities, Government Operations became Government Reform and Oversight, and Public Works and Transportation became Transportation and Infrastructure. As one Republican put it, "The old names implied a desire to perpetuate and expand the size and scope of government. The new names were needed to put our imprimatur on Congress and indicate the direction in which we're taking the institution."[33] Today, two of these same committees have slightly different names, including Education and the Workforce and Oversight and Government Reform, while Transportation and Infrastructure remains unchanged.

Gingrich also gave his freshmen firebrands unusual access to the inner circles of power. In a highly irregular move, the most powerful and exclusive committees of the House—Rules, Ways and Means, and Appropriations—got new freshmen members over the objections of their Republican chairs. As one grateful recipient observed,

> Newt really enjoys seeing some of us work because he sees the same rabble-rouser that he was a few years ago. Without Newt, the class wouldn't be such a dynamic class. Newt Gingrich asks: "What do the freshmen think?" And he's giving us more than anyone else would have.[34]

Such largesse paid off handsomely, as Gingrich was able to keep his fellow Republicans in line. Indeed, the Republican takeover of Congress coincided with the culmination of a rise in party-centered voting that began during the 1980s. Many were captivated by Ronald Reagan, who led a large, activist, conservative following. During the 1990s, the so-called Reaganites were succeeded by religious-minded conservatives who had strong anti-abortion, anti-gay, and anti-gun-control views. Following George W. Bush's election, Republicans were ready to follow Bush's lead—even if they had philosophical disagreements with the new president. For example, House majority leader Tom DeLay expressed regrets after he cast a vote for Bush's 2001 No Child Left Behind Education bill, saying, "I came here to eliminate the Department of Education." DeLay explained that his "yea" vote was cast only because he wanted to support Bush: "I'm ashamed to say it was just blatant politics."[35] The same pattern occurred throughout Bush's tenure. On the eve of the 2004 election, Republicans cast aside their doubts about Medicare and government spending and voted for a prescription drug program that would be added to the entitlement and would benefit seniors. Similarly, congressional Republicans were poised to act in unison with President Trump at the onset of his term—endorsing his healthcare bill in the House and supporting Trump's conservative nominee to the U.S. Supreme Court in the Senate.

Democrats, too, became more ideologically liberal. The continued exit of Southern conservatives from the party's congressional ranks, the introduction of social and cultural issues (such as abortion and gay rights), and their near-unanimous opposition to the Iraq War during George W. Bush's second term transformed congressional Democrats into a far more homogenous group. House Speaker Nancy Pelosi exemplified the transition. First elected in 1987, Pelosi compiled a liberal voting record, one that reflected the beliefs of the residents of her San Francisco district.[36] In 2012, Pelosi received an 80 percent rating from the liberally oriented Americans for Democratic Action (ADA).[37] In 2015, the House Democrats averaged an approval rating from the ADA of 85.3 percent, while House Republicans garnered a meager 2.5 percent. Forty-one House Democrats had perfect ADA scores of 100, while 171 House Republicans garnered scores of zero. The partisanship even spread to the Senate (which in many ways became much more like the House), as Senate Democrats averaged an ADA approval score of 89 percent, while Senate Republicans scored just 5 percent. Thirteen Senate Democrats had perfect scores of 100, while 27 Senate Republicans had scores of zero.[38]

Clearly, ideological purists from both parties have altered the way Congress conducts its business in both chambers. Those who once subscribed to the late Democratic House Speaker Sam Rayburn's wisdom that the best way to "get along" in Congress is to "go along" suddenly found themselves in the minority. House minority leader Bob Michel, an old-school Republican who was often chummy with his Democratic colleagues, first spotted the change. Of the 47 GOP newcomers elected in 1992, Michel concluded that "7 are thoughtful moderates, and the other 40 are pretty darn hardliners, some of them really hardline."[39] The Republican class of 1994 was even more zealous. Arizona freshman John Shadegg said his colleagues were not "interested in coming here to be reasonable and to settle for what they can get. They don't want to go along to get along."[40] Two congressional scholars, Thomas E. Mann and Norman J. Ornstein, write that the asymmetrical partisan warfare has affected Republican congressional members even more than Democrats:

> The Republican Party has become an insurgent outlier—ideologically extreme; contemptuous of the inherited social and economic policy regime; scornful of compromise; unpersuaded by conventional understanding of facts, evidence, and science; and dismissive of the legitimacy of its political opposition.[41]

The heightened sense of partisanship in the halls of Congress persisted throughout Barack Obama's presidency. Obama came to prominence promising to end the partisan politics that had gripped Washington, DC. But as soon as he was sworn in as president, partisanship asserted itself with a vengeance. During the healthcare debate in 2009, then-Republican senator Jim DeMint offered an insight into GOP thinking, saying that if Obama were defeated on this issue, "It will be his Waterloo. We will break him."[42] Senate Republicans unanimously opposed Obamacare, and only one House Republican voted for it. Repeal of Obamacare is the first item on the Republican Party's to-do list now that Donald Trump is President and the GOP is in control of Congress. Likewise, when it came to supporting Obama's economic stimulus, no Republicans in either the House or Senate supported it. According to a study conducted by the Brookings Institution, the 111th Congress that marked the start of the Obama presidency "is the most polarized in history. In both the House and Senate, the most conservative Democrat is more liberal than is the most liberal Republican."[43] More recent data find the parties sharply polarized, as conservative Southern Dixiecrats have all but disappeared from the shrinking Democratic congressional ranks, while moderate-to-liberal Republicans have also become nearly extinct.

Given this partisanship, it is not surprising that the party wars have intensified, leaving some members of Congress disillusioned and ready to leave. In 2010, Indiana Democrat Evan Bayh announced his retirement, arguing that the ideological polarization in the U.S. Senate had made that body dysfunctional: "For some time, I have had a growing conviction that Congress is not operating as it should." He continued, "There is too much partisanship and not enough progress—too much narrow ideology and not enough practical problem solving. Even at a time of enormous challenge, the people's business is not being done."[44] Bayh attempted a comeback in 2016, but failed to win support from Indiana voters after they learned that their former senator spent too little time in his home state and much of his time at a Washington, DC, lobbying firm.

## THE RISE OF THE PUBLIC SPEAKERSHIP

One consequence of the visible partisan warfare in Washington, DC, has been a more visible House Speakership. During the long reign of Democratic Party rule from 1954 to 1994, House Speakers ceded much of their power to committee chairs—many of them conservative Southern Democrats—who were the undisputed "kings of the hill." This suited most Speakers, as many of them were old-style operatives who worked behind closed doors. Sam Rayburn, one of the most powerful of the Democratic Speakers, had his famous "Board of Education" where favored members would gather to discuss pending business and make deals over bourbon and branch water. Once, when asked to appear on a Sunday talk show, Rayburn responded:

> I do appreciate your wanting me to be on *Meet the Press*, but I never go on programs such as yours. . . . The trouble about my going on one program is then I would have no excuse to say to the others that I could not go on their program. It is a chore that I have never relished and one that I doubt would be any good. . . . I would have to tell you what I tell all the others, and that is that I do not go on these programs.[45]

John McCormack and Carl Albert were far less powerful Speakers, yet, like Rayburn, they were ineffectual party spokespersons. In 1969, McCormack was mentioned on three network evening television newscasts (CBS, NBC, and ABC) a mere 17 times.[46] Media inquiries were so few that McCormack did not even bother hiring a press secretary. Carl Albert got a press secretary, but still refrained from assuming a public role. Thomas P. "Tip" O'Neill was much more visible, but his heightened recognition was due to a unique political situation: Republican control of the presidency and U.S. Senate in 1980 left O'Neill as the only viable Democratic Party spokesperson. O'Neill recognized his new position and added Chris Matthews to his staff (later host of MSNBC's *Hardball*). Said Matthews: "[O'Neill] would now be faced with the seemingly impossible task of defending his party's principles on that national, televised stage where the highly telegenic Ronald Reagan had long been professionally at home."[47] O'Neill began appearing regularly on the evening network newscasts and the Sunday morning talk shows. His successor, Jim Wright, sought O'Neill's visibility, but became much better known thanks to Newt Gingrich's charge that

Wright had violated congressional ethics rules. Wright resigned and was succeeded by Democrat Tom Foley. Although Foley appeared on the various Sunday talk shows, he was eclipsed by other Democratic Party spokespersons—most notably President Clinton.

All that changed with Newt Gingrich. In 1995, for the first time in history, the House Speaker delivered a nationally televised address to the American people. The following June, Gingrich shared a stage with President Clinton in a small New Hampshire town to debate the issues. Television, which had transformed the presidency, was working its magic on Congress. Gingrich became the first public Speaker in memory, as he freely acknowledged, "Each generation produces its own style of being effective. The most accurate statement of how I see the Speakership [is] somebody who could somehow combine grassroots organizations, mass media, and legislative detail into one synergistic pattern."[48] Gingrich redesigned the Speaker's office to accommodate his desire to "go public" by creating four media-oriented staff positions: press secretary, deputy press secretary, press assistant, and communications coordinator. Unlike his predecessors, Gingrich had little appetite for the machinations of the House floor—preferring to leave those duties to his number-two man, then-majority leader Dick Armey.

The effects of the new public Speakership were immediate: during his first three months in power, Gingrich was mentioned in 114 stories that ran on the three network nightly news programs. In 1996, Gingrich refused to seek the presidency, since his candidacy would require him to forsake his position as Speaker. But in 1998, disgruntled House Republicans were disappointed at their party's performance in that year's midterm elections, and forced Gingrigh's resignation.

An old saying has it that "imitation is the sincerest form of flattery." Democrats paid attention to Gingrich's skilled use of the media during the early months of his Speakership and emulated his tactics, if not his style. Toward that end, Democrats established a communications team that coordinated appearances on the House floor by party members and ensured that each Democrat "stayed on message." Although Nancy Pelosi did some interviews while serving as Speaker, she excelled in wielding power behind the scenes—preferring to leave the messaging to others and letting Barack Obama speak for the Democratic Party once he assumed the presidency. Today, both congressional parties have message groups and communication strategy teams, and they are intensely focused on getting their messages out to the public using every variety of social media available: Facebook, Twitter, Instagram, their party's congressional web pages, Google+, etc.

Social media has become a particularly important tool for party leaders in Congress. Paul Ryan has his own home page, Facebook, and Twitter accounts, as does Nancy Pelosi. Each seeks to tell their side of the party story to a web-connected audience. Increasingly, the Internet has become a forum for important Congress-related stories. There are numerous websites devoted to covering Capitol Hill, including *Politico*, *Roll Call*, and *The Hill*. Other websites, such as *The Huffington Post*, *Talking Points Memo*, the *Daily Kos*, the *Daily Beast*, and others, provide a steady stream of congressional information to their voracious readers.

# CONGRESS AND THE "LITTLE
# ARTS OF POPULARITY"

The demise of the Dixiecrat-Republican coalition in Congress and its replacement with a highly charged partisanship has met with a general public revulsion. Sensing the public's disgust with the intense partisanship, David Price, a respected North Carolina Democratic congressman, has called for a "subdued partisanship," but the passions that rule today's congressional parties make this an almost impossible goal to achieve.[49] It is not only the issues separating the two congressional parties that undermine bipartisanship, it is also the demeanor of both parties. Former Democratic House minority leader Dick Gephardt noted that "Democrats and Republicans don't even make eye contact when they pass one another in the halls of Congress, unless it's to exchange furious glares."[50] Similar complaints are heard on the Republican side. At a retreat of House Republicans in 2010, President Obama made a surprise appearance, and said:

> We've got to be careful about what we say about each other some-
> times, because it boxes us in in ways that makes it difficult for us to work
> together.... So just a tone of civility instead of slash and burn would be
> helpful. The problem we have sometimes is a media that responds only to
> slash-and-burn-style politics. You don't get a lot of credit if I say, "You know,
> I think Paul Ryan is a pretty sincere guy and has a beautiful family." Nobody
> is going to run that in the newspapers.[51]

But rather than engaging in the hard task of governing, many congressional partisans find it more enticing to be sought-after guests on cable television programs, such as MSNBC's *Hardball*, Fox's *Hannity*, Comedy Central's *The Daily Show*, and HBO's *Real Time with Bill Maher*. These shows often promote entertainment values (i.e., the fight) rather than political enlightenment. Even late-night television has become a forum for political debate, as party leaders appear on them to exchange quips with hosts Jimmy Fallon, Stephen Colbert, and Jimmy Kimmel.

Writing in *The Federalist*, Alexander Hamilton declared that the best legislators were those who vote their consciences and ignore pleas to do otherwise. Hamilton derided "the little arts of popularity"[52]—a dig at those who paid too much attention to the public opinion polls of their day—preferring strong congressional leaders who could muster support for unpopular positions whenever necessary. (Hamilton himself was instrumental in having the House support Jefferson's 1800 election as president over rival Aaron Burr.) On the other hand, Thomas Jefferson was much more sensitive to the need of lawmakers to pay attention to the folks back home—undoubtedly one reason why he was elected president and Hamilton was not. Given his predilection for viewing the country as a diverse collection of communities, Jefferson believed that legislators should act as delegates. In 1825, he wrote that the "salvation of the republic" rested on the regeneration and spread of devices like the New England town meeting.[53]

Hamilton's warning that legislators pay far too much attention to "the little arts of popularity" still rings true. Because public opinion polls often guide legislative behavior, and voters are increasingly polarized, the power of party leaders has grown. Cable television news and the Internet serve as means of both mobilizing and polarizing public opinion—a phenomenon that has spilled over into the Congress, where partisan leaders have more clout within their own parties. Even some political scientists are rethinking the wisdom of the responsible party doctrine. The late Nelson Polsby was one: "The trouble began when we political scientists finally got our wish—'responsible' political parties, instead of broad, nonideological coalitions. The idea was, of course, completely nuts from the start."[54] But nuts or not, the prospects for more unified (hence responsible) parties remain bright. Hamiltonian nationalism has bred its own form of national politics on whose stage congressional party leaders assume a dominant role.

The rise of Hamiltonian nationalism and national congressional leaders who constantly bicker with one another has produced a backlash. An October 2016 Gallup poll found 79 percent of respondents saying they disapproved of the way Congress is handling its job; just 18 percent approved.[55] After Trump won in 2016, it was clear that voters wanted the new president to work with Democrats in Congress and vice versa. Fifty-eight percent thought President Trump would "make a sincere effort to work with the Democrats in Congress to find solutions that are acceptable to both parties," and 58 percent believed congressional Democrats would do the same.[56] But in Washington, DC, expectations for bipartisan solutions remains low. As the parties become even more polarized and nationalized, some believe that the prospects for a third party are enhanced. That prospect will be explored in the next chapter.

# NOTES

1. Newt Gingrich, *Lessons Learned the Hard Way* (New York: HarperCollins, 1998), pp. 1, 2.

2. The ten items in the Contract with America were as follows: (1) The Fiscal Responsibility Act proposed a constitutional amendment requiring the president to submit, and the Congress to pass, a balanced federal budget for each fiscal year and would give the president a line-item veto over specific budgetary provisions in a bill passed by Congress; (2) the Taking Back Our Streets Act limited federal and state habeas corpus appeals, mandated minimum sentences for and victim restitution from those convicted of gun-related crimes, replaced recently passed crime-prevention programs with block grants for local law-enforcement programs, relaxed rules for admission of evidence at criminal trials, and would speed deportation procedures for aliens convicted of serious crimes; (3) the Personal Responsibility Act limited eligibility for the federal Aid to Families with Dependent Children (AFDC) program, denied AFDC benefits to teenage mothers, imposed work requirements for those receiving AFDC benefits, and transferred much of the responsibility for social welfare programs to the states; (4) the Family Reinforcement Act granted tax credits for adoption and for care of elderly dependents and increased penalties for sexual offenses against children; (5) the American Dream Restoration Act granted tax credits for families with children, reduced taxes on some married

couples, and expanded uses for Individual Retirement Accounts (IRAs); (6) the National Security Restoration Act restricted participation of U.S. forces in U.N. peacekeeping activities, subjected all funding for and participation in U.N. peacekeeping activities to congressional approval, and reinstated development of the "Star Wars" antiballistic missile defense system and other such systems; (7) the Senior Citizens Equity Act doubled the income level beyond which Social Security benefits are reduced, reduced taxes on upper-income recipients of Social Security, and created tax benefits for the purchase of private long-term healthcare insurance; (8) the Job Creation and Wage Enhancement Act cut the capital gains tax, increased the estate tax exemption, and imposed additional requirements for and restrictions on federal regulation; (9) the Common Sense Legal Reforms Act required the loser to pay the legal expenses of the winner in lawsuits filed in federal courts, reformed product liability laws, and limited lawsuits by shareholders against companies whose stock they hold; and (10) the Citizen Legislature Act proposed a constitutional amendment to limit tenure of senators and representatives to a maximum of 12 years. See House Republican Conference, *Legislative Digest*, September 27, 1994.

3.   Quoted in Linda Killian, *The Freshmen: What Happened to the Republican Revolution?* (Boulder, CO: Westview Press, 1998), p. 7.

4.   Alexander Hamilton, "Federalist 68," in Alexander Hamilton, James Madison, and John Jay, ed., *The Federalist* (New York: Mentor Books, 1961), p. 414.

5.   Donald J. Trump, Announcement Speech, New York City, June 16, 2015.

6.   See Charles O. Jones, *The Trusteeship Presidency: Jimmy Carter and the United States Congress* (Baton Rouge: Louisiana State University Press, 1988).

7.   Cited in Adam Cohen, *Nothing to Fear: FDR's Inner Circle and the Hundred Days That Created Modern America* (New York: Penguin Books, 2009), p. 40.

8.   Quoted in Jonathan Alter, *The Defining Moment: FDR's Hundred Days and the Triumph of Hope* (New York: Simon & Schuster, 2006), p. 251.

9.   Republican control of the Senate was short-circuited when Vermont senator Jim Jeffords left the GOP to become an independent and affiliated himself with the Democrats. For more on this, see Chapter 9.

10.   Quoted in John Heilemann and Mark Halperin, *Game Change: Obama and the Clintons, McCain and Palin, and the Race of a Lifetime* (New York: HarperCollins, 2010), p. 200.

11.   Capitol Journal, "In Crisis, Opportunity for Obama," *Wall Street Journal*, November 21, 2008. See http://online.wsj.com/article/SB122721278056345271.html. Accessed November 8, 2010.

12.   Woodrow Wilson, Inaugural Address, Washington, DC, March 4, 1913.

13.   Quoted in Stanley Kelley Jr., *Interpreting Elections* (Princeton, NJ: Princeton University Press, 1983), p. 127.

14.   See especially Richard Reeves, *President Nixon: Alone in the White House* (New York: Simon & Schuster, 2001).

15.   See John F. Hoadley, "The Emergence of Political Parties in Congress, 1789–1803," *American Political Science Review* 74 (1980): pp. 761, 768–769.

16.   Interestingly, the provision does not require that this person be an actual member of the House, although all Speakers have been members.

17.   Quoted in Jos Kraushaar, "Griffith Faults Pelosi for Switch," *Politico*, December 22, 2009. In 2010, Parker lost his bid for reelection, having been beaten by another Republican in the GOP primary.

18.   Aaron Blake, "Here Are the Republicans Who Voted Against John Boehner for Speaker," *Washington Post*, January 6, 2015.

19.   Deidre Walsh, Tom Lobianco, and Manu Raju, "Nancy Pelosi Reelected as House Democratic Leader," CNN.com, November 30, 2016. See www.cnn.com/2016/11/30/politics/house-democrat-election-results-nancy-pelosi-tim-ryan/. Accessed December 4, 2016.

20.   Quoted in Dale Vinyard, *The Presidency* (New York: Scribner's, 1971), p. 107.

21.   Committee on Political Parties, *Toward a More Responsible Two-Party System* (New York: Rinehart, 1950).

22.   Ibid., p. 15.

23.   Ibid., pp. 92, 94, 95.

24.   M. I. Ostrogorski, *Democracy and the Party System* (New York: Palgrave Macmillan, 1910), p. 380.

25.   Quoted in Austin Ranney, *The Doctrine of Responsible Party Government: Its Origins and Present State* (Urbana, IL: The University of Illinois Press, 1954), p. 96.

26.   Woodrow Wilson, "Leaderless Government," an address before the Virginia Bar Association, August 4, 1897, in *Public Papers,* vol. 1, pp. 336–359. Quoted in Austin Ranney, *The Doctrine of Responsible Party Government: Its Origins and Present State* (Urbana, IL: University of Illinois Press, 1954), p. 33.

27.   Quoted in David E. Price, *Bringing Back the Parties* (Washington, DC: Congressional Quarterly Press, 1984), p. 103.

28.   See Michael R. Beschloss, *Taking Charge: The Johnson White House Tapes, 1963–1964* (New York: Simon & Schuster, 1997), p. 64.

29.   Gerald M. Pomper, "Parliamentary Government in the United States?" in John C. Green and Daniel M. Shea, eds., *The State of the Parties: The Changing Role of Contemporary American Parties* (Lanham, MD: Rowman & Littlefield, 1999), p. 260.

30.   See John H. Aldrich and David W. Rohde, "The Transition to Republican Rule in the House: Implications for Theories of Congressional Politics," *Political Science Quarterly* 112 (Winter 1997–1998), p. 563. In fewer than 100 days, eight of the contract's ten items had been approved by the House, thanks to nearly unanimous support from the GOP freshmen. Only two measures failed: term limits, thanks to the opposition of Judiciary Committee chairman Henry Hyde; and a provision prohibiting the Pentagon from using funds for U.N. peacekeeping operations.

31.   These were Henry Hyde and Thomas Bliley.

32.   This was Robert Livingston of Louisiana.

33.   Nicol C. Rae, *Conservative Reformers: The Republican Freshmen and the Lessons of the 104th Congress* (Armonk, NY: Sharpe, 1998), p. 69.

34.   Ibid., pp. 70–71.

35.   Quoted in "Washington Wire," *Wall Street Journal,* July 27, 2001, p. A1.

36.   Pelosi won a special election in 1987 to fill the seat left by the late Sala Burton.

37.   See https://votesmart.org/interest-group/978/rating/6833#.WDyOSvkrJPY. Accessed November 28, 2016.

38.   See www.adaction.org/media/votingrecords/2015.pdf. Accessed November 28, 2016.

39.   Quoted in Aldrich and Rohde, "The Transition to Republican Rule in the House," p. 561.

40.   Ibid., p. 562.

41.   Thomas E. Mann and Norman J. Ornstein, *It's Even Worse Than It Was* (New York: Basic Books, 2016), p. xv.

42.  See Ben Smith, "Health Reform Foes Plan Obama's Waterloo," *Politico*, July 17, 2009.

43.  See William A. Galston, "Can a Polarized American Party System Be 'Healthy'?" *Brookings Institute Issues in Governance Studies*, April 2010, p. 4.

44.  Quoted in Adam Nagourney, "Democrats Reel as Senator Says No to Third Term," *New York Times*, February 15, 2010, p. 1.

45.  Quoted in Douglas B. Harris, "The Rise of the Public Speakership," *Political Science Quarterly* (Summer 1998), p. 198.

46.  Ibid., p. 195.

47.  Chris Matthews, *Tip and the Gipper* (New York: Simon and Schuster, 2013), p. 140.

48.  Quoted in Randall Strahan, *Leading Representatives: The Agency of Leaders in the Politics of the U.S. House* (Baltimore: Johns Hopkins University Press, 2007), p. 142.

49.  John Kenneth White, interview with David Price, Washington, DC, October 25, 2000.

50.  Richard Gephardt, *An Even Better Place: America in the 21st Century* (New York: Public Affairs, 1999), p. 18.

51.  Obama Remarks at House Republican Retreat, Baltimore, Maryland, January 29, 2010.

52.  Hamilton, "Federalist 68," p. 414.

53.  Quoted in Robert F. Kennedy, *To Seek a Newer World* (New York: Doubleday, 1967), p. 56.

54.  Quoted in Joe Klein, "The Town That Ate Itself," *New Yorker*, November 23, 1998, p. 80.

55.  Gallup poll, October 5–9, 2016. Text of question: "Do you approve or disapprove of the way Congress is handling its job?" Approve, 18 percent; disapprove, 79 percent; no opinion, 3 percent.

56.  Gallup poll, November 9–13, 2016. Text of question one: "In dealing with the problems facing the country, do you think Donald Trump will or will not make a sincere effort to work with the Democrats in Congress to find solutions that are acceptable to both parties?" Yes, 58 percent; no, 40 percent; no opinion, 2 percent. Text of question two: "Do you think the Democrats in Congress will or will not make a sincere effort to work with Donald Trump and the Republicans in Congress to find solutions that are acceptable to both parties in dealing with the problems facing the country?" Yes, 58 percent; no, 39 percent; no opinion, 3 percent.

# 9

# Third Parties in the Trump Era

The year 2016 should have been a great year for third-party candidates. That year, the major parties nominated two historically weak presidential candidates whom voters saw as exceptionally flawed. The Democratic nominee, Hillary Clinton, was distrusted by voters following revelations that she kept an email server at her home where classified government secrets were housed during her tenure as secretary of state. The fact that Clinton was not charged by the FBI, coupled with criticism by its director that she was "extremely careless" in handling national security information, did nothing to ameliorate concerns about her veracity and penchant for secretiveness. Those doubts were brought into sharp relief when the FBI director, James Comey, on the eve of the election, announced that the Clinton investigation was being reopened after emails between the former secretary of state and a loyal staffer were found on that staffer's estranged husband's computer. Although the director further clarified his findings just 48 hours before the polls closed and announced no change to his initial finding not to prosecute Clinton, voters were hardly assuaged: 45 percent said Clinton's use of a private email server bothered them "a lot"; 61 percent said she was "not honest and trustworthy"; and 54 percent had an unfavorable view of her.[1]

The Republican nominee, Donald J. Trump, fared even worse: 60 percent of voters said he was "not qualified" to serve as President; 63 percent believed he did not have the right temperament to be commander in chief; 63 percent thought he was "not honest and trustworthy"; 60 percent had an unfavorable view of him; and 50 percent said his treatment of women bothered them "a lot."[2] Not surprisingly, just 13 percent were "excited" about the prospect of a Trump presidency; 27 percent were "optimistic"; 20 percent were "concerned"; and 36 percent were "scared."[3] Given a choice between a dishonest candidate and an unqualified one, it wasn't surprising that 59 percent of voters pronounced themselves to be unhappy with the whole process.[4] And it also wasn't surprising that 65 percent said they would consider voting for a third-party candidate just because they disliked both major-party candidates.[5]

With all that, third-party candidates failed to muster much support at the polls. The Libertarian Party managed to win a paltry 3.3 percent of the votes cast. This happened despite the fact that the Libertarian Party nominated two former moderate Republican governors, Gary Johnson of New Mexico for President and William Weld of Massachusetts for Vice President. Both presented themselves as fiscally conservative and socially liberal, positions that they believed would appeal to Millennials and moderates of all ages. But Johnson was an especially flawed candidate who became the subject of tremendous ridicule when he could not identify Aleppo as the Syrian city enduring an ongoing humanitarian crisis. Another candidate, Dr. Jill Stein, the nominee of the Green Party, tried to win over disillusioned Bernie Sanders supporters, who had placed their hopes in his failed candidacy. But Stein did even worse, winning just 1 percent of the votes cast.

Neither the ballot box nor Washington, DC is a hospitable environment for third parties. Institutionally, everything in Congress is organized around the two major parties. The caucus (or conference, as it is called by Republicans) is a gathering of every elected congressional Democrat or Republican within their respective chamber. These organizations select the leaders of Congress—including the Speaker of the House, the majority and minority leaders, and whips. They also debate legislative policies, map out strategies on pending bills, provide valuable information to their members, and approve committee assignments. Without the aid of caucus leaders, new members can expect to be placed on undesirable committees that are of little importance back home. Non-caucus members accumulate no committee seniority, thereby dashing any hopes of one day becoming a committee or subcommittee chair. While three senators were elected without running on a major-party label—Bernie Sanders of Vermont, Angus King of Maine, and Lisa Murkowski of Alaska—all have cast their lots with the major parties (Sanders and King with the Democrats and Murkowski with the Republicans), knowing that to stay outside of the major-party organizations offers them little in the way of access to power. In the House, there are currently no independent or third-party members.

Such partisan structures derive naturally from the stranglehold the major parties exercise over our political institutions and reflect the dominant role of the major parties in American political life. Nonetheless, third parties do form, occasionally endure, and in rare instances exercise an important influence on our politics. It seems paradoxical that a political system so thoroughly dominated by two major parties would spawn minor parties. Yet minor parties have been a consistent feature in the American political landscape. In this chapter, we'll explore why.

*Third party* or *minor party* (the terms can be used interchangeably) refers to entities that have formal organizational structures and procedures. Like major parties, minor parties write platforms, nominate candidates for office, and have formal officers (e.g., a state party chair). They persist for long periods of time— far longer than one election. *Splinter candidacies* differ from minor parties in that they are "one-hit wonders" that happen when candidates with a following who are displeased with the major parties, or who are unable to win a nomination from one of them, decide to go it alone. Notable splinter presidential candidates have included J. Strom Thurmond in 1948, who deplored Harry S. Truman's embrace of a pro–civil rights Democratic platform; George C. Wallace in 1968, who rejected Lyndon B. Johnson's support for civil rights; and John B. Anderson in 1980, who disagreed with the conservative policies of Republican nominee Ronald Reagan. Each was either a prominent Democrat (Thurmond, Wallace) or a Republican (Anderson) prior to his independent bid for the White House.

## THE THIRD-PARTY PARADOX

We have seen how the Democratic–Republican duopoly is an enduring feature of American political life. Minor parties, in contrast, have struggled for recognition and votes, yet they compete all the same. In the 2016 election, Libertarian Party candidate Gary Johnson appeared on all 50 state ballots, while Green Party candidate Jill Stein's name was listed on 44 of them.[6] Despite this notable achievement, only 21 percent of voters said they would even consider voting for Johnson at the onset of the fall campaign, while 12 percent said the same about Stein. The same survey found 61 percent saying they *would not* consider voting for Johnson (with 44 percent saying that they would "strongly" not consider him), while 66 percent said they *would not* consider casting a ballot for Stein (with 47 percent responding that they would "strongly" rule out such a prospect).[7] Some years ago, political scientist Clinton Rossiter coined an aphorism that still remains valid:

> The most momentous fact about the pattern of American politics is that we live under a persistent, obdurate, one might almost say tyrannical, two-party system. We have the Republicans and we have the Democrats, and we have almost no one else... in the struggle for power.[8]

At the state and local levels, third-party competition makes some sense, as third-party candidates have had some success in statewide races. In the last quarter century, independents have won the governorships of Maine, Connecticut, Minnesota, and Rhode Island, and have run credible campaigns in other states. In 1990, former Connecticut senator Lowell Weicker left the Republican Party to form "A Connecticut Party" and was elected governor of that state, serving for one term. Four years later, independent Angus King, a former Democrat, was elected Maine's governor and served for two terms. In 1998, the Reform Party scored a stunning victory when former professional wrestler Jesse Ventura won the

Minnesota governorship. In 2010, one-time Republican senator Lincoln Chafee beat the Republican and Democratic candidates (who placed second and third, respectively) to win the governorship of Rhode Island as an independent. (Chafee later became a Democrat.) In 2010 and 2014, an independent candidate in Maine ran a strong third in that state's gubernatorial contest, tipping the governorship to the Republican candidate, Paul LePage.[9]

At the national level, the story is different. When third-party candidates exert influence at the national level, it is usually in a spoiler role made available to them through the temporary fracturing of Republican or Democratic Party coalitions. In 1992, billionaire businessman Ross Perot ran for president as an independent. In the general election, Perot captured 19 percent of the vote—the largest percentage won by a candidate without a major-party affiliation since former Republican president Theodore Roosevelt ran as a third-party candidate in 1912. Four years later, Perot made a second foray into presidential politics as the candidate of the Reform Party. Although winning just 8 percent of the vote—less than half of what he received in 1992—Perot garnered the largest share of votes given to third-party or independent candidates in consecutive elections in the twentieth century. In 2000, Green Party presidential candidate Ralph Nader castigated Bill Clinton for not seriously pursuing campaign finance reform and becoming too closely associated with corporate interests. Nader won backing from progressives who were disenchanted with what they saw as the conservative direction the Democratic Party had taken under Clinton. Thanks to their support, Nader won 2.7 percent of the popular vote—enough to tip a close presidential election to George W. Bush. And in 2016, Gary Johnson and Jill Stein won 3.2 percent and 1 percent of the vote, respectively. These candidates made a difference in Michigan, Wisconsin, and Pennsylvania, as they collectively won more votes than Donald J. Trump's margin of victory in each state. (If these states had flipped to Hillary Clinton, she would have won the Electoral College in addition to winning the popular vote.) Despite such notable showings, third parties confront several difficulties—including institutional barriers, the tides of history, and the constraints imposed by the U.S. political culture. In this chapter, we pose several questions:

◆ Why have third parties generally failed at the polls?
◆ Which parties have captured the public's attention, and why were they relatively successful?
◆ How does our system's adherence to a two-party model square with the Jeffersonian and Hamiltonian views of democracy?

# INSTITUTIONAL AND CULTURAL BARRIERS TO THIRD PARTIES

A number of institutional and cultural factors make it difficult for third parties to compete with Republicans and Democrats. In some instances, these barriers are intentional, placed there by the major parties for the express purpose of maintaining their dominance. In other cases, the barriers are rooted in American political culture and development. Institutional barriers include single-member electoral districts, the Electoral College, the executive-centered nature of American governance, ballot access restrictions, direct primaries, campaign finance laws, and restrictions placed on third parties barring participation in the presidential debates. Cultural barriers include a historical tendency toward finding compromise and a decidedly centrist approach to politics, which has reinforced the dominance of two large political parties capable of finding supporters in the middle of the political spectrum.

## INSTITUTIONAL BARRIERS TO THIRD PARTIES

In some democracies—including Austria, Germany, Japan, and Israel—a voting system known as proportional representation is used to elect legislative candidates who, in turn, choose the leader of the government. This system has two important components that influence party formation. First, more than one elected official is sent to the national or provincial assembly from each legislative district. Second, the number of representatives elected is directly proportional to the votes that a party receives on Election Day. If, for example, the Socialist Party of Austria receives 20 percent of the ballots and a district has five members, then the Socialists can expect to send one member to parliament from that district. The key element that fosters minor-party activity is that there are benefits even when the party does not win a plurality of votes. Extremist or rigidly ideological parties are encouraged to participate, because the multi-member proportional representation system all but guarantees that they will win a few seats. This is in sharp contrast to the United States, which relies on a winner-take-all single-member district system for choosing most of its officeholders. No matter how hard a party might work, there is no payoff unless a candidate receives a plurality of votes on Election Day. Only one person is sent to the legislature.

To better illustrate the contrast between the multi-member proportional representation system and the winner-take-all single-member district method, imagine a situation in which four parties are competing for a single seat. Let's say that Party A is at the far left of the ideological spectrum (the most liberal); Party B, left-of-center; Party C, right-of-center; and Party D, at the far right (the most conservative). In this hypothetical election, Party A wins 20 percent of the votes; Party B, 30 percent; Party C, 27 percent; and Party D, 23 percent. Under the proportional system, each party has roughly the same number of legislators in the national assembly, with a small edge going to Party B. Under the winner-take-all single-member district system, only Party B would send legislators to the capitol. The British, who use the winner-take-all method, liken such electoral outcomes to horse races and have characterized their system as being "first past the post."

In a winner-take-all single-member district system, there are strong incentives for political parties located near each other on the ideological spectrum to merge. Using the previous example, operatives from Party C might say to Party D, "You know, we don't agree on everything, but we think alike. If we joined forces, we could surely overtake Party B. After all, they netted only 30 percent of the vote in the last election, whereas together we grabbed 50 percent." Under these rules, Party C's operatives know that it does not matter whether there are 4, 14, or 40 parties vying for support. When the laws dictate a winner-take-all single-member district system, there is no payoff for coming in second.

Another institutional barrier limiting minor-party success in the United States is the Electoral College. Recall that the Electoral College was designed by the Framers of the Constitution to nominate and elect a nonpartisan president (see Chapter 4). Two aspects of the Electoral College hinder minor-party success. First, each state is granted a number of electors equal to its total federal representatives in Congress (both House and Senate members combined). Although the Constitution is silent on how each state should apportion these electors, most employ a winner-take-all scheme whereby the candidate who receives a plurality of votes receives all of that state's electors.[10] Second, under the Electoral College rules, the winning presidential candidate must receive an absolute majority of the electoral votes cast—currently 270 out of 538. (In 2016, Donald Trump received 306 electoral votes to Hillary Clinton's 232.) If no candidate wins an electoral majority, the House of Representatives chooses the president by having each state's delegation cast one vote. This happened only once, in the disputed presidential election of 1824, when the House chose John Quincy Adams (see Chapter 2). Today, it is hard to imagine that a body composed entirely of Democrats and Republicans would select a third-party candidate— especially if that person did not garner more than 50 percent of the popular vote.

The way the Electoral College punishes third-party candidates is illustrative of the problems confronting alternatives to the major parties in a single-member district system. In 1912, Theodore Roosevelt was unable to wrest the GOP nomination from William Howard Taft, so he left the GOP to form the Progressive (Bull Moose) Party. The former president finished second with 27 percent of the popular vote. But in the Electoral College, Roosevelt captured just 17 percent of the electoral votes cast. Ross Perot met a similar fate in 1992. His 19 percent of the popular vote was the third largest in U.S. history—behind Roosevelt and another former president, Millard Fillmore—but because his supporters were spread uniformly across the country and not concentrated in particular states, Perot was unable to garner a single electoral vote.[11] In 2016, both Gary Johnson and Jill Stein won *zero* electoral votes.

Besides the Electoral College, another reason for the persistence of the two-party system is that the U.S. polity is executive centered. Voters expect their executives—be they mayors, governors, or presidents—to exercise vast powers. When a great deal of power is given to one person, and citizens accept this arrangement as legitimate, there are strong incentives for elites to form broad-based parties capable of winning an executive position. For their part, voters do not want to "waste their vote" on a third-party candidate who is unlikely to win, because there is so much at stake. The "I don't want to waste my vote" phenomenon was very much in evidence in 2016. According to one survey, 52 percent said they would not cast a ballot for a third-party candidate because "it would be a waste of your vote."[12] This sentiment helped to reduce the starting margins for the significant third-party contenders, the Libertarian Gary Johnson and Green Party nominee Jill Stein. At the start of the fall campaign, Johnson was winning 9 percent of the national vote, hoping he could approach the 15 percent mark required to be on the presidential debate stage with Donald Trump and Hillary Clinton.[13] But by Election Day, Johnson's support had declined by two-thirds—partly due to his flaws as a candidate, and partly to the overwhelming belief that the presidency was a choice between Clinton and Trump. The two-party system has flourished behind the widespread presumption that the presidency is a binary choice, and the willingness of Democratic and Republican leaders to exploit such predispositions.

Regulations to limit ballot access further restricts minor-party development. Getting a new party on the ballot and keeping it there poses extraordinarily difficult legal challenges. The major parties do not have this problem, as they have automatic ballot access by virtue of their dominance. For example, some states stipulate that a party whose gubernatorial candidate wins 10 percent of the vote is automatically listed on the next election ballot. Because Democrats and Republicans almost always garner that many votes, they have virtually automatic ballot access.

Another strong institutional force limiting minor-party success is the direct primary. In most other political systems where nominations are controlled by party elites, intra-party dissidents often leave to form their own parties. In the United States, the direct primary system has the effect of channeling dissent into the two major parties.[14] Frustrated voters can support a maverick candidate in a primary—or become candidates themselves, as happened in 2016 when Bernie Sanders left his long-standing position outside of the two major parties to compete in the Democratic Party's presidential contest, the first time Sanders ever sought a major-party nomination.

The presidential campaign finance system poses another institutional barrier to minor-party success. The Federal Election Campaign Act (FECA) stipulates that a presidential candidate is eligible for public funds, provided that the party's nominee receives a given percentage of votes in the previous election. For "major parties," a 25 percent threshold is required. If this goal is met, then the nominee is entitled to full funding (although neither major party has accepted this money since 2012).[15] For minor-party candidates, the threshold is only 5 percent, but the amount they receive from the federal government is far less than what their Democratic or Republican counterparts get. Ross Perot, who won 19 percent of the vote in 1992, was given $29 million in public funds in 1996—less than half of what Bill Clinton and Bob Dole received. Ralph Nader, who won 2.7 percent of the popular vote as the 2000 Green Party candidate, was not eligible for federal funds in 2004. And neither Gary Johnson (despite his fervent hopes) nor Jill Stein qualified for future federal funding of their party's campaigns in 2020. The inability of the minor parties to receive a share of public funding is a prime example of how those who write the rules (Democrats and Republicans) oppose changes that would benefit others. The financial obstacle has only increased since the Supreme Court's decision in *Citizens United vs. Federal Election Commission* in 2010. Today, the cost for seeking the presidency is in excess of $1 billion for each major party, causing them to rely on scarce dollars from consumers and mega-dollars from wealthy donors. Minor parties have little access to either monetary source, and without help from the federal government, they are left to gain as much "free media" as the cable networks are willing to give them (often very little).

Even though money is a chief obstacle confronting minor-party candidates, it is not the only one. In 1996, the Commission on Presidential Debates (a private organization) ruled that Ross Perot was not a serious contender, and banned him from the televised debates featuring major-party nominees Bill Clinton and Bob Dole. Perot argued that he could not win unless he was allowed to debate the other candidates. But the commission, which was composed of Democrats and Republicans, lent an unsympathetic ear to Perot's complaint. Much the same thing happened in 2000, when the Commission on Presidential Debates ruled Green Party candidate Ralph Nader ineligible. The commission even denied Nader a seat in the audience for the first George W. Bush–Al Gore face off, causing Nader to loudly complain about unfair treatment. In 2016, Libertarian Gary Johnson pinned his hopes on securing a slot in at least one of the three presidential debates. But that appearance was dependent on Johnson winning 15 percent support in the public opinion polls, a threshold set by the commission that Johnson could not meet. Green Party candidate Jill Stein was not even a contender for appearing on the debate stage as her support was mired in the low single digits. Taken together, the legal and structural mechanisms erected by the major parties and their supporters stack the deck against minor parties.

## CULTURAL BARRIERS TO THIRD PARTIES

Institutional constraints like single-member districts, the Electoral College, direct primary laws, and ballot access restrictions perpetuate the existence of the two-party model in the United States. Cultural barriers also present an additional barrier to third-party development. A nation's political culture encompasses the fundamental values and beliefs that influence society within which political behavior and government policies are bound. It is the umbrella under which political activities take place and where public questions are resolved. Several core values of American political culture help maintain a two-party system, including adherence to peaceful resolutions of conflicts, acceptance of compromise and incremental change, and a strong endorsement of the nation's governing framework.

Americans peacefully accepted the constitutional arrangements that the Framers instituted in 1787, and, in 1801, peacefully accepted the transfer of power from the Federalists to the Democratic-Republicans—a transfer of power that remains a rarity in today's world. From these origins, Americans came to expect that power would be peacefully passed between rival parties following legitimately held elections, which has had a moderating influence on public opinion that serves as a point of pride for many Americans. Despite recent controversies where the popular-vote winner did not become president (Al Gore in 2000 and Hillary Clinton in 2016), Americans accepted the election result, even though many took to the streets after the 2016 winner was declared to protest Donald Trump's misogyny and campaign against minorities.

The late James MacGregor Burns once noted that the peaceful transition of power from one party to another constituted an additional liberty beyond those explicitly granted in the U.S. Constitution. This liberty was secured in 1800 when Federalist John Adams ceded a contested election to Democrat Thomas Jefferson, an opponent Adams found extremely distasteful and with whom an estrangement existed that was to last decades.[16] Adams could have summoned the military, or his followers could have taken to the streets, to overturn the victory of the opposition Democrats. The fact that Adams and his fellow Federalists accepted the contested result established the expectation of the peaceful transition from a party-in-power to its opposition. As Burns concluded:

> A crucial liberty, one that had not been tested during the twelve-year hegemony of Federalist government, was established in the election of 1800—the freedom of the opposition not only to oppose, but to prevail peacefully. Not only did this constitute evidence to the world that the American polity was far more stable than it may have appeared, it was a notice to future American political leaders that they need not contemplate coups or venture violence in order to succeed. Much to the contrary, the path to political power in the United States was shown to lead directly to and through the ballot box, ensuring for generations to come the freedom of meaningful political opposition and the regular, orderly, peaceful transfer of political power.[17]

This is one reason why Americans extol their governing system, built around two-party competition, as the best ever devised. During the depths of the Great Depression, pollsters asked,

> Which one of the following most nearly represents your opinion of the American form of government? (a) Our form of government based on the Constitution is as near perfect as it can be and no important changes should be made in it; (b) the Constitution has served its purpose well, but it has not kept up with the times and should be thoroughly revised to make it fit present day needs; or (c) the systems of private capitalism and democracy are breaking down and we might as well accept the fact that sooner or later we will have to have a new form of government.[18]

Sixty-four percent said our political system is "as near perfect as it can be"—including 58 percent who were classified as being "poor."

American attitudes are also decidedly centrist. Louis Hartz, a political theorist best known for his commentary on the uniqueness of the U.S. political culture, maintains that there is a national consensus centered on individual freedoms. "It is a remarkable force," Hartz writes, "this fixed, dogmatic liberalism of a liberal way of life. It is the secret root from which have sprung many of the most puzzling aspects of American cultural phenomena."[19] Englishman G. K. Chesterton wrote in 1920 that the United States was founded on a "creed." He elaborated, "That creed is set forth with dogmatic and even theological lucidity in the Declaration of Independence; perhaps the only piece of practical politics that is also theoretical politics and also great literature."[20] This creed allows little tolerance for extremes. Lewis Cass, the 1848 Democratic nominee for president, once told a Tammany Hall audience that he was "opposed to all the isms of the day . . . to communism and socialism, and Mormonism; to polygamy and concubinage, and to all the humbugs that are now rising among us."[21] Abraham Lincoln warned that if the Declaration of Independence were amended to read that "all men are created equal, except Negroes, and foreigners, and Catholics," then "I should prefer emigrating to some country where they make no pretense of loving liberty—to Russia, for instance, where despotism can be taken pure, and without the base alloy of hypocrisy."[22] Karl Marx acknowledged communism's failure in the United States, blaming it on "the tenacity of the Yankees," citing their "theoretical backwardness" and their "Anglo-Saxon contempt for all theory."[23]

Additionally, historical constraints have reinforced the American cultural predisposition toward two-party dominance. Consider the words of political scientist V. O. Key on the connections between the formative years for political parties and the contemporary party system:

> Human institutions have an impressive capacity to perpetuate themselves or at least to preserve their form. The circumstances that happened to mold the American party system into a dual form at its inception must bear a degree of responsibility for its present existence.[24]

As noted in Chapters 1 and 2, the narrowness of U.S. political arguments has been attributed to its two most important party founders, Alexander Hamilton and Thomas Jefferson. The struggle between Hamiltonian nationalism and Jeffersonian localism that has been waged continuously throughout American history creates a sense of déjà vu—issues change, but not the essential nature of the conflict about the proper place for the federal government. Journalist Walter Lippmann put it this way:

> To be partisan. . . as between Jefferson and Hamilton is like arguing whether men or women are more necessary to the procreation of the race. Neither can live alone. Alone—that is, without the other—each is excessive and soon intolerable.[25]

# SIGNIFICANT THIRD PARTIES
# IN U.S. HISTORY

Although history has not been kind to minor parties, several have changed the direction of political debate and influenced the outcomes of elections. From the Anti-Masons of the 1820s through Gary Johnson's Libertarian Party and Jill Stein's Green Party candidacies in 2016, the history of American two-party competition has been periodically influenced by the emergence of third parties that were too weak to win elections, but influential enough to shape them.

***The Anti-Mason Party.*** The first significant minor party emerged shortly after the Era of Good Feelings ended in 1824. For decades prior to the Revolution, nearly every large community had a Masonic Lodge, or what was called a Freemason organization. These secretive clubs were composed of middle- and upper-class white Protestants, often the leading businessmen of their communities, who were interested in the issues of the day and had a strong belief in moral self-improvement. Prominent Masons included George Washington, Henry Clay, and Andrew Jackson. According to historian Phyllis F. Field, "In a nation with high rates of geographic mobility, Masonry provided a convenient way for nomadic American middle-class men to integrate themselves quickly into a new community and feel at home there."[26]

But Masonic elitism and secret rites created a public backlash—especially among religious fundamentalists. Following the mysterious disappearance of New York Freemason William Morgan in 1826, after he threatened to reveal the secret rituals of the group, the anti-Mason movement was born. Anti-Masons maintained that the secretive cliques were conspiring against the working class and, through their bizarre rituals such as frequent cross burnings, were a threat to Christianity. Within four years of their humble beginnings in 1826, the anti-Masons became a powerful political force. In 1831, they held a presidential nominating convention—a novel idea for its day—and chose as their candidate former attorney general William Wirt. Wirt proved to be an ineffectual campaigner, and the Anti-Mason Party finished a distant third in the 1832 presidential election with 100,000 votes (8 percent) behind Democrat Andrew Jackson and Whig Party candidate Henry Clay. However, Wirt finished first in Vermont, winning that state's seven electoral votes—the first time a third-party candidate had garnered any support in the Electoral College. The Anti-Masons fared better in state contests, winning the governorships of Vermont and Pennsylvania, and several congressional and state legislative seats in New York, Vermont, Pennsylvania, Rhode Island, and Connecticut. Their most significant policy achievement was the passage of a national law outlawing extrajudicial oaths of office.

By the mid-1830s, the Anti-Mason Party began to fade. Part of its demise was due to the fact that President Andrew Jackson endorsed policies that gave political leverage to working-class voters. More than anything else, the Anti-Mason Party disappeared because the Freemason movement was out of step with the democratic impulses of the 1830s. There was less public concern about elitism in the years after Jackson's election and his brand of Jacksonian Democracy.

***The Free-Soil Party.*** Several anti-slavery groups nipped at the edges of the political system prior to the 1840s. The most notable of these were the Barnburners, the Conscience Whigs, and the Liberty Party. Controlled by extremists and religious fanatics whose ideas about ending the interstate slave trade were considered radical—even in a time of rising opposition to slavery—these groups were relatively short-lived.

The Free-Soil Party had better luck. The impetus for this party's founding in 1848 was the debate over the Wilmot Proviso, which limited the extension of slavery into the new western territories. Operating on a platform of "free soil, free speech, free labor, and free men," the Free-Soil Party combined opposition to slavery with a desire for cheap western land. As the Free-Soil Party gained followers, it became more pragmatic than its abolitionist predecessors. It advocated policies that would allow blacks to vote and attend school. At the same time, Free-Soilers bowed to existing racial prejudices by arguing that the Wilmot Proviso would keep blacks in the South.[27] Free-Soilers did not endorse the abolition of slavery, nor did they denounce either the Fugitive Slave Act or the three-fifths clause of the U.S. Constitution (which counted blacks as "three-fifths" of a person for the purpose of determining how they would be represented in the House of Representatives). Other planks that broadened the Free-Soil Party's appeal included cheaper postage rates, reduced federal spending, tariff reform, the election of all civil officers, and free homesteading in the west.[28]

In 1848, the Free-Soil Party held a convention in Buffalo, New York, with nearly 20,000 delegates and spectators in attendance. Hopes were high when they nominated former president Martin Van Buren for president and Charles Francis Adams, son of John Quincy Adams and grandson of John Adams, for vice president. Despite the ticket's high name recognition, Van Buren and Adams won just 10 percent of the popular vote and failed to carry a single state. Congressional results were equally disappointing, as the party won a mere 12 seats. Shortly after the 1848 election, the Free-Soil Party disappeared. Most Free-Soilers returned to the parties they previously supported, albeit with a renewed determination to change their parties' respective stands on slavery-related issues. This movement back to the major parties caused considerable strife that led to the current two-party alignment. Republicans replaced the Whigs, and Democrats became the party of the South.

***The American (Know-Nothing) Party.*** For many Americans living in urban areas, immigration was a primary concern prior to the Civil War. A vast number of working-class, native-born Protestants were deeply troubled by the heavy influx of Irish Catholics beginning in the early 1840s. Jobs, cultural differences, and the transformation of the United States into an ethnic polyglot became contentious political issues. In 1854, the American Party emerged in response to these anxieties. Originally organized around two groups known as the Supreme Order of the Star Spangled Banner and the National Council of the United States of America, adherents were dubbed the Know-Nothings after a reporter asked a member about their secret meetings, only to be told that he "knew nothing." The party's core philosophy was simple: "Americans should rule America. . . . Foreigners have no right to dictate our laws, and therefore have no just ground to complain if Americans see proper to exclude them from offices of trust."[29] The Know-Nothing platform included planks mandating that immigrants live in the United States for 21 years before being allowed to vote; that they never hold public office; and that their children should have no rights unless they were educated in public schools. Taking aim at Catholics and their allegiance to the pope, the Know-Nothings declared, "No person should be selected for political station (whether of native or foreign birth), who recognizes any alliance or obligation of any description to foreign prince, potentate or power."[30]

The popularity of the Know-Nothings is one of the darker tales in U.S. history. In 1854, the party achieved extraordinary success by capturing scores of congressional and state legislative seats, mostly in the Northeast. In Massachusetts, where immigrants were pouring in at a rate of 100,000 per year, the Know-Nothings won an astounding 347 of 350 state house seats and all of the state senate, congressional, and statewide contests, including the governorship. In New York, they elected 40 members of the state legislature and took control of the governorship. The party also won the governorships of Rhode Island, New Hampshire, and Connecticut.

In 1856, the Know-Nothings became caught up in the politics of slavery. At the party's convention in Philadelphia, Northern delegates wanted to nominate a presidential candidate who opposed the extension of slavery into the new western territories. Southerners blocked the move, and Northern delegates bolted out of the convention hall. The remaining Southern delegates nominated former president Millard Fillmore as their candidate for president and Andrew Jackson Dodelson of Tennessee for vice president. The Fillmore-Dodelson ticket captured 875,000 votes, or 21 percent of the popular vote, and eight Electoral College votes (from the state of Maryland). After two stunning showings at the polls, the Know-Nothings faded rapidly. Passage of the 1854 Kansas-Nebraska Act accentuated the slavery issue and created deep sectional divisions. The Republicans—a Northern, antislavery party—burst on the scene, and most Northern Know-Nothings joined their ranks. In the South, the Know-Nothings were absorbed by the former Whigs. By 1860, the Know-Nothings were no more.

***The Greenback and Populist (People's) Parties.*** During the early 1870s, the nation entered hard times and Midwestern farmers suffered from plummeting crop prices. Railroads were the only means by which to ship Midwestern farm goods to major markets in the East, and privately owned companies charged exorbitant rates. Adding to the farmers' plight was a deflation of the currency, which made it difficult for them to pay their high bills.

The first efforts to organize agricultural interests culminated in the formation of hundreds of local organizations called farmers' alliances, or granges. Mixing political and social activities, the granges united farmers into a cohesive voting bloc. Many who belonged to the granges were supportive of a third party, and after the economic panic of 1873, the Greenback Party was created. The Greenback Party proposed an inflated currency based on cheap paper money known as "greenbacks" that were first introduced during the Civil War.[31] Their argument was simple: by making the greenback legal tender, there would be enough money in circulation to ease the burden of indebted farmers and laborers. The Greenback Party was also known as the Greenback-Labor Party.

In 1878, Greenback congressional candidates won more than one million votes and 14 U.S. House races. Two years later, they nominated General James Weaver of Iowa as their presidential candidate. By that time, however, the national economy had improved, and the Greenback Party lost its initial appeal. Weaver won just 300,000 votes, and the Greenbacks sent just eight members to Congress. In 1884, the Greenbacks found their presidential support cut almost in half.

Overproduction and increased world competition led to another agricultural crisis in the early 1890s. The remaining Greenbacks merged with a new party called the Populists, or People's Party, in 1891. Unlike the Greenbacks, the Populists' demands were more radical and far-reaching: "We meet in the midst of a nation brought to the verge of moral, political, and material ruin. . . . From the womb of governmental injustice, we breed the two great classes—tramps and millionaires."[32] Among other things, the Populist platform proposed public regulation of railroads and telegraphs; free coinage of silver and gold (as a means to increase currency in circulation); creation of postal savings banks; prohibition of alien ownership of land; a graduated federal income tax; direct election of U.S. senators; and a reduction of the workday to eight hours. The Populists readily won adherents in the Midwest, West, and even the South. One historian summarized the new party's appeal this way: "The Populist Party was the embodiment of an attitude, a way of looking at life that had been prevalent for almost 20 years, and a general position taken against concentrated economic power."[33] The Populists selected former Greenback James Weaver as their 1892 presidential nominee. Weaver won just 8 percent of the popular vote (about a million votes) and 22 Electoral College votes. Nearly all of his support came from western states. In effect, the Populists split the Republican vote, giving Democrat Grover Cleveland a chance to capture the presidency. Democrats also won control of both houses of Congress—a rarity in this Republican-dominated era. Populist strength grew in 1894, when they won nearly 1.5 million votes and elected six U.S. senators and seven House members, all from the West.

Then, in 1896, something unusual happened: both the Populists and the Democrats nominated William Jennings Bryan for president. Bryan endorsed many Populist planks—most notably, the elimination of the gold standard. At the Democratic National Convention, Bryan gave one of the most famous speeches in the history of U.S. oratory, the so-called "Cross of Gold" speech. After the Democratic Convention, the Populists—also moved by Bryan's "Cross of Gold" speech—chose him for president.[34] Although Bryan lost, many of the Populist Party's proposals were accepted by both parties and incorporated into law during the twentieth century.

***The Progressives: 1912–1924, 1948, and Today.*** In Chapter 3, we outlined the rationale behind the Progressive movement, its numerous successes against machine-dominated locales, and its eventual coalescence into a third party in 1912 behind former President Theodore Roosevelt. Calling for a "new nationalism," Roosevelt bolted the Republican Convention to form the Progressive (or Bull Moose) Party, running on a platform that promised stricter regulation of corporations; downward revision of tariffs; popular election of U.S. senators; women's suffrage; and support for the referendum, ballot initiatives, and recall. With 27 percent of the popular vote and 88 Electoral College votes, Roosevelt finished in second place behind Democrat Woodrow Wilson. William Howard Taft, the Republican nominee, finished third—the first time that had happened to a GOP presidential candidate since the party's inception.

Certainly, the high point of the Progressive movement was Roosevelt's strong showing in 1912. Thereafter, President Woodrow Wilson pursued a Progressive agenda—including passage of new antitrust laws, banking regulations, and scores of business reforms. But the Progressive Party did not die completely, especially in states with strong populist traditions. In 1924, Robert La Follette—a former U.S. representative, U.S. senator, and governor of Wisconsin—became the Progressive Party's presidential nominee. La Follette was an articulate champion of labor reform, business regulation, a graduated income tax, and a constitutional amendment providing for direct election of judges to the federal courts. His party's platform proposed public ownership of the nation's water power, strict control and conservation of all natural resources, farmers' cooperatives, and legislation to make credit available to farmers and small businessmen. La Follette captured 17 percent of the popular vote (4.8 million ballots), but won only 13 Electoral College votes (all from his home state of Wisconsin). With his death in 1925, La Follette's brand of progressivism died as well. Though his children and grandchildren became active in politics and continued to push the Progressive agenda, they did not attract much attention beyond the Wisconsin borders.

In 1948, the Progressive Party reemerged. That year, a left-wing group led by former vice president Henry A. Wallace bolted from the Democratic Party. At issue was President Harry S. Truman's "get tough" policy toward the Soviet Union, which Wallace strongly opposed. The Progressive Party accused Truman of being vociferously anti-communist, which they said stemmed from "the dictates of monopoly and the military" and resulted in "preparing for war in the name of peace."[35] To the utopian-minded Progressives, peace was "the prerequisite of survival":

> There is no American principle of public interest, and there is no Russian principle of public interest, which would have to be sacrificed to end the Cold War and open up the Century of Peace which the Century of the Common Man demands.[36]

Given these views, the Progressive Party called for a wholesale reversal in how the U.S. government dealt with domestic communism. The party favored eliminating the House Un-American Activities Committee, claiming it had vilified and prosecuted citizens "in total disregard of the Bill of Rights." It also rejected any ban of the U.S. Communist Party or the required registration of its members, likening such legislation to the Alien and Sedition Acts.

In July 1948, the Progressive Citizens of America selected Wallace as its presidential candidate. As the Progressive Party standard-bearer, Henry Wallace drew large crowds—including many young liberals, blue-collar workers, and African Americans. His liberal supporters worried Truman, who would need them to win, and Truman attempted to link Wallace with the U.S. Communist Party. At campaign stops, Truman vowed, "I do not want and I will not accept the political support of Henry Wallace and his communists."[37] Wallace's public statements made Truman's task an easy one. A Gallup poll taken shortly before the Progressive convention found 51 percent agreed that the Progressive Party was communist dominated.[38]

Despite Wallace's political shortcomings, he influenced the election result. When the ballots were counted, Wallace received 1,157,172 votes (slightly more than 2 percent). This was enough to throw three states to GOP presidential nominee Thomas E. Dewey: New York, Maryland, and Michigan. If Wallace had done somewhat better in California and had not been kept off the Illinois ballot, the 1948 contest might have been decided in the House of Representatives.

Progressive ideas have been a recurring force in U.S. politics, although progressivism has assumed different meanings in different eras. Originally, its focus was centered in the religious belief that the human condition could be infinitely improved. By the end of the nineteenth century, progressivism meant ridding the political system of corrupt influences. At the turn of the twentieth century, Progressives wanted greater participation by average citizens in governmental affairs, and they believed government could be improved by bringing scientific methods to bear on public problems. In the late twentieth century, a new progressivism emerged in the image of nineteenth-century progressivism, around the desire to rid the political process of the influence of big money in order to make it more responsive to ordinary voters. In 1991, the Progressive Caucus was created in the House of Representatives. Today, it has 75 members (including one U.S. Senator and all of them Democrats), making it the largest group within the House Democratic caucus.[39] Its core principles are "(1) fighting for economic justice and security for all; (2) protecting and preserving our civil rights and civil liberties; (3) promoting global peace and security; and (4) advancing environmental protection and energy independence."[40] Given the reduced Democratic ranks in the House during the Obama years, the Progressive Caucus has assumed a greater voice in party affairs.

***States' Rights Party (1948) and the American Independent Party (1968).*** After the Civil War, the roots of the Democratic Party became deeply planted in the South. During the 1930s, Franklin D. Roosevelt broadened the Democratic coalition to include labor, middle- and lower-class urban residents, Catholics, African Americans, and Jews, transforming the Democratic Party into a majority coalition. Relations between progressive Northern Democrats and conservative Southern Democrats became a "marriage of convenience." Northern Democrats controlled the White House, thanks to their Southern partners, and Southern Democrats chaired important congressional committees, thanks to their party's majority status and adherence to the seniority rule.

By the late 1940s, the marriage between Northern and Southern Democrats was in trouble. Civil rights split the two factions apart in 1948. That year, the Democratic Convention adopted a strong pro-civil rights plank. Many Southern delegates walked out and reconvened in Birmingham, Alabama. The gathering adopted the name States' Rights Party and quickly became known as the Dixiecrat Party, given its overwhelming Southern base of support. The convention reiterated a plank extracted from the 1840 Democratic Party platform:

> Congress has no power under the Constitution to interfere with or control the domestic institutions of the several states, and. . . such states are the sole and proper judges of everything appertaining to their own affairs and not prohibited by the Constitution.[41]

This so-called states' rights argument was designed to keep the existing racial segregation intact.

The delegates nominated J. Strom Thurmond, then governor of South Carolina, as their presidential candidate. On Election Day, Thurmond garnered 1.1 million votes (2.4 percent) and won 38 Electoral College votes from five Southern states. The party closed shop after the election, and Thurmond went on to have a successful political career. In 1954, Thurmond won a write-in Senate campaign after the state Democratic Party rejected him.[42] Ten years later, Thurmond formally switched his party registration from Democratic to Republican. In 2002, he retired from the U.S. Senate as a Republican at age 100, and he died a year later on June 26, 2003.

The final blow to the post-Civil War Democratic coalition came in 1968. Once again, the breakdown centered upon efforts to broaden legal protections for African Americans. The American Independent Party was established in 1968 as the personal organization of Alabama governor George C. Wallace. Wallace was elected governor in 1962 as a Democrat and ardent segregationist. A year later, Wallace entered the national spotlight when the federal government ordered the integration of public colleges. In a televised display of defiance, Wallace and his state troopers blocked access to the University of Alabama to two incoming African American students before eventually stepping aside.

After an unsuccessful (but impressive) primary campaign against Lyndon B. Johnson in 1964, Wallace abandoned the Democratic Party in 1968 to form his own party, which followed his get-tough, law-and-order, segregationist beliefs. With old-time populist themes and a powerful gift for oratory, Wallace won nearly 10 million ballots—13.5 percent of the total votes cast. His 46 electoral votes from five Southern states were more than Republican nominee Barry M. Goldwater received in 1964. Much of Wallace's Southern strength came from former Democrats, who used the Wallace candidacy as a way station before entering the Republican Party. In 1972, Richard M. Nixon won the vast majority of the 1968 Wallace backers, and during the 1980s, Wallace voters began supporting Republicans for other offices such as governor, members of Congress, and state legislature. Wallace, meanwhile, reentered Democratic presidential politics in 1972, only to be shot and permanently paralyzed at a rally in Laurel, Maryland. Although he later won the Alabama governorship as a Democrat, Wallace's days in presidential politics were over. His American Independent Party and its offshoot, the American Party, continued to nominate candidates for a while before fading into obscurity.

***The Reform Party.*** The difference between minor parties and splinter candidacies is clearly evident when comparing Ross Perot's 1992 run for the presidency with his second try four years later. In his first effort, Perot did not field candidates for other offices, affirming his independence from all officeholders and parties. Using his hefty pocketbook to finance his campaign, Perot ran on a platform that stressed the importance of a balanced budget during a time of economic difficulty and the need to enact major campaign finance reforms. His foremost strength was his charisma and can-do attitude. After winning an impressive 19 percent of the vote,

Perot remained active by organizing a new political party centered on the issues of a balanced budget and campaign finance reform. The Reform Party was born, and by 1996 it qualified to run a slate of candidates in all 50 states. It had a national organization, developed formal rules, and even held a convention to nominate its presidential candidate, who, not surprisingly, was Perot. This time, however, Perot accepted federal funds, thus saving him from once again having to finance his own campaign. Perot received only 8 percent of the vote, a signal that the days of the Reform Party were numbered.

Although the party received $12.6 million from the federal government for the 2000 general election based upon Ross Perot's 1996 showing, the money made the party a target for would-be presidential candidates, some of whom were far removed from the party's original emphasis on eliminating federal deficit spending. Donald Trump became a member of the party and established an exploratory committee in 1999 before eventually dropping out of the contest. Trump was supported by Reform Party governor Jesse Ventura of Minnesota, but dropped out of the race after determining that the Reform Party had become dysfunctional. Patrick J. Buchanan, who unsuccessfully sought the Republican presidential nomination in 1992, successfully became the Reform Party nominee after defeating John Hagelin, who had been the 1996 Natural Law Party's candidate for president. The contest over the Reform Party nomination split the Perot movement in two. In a convention marred by fisticuffs, both Buchanan and Hagelin claimed to have enough support to clinch the Reform Party's presidential nomination. Ultimately, the Federal Election Commission decided that Buchanan was the legitimate nominee and awarded him the $12.6 million. Disgusted at the turn of events, Perot refused to back Buchanan and endorsed Republican George W. Bush. Meanwhile, Jesse Ventura, who had been the Reform Party's greatest success story after winning the governorship of Minnesota, left the party, calling it "hopelessly dysfunctional."[43] In November 2000, Buchanan fared poorly, winning fewer than 1 million votes out of more than 100 million cast. With the exits of Ross Perot, Donald Trump, and Jesse Ventura, the Reform Party faded into obscurity.

***The Green Party.*** During Bill Clinton's tenure as president, some Democrats became restive, seeing Clinton as a self-styled "new kind of Democrat" who eschewed the party's traditional New Deal liberalism. Many liberals complained that with the presidency in Democratic hands, they had little to show for it. In 1996, the Green Party echoed these sentiments and selected Ralph Nader as its presidential candidate. Nader did not actively seek the presidency; rather, he let his name appear on the ballot and made no campaign appearances. Even so, Nader's presence cost Clinton a victory in Colorado.

Things were different in 2000. With Republicans in control of Congress, Bill Clinton was compelled to strike deals with them, telling confidants, "Strategically, I want to remove all divisive issues for a conservative [Republican presidential] candidate, so all the issues are on progressive terrain."[44] But Nader and the Greens complained that far from being progressive, both Clinton and the Republicans sided with corporate interests. Nader decided to confront the Clinton–Gore administration in 2000, charging that its obsession with deficit reduction and not using the powers of government more forcefully—especially when it came to protecting the environment and promoting campaign finance reform—had transformed the Democrats into a "me-too" party that emulated the Republicans. Nader and the Greens especially took umbrage at the failure to enact campaign finance reform, which to them was proof-positive of how strongly corporations and Wall Street controlled what happened inside the federal government.[45]

Nader won 2.73 percent of the total popular votes cast for president, making him a "spoiler" in the race. The 97,488 votes Nader received in Florida made a real difference, given that George W. Bush's statewide margin was 537 votes out of nearly 6 million cast. Nader had a similar effect in New Hampshire, where he received 22,198 votes, enough to cost Democrat Al Gore a victory in the state where Bush edged Gore by just 7,211 votes. If Nader had not been in the race, it is very likely that Gore would have won a majority of electoral votes and would have been the nation's 43rd president.[46]

Democrats were well aware of their missed opportunity to win the White House in 2000, and they made sure that their supporters were not tempted to vote for Ralph Nader in 2004. That year, Nader did run again, but received less than 1 percent of the vote. By 2008, Nader abandoned the Green Party and ran as an independent, garnering 739,278 votes—the most of any of the third-party candidates, but still just one-half of 1 percent of the total votes cast. With that, Nader no longer lent his name to any third party or independent effort, and left presidential politics to others.

In 2016, the Green Party enjoyed a resurgence, having been energized by the failed Democratic bid made by Vermont senator Bernie Sanders. When Sanders capitulated to Hillary Clinton, many of his supporters were attracted to the Green Party nominee, Dr. Jill Stein. Stein cast herself as a Sanders ally, telling supporters that "the Bernie Sanders movement lives on outside the Democratic Party."[47] Like Sanders, Stein castigated the power exercised by Wall Street, supported a measure to eliminate student debt, endorsed the Black Lives Matter movement, opposed Donald Trump's plan to build a wall on the U.S.-Mexican border, and called for clean, renewable energy sources.[48] Both Hillary Clinton and Bernie Sanders made strong arguments for would-be Green Party supporters not to waste their votes on a third-party candidate. Sanders explicitly told supporters that while the Green Party is "focusing on very, very important issues. . . you're going to end up having a choice. Either Hillary Clinton is going to be president, or Donald Trump."[49] As late as early October, polls showed Stein capable of winning 3 percent of the national vote.[50] But as Election Day loomed, Stein's vote share fell to a mere 1 percent. Still, Stein's presence arguably made a difference in two states—Michigan and Wisconsin—where the Green Party nominee won more votes than Donald J. Trump's margin of victory, prompting Hillary Clinton's supporters to argue she would have won both states, even though that would have left her short of the necessary 270 votes in the Electoral College. Stein raised money after the election to finance recounts in these two states (plus

Pennsylvania), and was successful in obtaining a recount in Wisconsin, but her efforts did not change the election outcome.

## AN EXPLOSION OF MINOR PARTIES

Despite the numerous barriers to third-party formation, there has been an explosion of minor parties in the United States. One study of minor-party candidacies reveals interesting details about their motivation for taking an independent political path.[51] The vast majority belonged to one of the major parties before striking out on their own. In fact, 14 percent had actually belonged to both parties at one time in the past. Most cited the failure of two-party politics—claiming that the Democrats and Republicans were ineffective, elitist, committed to the status quo, and corrupt. However, although they were disillusioned with the two parties, nearly all believed in the party system. Demographically, most minor-party candidates were well educated and affluent: 77 percent had personal incomes over $40,000 per year, and 33 percent made over $60,000 annually. In many respects, Donald Trump fits this profile, having changed his party affiliation six times over the course of his lifetime, including having once been a registered Democrat, member of the Reform Party, and an unaffiliated voter before becoming a registered Republican.[52]

Perhaps the most significant finding is that like their nineteenth- and twentieth-century predecessors, today's third parties emerge out of the sense that neither major party is addressing the concerns of ordinary voters. Abolitionist parties developed because of slavery, the Populists and Greenbacks because of economic issues, the Progressives because of corruption, and segregationist parties in response to pending civil rights legislation. Today, third parties have been drawing notice from people who are increasingly discouraged by the status quo.

Nowhere is this more evident than in the Tea Party movement, which has attempted to move the Republican Party in a more conservative populist direction. Tea Party followers have been extremely concerned about the size of the federal deficit, support tax reductions, and oppose an expanding U.S. government, especially during the Obama years. But the Tea Party lacks a formal party structure. Despite the word "party" in its name, the "Tea Party" does not operate as a formal third party, preferring instead to influence Republican primaries by supporting candidates who empathize with their cause and providing them with considerable financial support. Matt Ney, a Tea Party activist, described his Tea Party group's focus: "We're not wanting to be a third party. We're not wanting to endorse individual candidates ever. What we're trying to do is be activists by pushing a conservative idea."[53] The Tea Party exerted considerable influence on the Republican Party during the low-turnout midterm elections of 2010 and 2014. In five states, Tea Partiers were able to nominate their preferred Senate candidates.[54] And in 2016, many Tea Party sympathizers (though not all) were attracted to the two GOP finalists: Donald Trump and Ted Cruz, the latter owing his election as a senator to support received from the Tea Party.

# MORE POSITIVE VOTER ATTITUDES TOWARD MINOR PARTIES

Throughout history, political parties have fallen in and out of favor with voters. When a 1938 Roper poll asked voters what parties they would like to see competing in the next presidential race, a plurality answered only a Republican and a Democrat.[55] Today, the idea of having some choice other than the Democrats or Republicans is popular. This sentiment is not surprising, given the persistent voter anger toward the two major parties. Today, only 28 percent believe the major parties "do an adequate job of representing the American people," while 71 percent believed a third party is needed.[56] But the historical, institutional, and cultural obstacles to third-party formation suggest it will be difficult for a viable third party to emerge and satisfy these wishes.

# JEFFERSON, HAMILTON, AND THE FUTURE OF THIRD PARTIES IN AMERICA

Scores of institutional barriers—including the winner-take-all electoral system, the Electoral College, barriers to ballot access, and a host of historical and cultural forces—push the U.S. polity toward a two-party model. Yet minor parties have played a critical role at key moments before fading into the history books. Thus, to ignore minor parties is to overlook a crucial factor in the evolution of the American party system.

One way to understand the paradox of third-party institutions that repeatedly emerge (but never win national elections) is to return to the fundamental split between Hamiltonian nationalism and Jeffersonian localism. American political parties rest on a Hamiltonian foundation—meaning that party elites at the state and national levels control the inner workings of their respective parties. For these folks, community-based party organizations and grassroots activism are directed toward winning elections. Policy innovation is usually sluggish, as party operatives retreat to proven themes that win at the polls. Yet the desire for a Jeffersonian-style party system centered around deep-seated policy concerns is a powerful and recurring counter-force. Minor parties burst on the scene when a sizable segment of the electorate feels that the Hamiltonian-style parties are not adequately addressing important issues. Third parties become a manifestation of voter desire for a policy-driven politics. Invariably, the two-party Hamiltonian-style party system reacts and reasserts itself by addressing the concerns that precipitated the third-party split.

Several scholars have explored the idea that minor parties help shape the party system in a way that major parties cannot. Theodore J. Lowi, a former president of the American Political Science Association, writes,

> New ideas and issues develop or redevelop parties, but parties, particularly established ones, rarely develop ideas or present new issues on their own. . . . Once

a system of parties is established, the range and scope of policy discussion is set, until and unless some disturbance arises from other quarters.[57]

The "disturbance" Lowi speaks of is the development of aggressive third parties. Lowi notes there have been four historical eras where Democrats and Republicans have been especially innovative: (1) 1856–1860; (2) 1890–1900; (3) 1912–1914; and (4) 1933–1935. In these years, party leaders became more susceptible to mass opinion as a result of third-party competition. Once the policy innovations were achieved, however, third parties withered away. Using the Hamilton–Jefferson model, third parties have periodically shaken the system and have temporally shifted it toward Jeffersonian localism.

How will third parties fare in an era when Americans say they are dissatisfied with Democrats and Republicans alike? Certainly, today's social networking capability makes it easy for minor-party leaders to connect with potential supporters at a minimal cost. In this respect, the minor parties may find it easier to do business in the twenty-first century than ever before. It is possible that if more minor-party candidates can overcome the odds against them, more voters will act upon their pro–third-party proclivities, thereby setting aside any concern they are wasting their votes by supporting third-party candidates. And as we have seen, although the success of third-party candidates has been limited, more are jumping into the fray and getting at least some media attention.

Nevertheless, the obstacles that prevent the creation of a viable multi-party system remain daunting. Over the past three decades, we have witnessed a centralization and professionalization of electoral politics that have accentuated a profound shift toward Hamiltonian nationalism. Major-party candidates realize that they must amass huge war chests, with successful presidential campaigns having to raise $1 billion (or be self-funded). This extraordinary level of funding that is needed just to become competitive is beyond the reach of most third parties, despite the fervent backing of their most ardent supporters. Given the increased professionalization of U.S. politics, it is likely that minor parties will continue to exert their greatest influence at the margins, even if such marginal influences are at times profound.

# NOTES

1.  Edison Research, exit poll, November 8, 2016.
2.  Ibid.
3.  Ibid.
4.  NBC News/*Wall Street Journal*, poll, November 3–5, 2016. Text of question: How satisfied are you with the choice of candidates for president—very satisfied, fairly satisfied, not very satisfied, or not that satisfied?"Very satisfied, 12 percent; fairly satisfied, 28 percent; not very satisfied, 31 percent; not that satisfied, 28 percent; not sure, 1 percent.
5.  Quinnipiac University, poll, August 18–24, 2016. Text of question: "Would you say that you would consider voting for a third party candidate (in the 2016 presidential

election) more because you like one of the third party candidates, or more because you dislike both major party candidates?" Like third party, 23 percent; dislike major party, 65 percent; don't know/no answer, 12 percent.

6.  Stein was not listed on the ballot in South Dakota, Oklahoma, and Nevada. She was also not listed on the ballots in North Carolina, Georgia, and Indiana, although voters in all three states could write in her name.

7.  George Washington University Battleground 2016 survey, August 28–September 1, 2016. Text of first question: "Now thinking about the 2016 presidential election in a different way, no matter who you chose on the previous questions, please tell me, if yes, you would consider voting for this person for president or no, you would not consider voting for this person for president. Gary Johnson. Would that be strongly would consider, would not consider, or just a somewhat?" Yes, would consider strongly, 7 percent; yes, would consider somewhat, 14 percent; no, would not consider somewhat, 17 percent; no, would not consider strongly, 44 percent; don't know/refused, 17 percent. Text of second question: Now thinking about the 2016 presidential election in a different way, no matter who you chose on the previous questions, please tell me, if yes, you would consider voting for this person for president or no, you would not consider voting for this person for president. Jill Stein. Would that be strongly would consider, would not consider, or just a somewhat?" Yes, would consider strongly, 2 percent; yes, would consider somewhat, 10 percent; no, would not consider somewhat, 19 percent; no, would not consider strongly, 47 percent; don't know/refused, 22 percent.

8.  Clinton Rossiter, *Parties and Politics in America* (Ithaca, NY: Cornell University Press, 1960), p. 3.

9.  Eliot Cutler finished second in the 2010 race, garnering 36 percent of the vote, while the Democratic candidate won just 19 percent. Four years later, Cutler finished third with 8 percent of the vote.

10.  Only Maine and Nebraska do not employ a winner-take-all electoral vote system, preferring to allot their electoral votes according to which candidate wins a particular congressional district. In 2008, Barack Obama received one electoral vote from Nebraska because he carried the congressional district that included the city of Omaha. In 2016, Donald Trump received one electoral vote in Maine because he won a congressional district there.

11.  In 1856, Fillmore was the presidential candidate of the Know-Nothing Party, receiving 22 percent of the popular vote.

12.  Quinnipiac University, poll, August 18–24, 2016. Text of question: "Would you say that you would consider not voting for a third party candidate more because you don't like any of the third party candidates, more because it would be a waste of your vote, or more because you don't want to risk either Hillary Clinton or Donald Trump getting elected?" Dislike third party, 16 percent; waste of vote, 52 percent; risk major party win, 24 percent; don't know/no answer, 7 percent.

13.  CNN/Opinion Research Corporation, poll, September 1–4, 2016. Text of question: "Suppose that the (2016) presidential election were being held today and you had to choose between Hillary Clinton and Tim Kaine as the Democratic party's candidates, Donald Trump and Mike Pence as the Republican party's candidates, Gary Johnson and Bill Weld as the Libertarian Party's candidates, and Jill Stein and Ajamu Baraka as the Green Party's candidates. Who would you be more likely to vote for? (If None/Don't know, ask:) As of today do you lean more toward Clinton and Kaine, Trump and Pence, Johnson and Weld, or Stein and Baraka?" Clinton/Kaine (including leaners), 44 percent; Trump/Pence (including leaners), 41 percent; Johnson/Weld (including leaners), 9 percent; Stein/Baraka (including leaners), 3 percent; none (volunteered), 3 percent.

14.  This argument is made in John F. Bibby and L. Sandy Maisel, *Two Parties—Or More? The American Party System* (Boulder, CO: Westview Press, 1998), p. 58.

15. Barack Obama became the first major-party nominee not to accept federal funding in 2008, as Obama was able to raise a total of $747.8 million for his entire campaign. Today, the Federal Election Campaign Act is essentially null and void, as neither major party is willing to accept public funding for either the primaries or the general election.

16. Adams was so distraught at the election result that he refused to attend Thomas Jefferson's swearing-in and sulked off to his native Braintree, Massachusetts, at 4 a.m. on inauguration day.

17. James MacGregor Burns, *Cobblestone Leadership: Majority Rule, Minority Power* (Norman, Oklahoma: University of Oklahoma Press, 1990), p. 29.

18. Survey conducted by the Roper Organization, December 1939. The results were taken among "whites only." There were no dollar definitions as to what constitutes "poor" in this survey.

19. Louis Hartz, *The Liberal Tradition in America: An Interpretation of American Political Thought Since the Revolution* (New York: Harcourt Brace, 1955), p. 7.

20. Quoted in Everett Carll Ladd, *The American Ideology: An Exploration of the Origins, Meaning, and Role of American Political Ideas* (Storrs, CT: Roper Center for Public Opinion Research, 1994), p. 32.

21. Quoted in John Gerring, "A Chapter in the History of American Party Ideology: The Nineteenth Century Democratic Party, 1828–1892." Paper presented at the Northeastern Political Science Association, Newark, New Jersey, November 11–13, 1993, pp. 36–37. Cass made these remarks on September 2, 1852.

22. See Roy P. Basler, ed., *The Collected Works of Abraham Lincoln* (New Brunswick, NJ: Rutgers University Press, 1953), p. 323.

23. Cited in Seymour Martin Lipset, "Why No Socialism in the United States," in Seweryn Bailer and Sophia Sluzar, eds., *Radicalism in the Contemporary Age* (Boulder, CO: Westview Press, 1977), p. 40.

24. Quoted in Daniel M. Shea, ed., *Mass Politics: The Politics of Popular Culture* (New York: St. Martin's Press, 1999), p. 207.

25. Quoted in James Reston, "Liberty and Authority," *New York Times,* June 29, 1986, p. E23.

26. Phyllis F. Field, "Masons," in L. Sandy Maisel, ed., *Political Parties and Elections in the United States: An Encyclopedia* (New York: Garland, 1991), pp. 641–642.

27. Robert J. Spitzer, "Free-Soil Party," in Maisel, *Political Parties and Elections,* pp. 409–410.

28. Edward W. Chester, *A Guide to Political Platforms* (New York: Archon Books, 1977), p. 58.

29. See Elinor C. Hartshorn, "Know-Nothings," in Maisel, *Political Parties and Elections,* pp. 549–550.

30. See Chester, *A Guide to Political Platforms,* p. 70.

31. Earl R. Kruschke, *Encyclopedia of Third Parties in the United States* (Santa Barbara, CA: ABC-Clio, 1991), p. 71.

32. Quoted in Chester, *A Guide to Political Platforms,* pp. 121–135.

33. Frederick J. Augustyn Jr., "Populists (People's) Party," in Maisel, *Political Parties and Elections,* pp. 849–850.

34. But in a strange twist, the Populists refused to endorse the Democratic vice presidential candidate, Arthur Sewall, a banker from Maine.

35. "Progressive Party Platform, 1948," in Kirk H. Porter and Donald Brace Johnson, eds., *National Party Platforms: 1840–1968* (Urbana, IL: University of Illinois Press, 1970), p. 437.

36. Ibid., p. 439.

37. Quoted in A. James Reichley, *The Life of the Parties: A History of American Political Parties* (New York: Free Press, 1992), p. 297.

38. Gallup poll, June 16–23, 1948. Text of question: "Do you think that the Henry Wallace third party is run by Communists?"

39. Chris Moody, "Election Results Confirm House Democratic Caucus in 2011 Will Be Smaller, But More Liberal," *Daily Caller*, November 4, 2010.

40. See https://cpc-grijalva.house.gov/index.cfm?sectionid=74&sectiontree=2,74. Accessed November 25, 2016.

41. Kruschke, *Encyclopedia of Third Parties in the United States*, p. 183.

42. Thurmond's record stood until 2010, when Lisa Murkowski won reelection to her U.S. Senate seat from Alaska on a write-in campaign. Murkowski had been defeated in the Republican primary after former governor Sarah Palin endorsed Murkowski's challenger, Joe Miller.

43. Quoted in "Ventura Leaves Reform Party," *PBS Online NewsHour*, December 10, 2002.

44. Quoted in Michael Waldman, *Potus Speaks: Finding the Words That Defined the Clinton Presidency* (New York: Simon and Schuster, 2000), p. 181.

45. See Nader, *Crashing the Party*, p. 289.

46. Gore won 266 electoral votes to Bush's 271 electoral votes (one more than needed for a majority). One elector in Washington, DC, did not vote for Gore in order to protest DC's lack of statehood.

47. Jill Stein, Acceptance Speech, Green Party Convention, Houston, Texas, August 6, 2016.

48. Ibid.

49. Quoted in Eric Levitz, "Sanders Suggests That Voting for a Third-Party Candidate Who Can't Win Probably Not Best Way to Stop Trump," *New York Magazine*, July 26, 2016. See http://nymag.com/daily/intelligencer/2016/07/bernie-gives-supporters-red-light-on-green-party.html. Accessed November 26, 2016.

50. Fox News, poll, October 3–6, 2016. Text of question: "If the 2016 presidential election were held today, how would you vote if the candidates were Democrats Hillary Clinton and Tim Kaine, Republicans Donald Trump and Mike Pence, Libertarians Gary Johnson and Bill Weld, and Green Party candidates Jill Stein and Ajamu Baraka? (If don't know ask:) Well, which way do you lean?" Democrats Hillary Clinton and Tim Kaine including leaners, 42 percent; Republicans Donald Trump and Mike Pence including leaners, 40 percent; Libertarians Gary Johnson and Bill Weld including leaners, 7 percent; Green Party candidates Jill Stein and Ajamu Baraka including leaners, 3 percent; other (volunteered), 1 percent; wouldn't vote (volunteered), 2 percent; don't know, 6 percent.

51. Christian Collet and Jerrold Hansen, "Minor Party Candidates in Subpresidential Elections," in John C. Green and Daniel M. Shea, eds., *The State of the Parties: The Changing Role of Contemporary American Parties*, 2nd ed. (Lanham, Maryland: Rowman & Littlefield, 1997), Table 15.1.

52. See Michael Kranish and Marc Fisher, *Trump Revealed: An American Journey of Ambition, Ego, Money, and Power* (New York: Scribner, 2016), pp. 290–291.

53. Quoted in Amy Gardner, "Gauging the Scope of the Tea Party Movement in America," *Washington Post*, October 24, 2010, p. A-1.

54. These were Nevada, Delaware, Colorado, Indiana, and Missouri.

55. Roper Organization, poll, May 1938. Text of question: "Which parties would you like to see competing in the next presidential race. . . . Republican and Democrat only. . . .

Republican and Democrat and minor parties as before. . . . Republican, Democrat, and a new strong third party. . . . Two new parties with all conservatives voting together and all liberals voting together?" Republican and Democrat, 44 percent; Republican and Democrat and minor parties as before, 21 percent; Republican, Democrat, and a new strong third party, 13 percent; two new parties with all conservatives voting together and all liberals voting together, 6 percent; don't know, 15 percent.

56.   Associated Press, NORC Center for Public Affairs Research, poll, July 9–12, 2016. Text of question: "In your view, do the Republican and Democratic parties do an adequate job of representing the American people, or do they do such a poor job that a third major party is needed?" Parties do an adequate job, 28 percent; third party is needed, 71 percent.

57.   Theodore J. Lowi, "Toward a Responsible Three-Party System," in John C. Green and Daniel J. Coffey, ed., *The State of the Parties: The Changing Role of Contemporary Party Organizations* (Lanham, Maryland: Rowman and Littlefield, 2011), p. 47.

# Conclusion

# Hamilton's Moment of Zen

We started this book by noting how Alexander Hamilton and Thomas Jefferson passionately disagreed about the proper course for governing their new nation, leading them to confront each other during George Washington's cabinet meetings. By 1800, each had established a political party and carried the battle of ideas from behind closed doors into the electoral arena. The origins of the U.S. party system can be traced to their heated debate. Yet the two men remained civil, honorable adversaries. After all, they worked closely on a deal placing the nation's capital on the banks of the Potomac River as Jefferson hoped, and Hamilton won Jefferson's backing for a tax and spending plan designed to boost the fortunes of the business class. In fact, Jefferson so admired Hamilton that he had a bust of his opponent placed at the front hall of his home, Monticello; the bust faced one of Jefferson, reflecting Jefferson's acknowledgment that both were opposites in life.

If we could resurrect these two important figures from our nation's past, they would certainly marvel at the changes that have taken place. They never could have envisioned the omnipotence of the federal government; the relative equality afforded to African Americans, women (including the right of both groups to vote), and gays (including the right to marry); the rise of nearly instantaneous communications; and the high-tech nature of contemporary campaigns. Nonetheless, some things would be surprisingly familiar—especially the broad outlines of the federal government that each helped fashion more than two centuries ago, and the public's enduring commitment to the ideas of liberty, individualism, hard work, self-reliance, and self-governance. Alexis de Tocqueville's observation that the public desire for "standing alone," and believing that the future lies in one's individual efforts, continues to be a centerpiece of political thought, even as more Americans believe the American Dream is harder to attain than ever before.[1]

The contrasting impulses between Hamilton's desire for a strong national government and Jefferson's preference for localism and individual self-reliance are evident in today's public opinion. As has been true throughout our history, contemporary Americans are caught in a paradox: they want the federal government to act when it must, but also prefer it stay out of those things best left to individuals and businesses. Today, only 22 percent express a great deal of confidence in the federal government.[2] This profound public distrust is matched by the 54 percent who believe "government is doing too many things better left to businesses and individuals," while just 41 percent think "government should do more."[3] Similarly, 67 percent say the federal government has far too much influence in the daily lives of individuals, and an equal percentage would react positively to any candidate who proposed to immediately cut government spending and pass a constitutional amendment requiring a balanced budget.[4]

At the same time, Americans want the federal government to *do more*: 64 percent want more federal funding for scientific research that would develop new gene therapy treatments;[5] 53 percent say government should spend more on building and improving roads, highways, and interstates;[6] 46 percent think there should be more government regulation of financial institutions;[7] a 37 percent plurality want more spending for national defense and military purposes;[8] and only 16 percent believe government spending should be cut for entitlement programs such as Medicare and Medicaid.[9] Following the election of Donald Trump, many of his supporters worried he would abolish Obamacare. Said one whose husband is waiting for a liver transplant: "I guess I thought that, you know, [Trump] would not do this. I mean, what are you to do then if you cannot pay for the insurance?"[10] According to conservative writer Salena Zito, many Trump voters took him seriously, but not literally.[11] Abolishing Obamacare, converting Medicare into a voucher program, cutting Social Security, or otherwise altering existing entitlement programs is fraught with danger for the newly empowered Republican majorities in Congress and the White House. Whether Democrats or Republicans control either the presidency or Congress in the years ahead, more government is expected. This follows a historic pattern. At the conclusion of Ronald Reagan's presidency, conservative columnist George F. Will noted that Reagan's acceptance of the welfare state had left Republicans "free to talk like Jeffersonians, celebrating that government which governs least." But, Will added, "they live in, and want to be the dominant party in, Hamilton's America."[12] Will's observation has particular resonance as we begin a unified Republican government under the presidency of Donald Trump.

When it comes to the extra-constitutional device known as political parties, Hamilton's triumph is even more complete. Just as the federal government has become more powerful, so, too, has the U.S. party system, with its hierarchal structure and professional politicians overseeing aggressive national party organizations. Hamiltonian nationalism has created a largely top-down party system managed by elites, which has emerged at the expense of Jefferson's idea of a community-based politics. Recall that Jeffersonian localism is based on the idea that, given its size and diversity, the United States can only be viewed as a series of relatively independent communities. In Jefferson's view, power is vested at the local level and great trust is placed in the hands of ordinary citizens. Party politics is best undertaken by amateurs, whose virtue and commitment are to ideas benefitting the local citizenry. Jeffersonian localism places a premium on policy coherence and intra-party democracy. It is a bottom-up political system wherein individuals are at the center of a politics of ideas designed to reorient the government in a particular direction.

Today, Jefferson's approach is best expressed by netroots activists who toil online to replace a top-heavy, professional Democratic and Republican Party with a more mass-based apparatus centered in Internet communities. But their view of localism is something Jefferson would have trouble fathoming: virtual networks of people dispersed throughout physical communities across the country and even around the world. Today, the very meaning of the word "local" has been challenged by new technologies that create community without proximity, even as the appeal of Jefferson's ideas lives on.

This recent dominance of Hamiltonian nationalism over Jeffersonian localism has come after two centuries of struggle. Throughout this period, the two surviving major parties, Democrats and Republicans, each took a turn as guardians of the Hamiltonian or Jeffersonian approach. During the Civil War and Industrial Revolution, the newly formed Republican Party became closely identified with Hamiltonian nationalism, as it sought to give the federal government the necessary tools to fight the Civil War, end slavery, and transform an agricultural society into an industrial one. Democrats, largely dominated by their southern wing, spoke of states' rights as code for continuing the separation between blacks and whites. Franklin D. Roosevelt, Harry S. Truman, John F. Kennedy, Lyndon B. Johnson, and Barack Obama aligned the Democratic Party with the Hamiltonian idea that the national government must overcome the Great Depression and be strong enough to lead the nation through World War II, the cold war, the fight for civil rights, and the Great Recession.

From the 1930s to the 1960s, Americans believed in the simple proposition that big government worked. When pollster George Gallup asked in 1936, "Which theory of government do you favor: concentration of power in the federal government or concentration of power in the state government?" respondents chose the federal government by a 56 percent to 44 percent margin.[13] In the intervening years, those attitudes have dramatically changed. When the Gallup Organization asked the same question in 2016, only 37 percent favored a concentration of power in the federal government, while 55 percent preferred power be concentrated in state government.[14] This swing toward Jeffersonian localism and away from Hamilton's idea of greater power for the federal government was aided by several conspicuous failures—including a lost war in Vietnam accompanied by the twin economic evils of high inflation and unemployment during the 1970s; stalemated wars in Iraq and Afghanistan; a widespread belief that federal bailouts of the banking and automotive industries benefitted the few, not the many; and stagnated wages that failed to rise, even as the economy improved during the Obama years.

And yet, there has been a vast Hamiltonian-like expansion of government in both foreign and domestic affairs. Declaring a state of emergency on September 11, 2001, George W. Bush authorized $40 billion in emergency spending, with $20 billion earmarked for restoring New York City, and an additional

$15 billion to bail out faltering airlines. Bush also created a new cabinet-level Department of Homeland Security and added a prescription drug benefit to Medicare. A study conducted by the CATO Institute found George W. Bush to be the biggest spender since Lyndon B. Johnson.[15] The Great Recession that greeted Barack Obama upon his taking office in 2009 also caused a spike in government spending. Obama approved a $787 billion stimulus program designed to put people back to work and jump-start the economy. Later, the Obama administration devoted billions to bailing out the U.S. automobile industry. In 2010, President Obama signed into law the Patient Protection and Affordable Care Act, the statute creating Obamacare, that established federal marketplaces where individuals could purchase health insurance, often at subsidized prices. While Americans debated the efficacy of these programs, there remained a prevailing consensus that in times of crisis, the federal government must "do something." At the onset of the Trump administration, the newly sworn President is requesting Congress approve a massive expenditure to rebuild the nation's highways, airports, and railroads—a proposal that has a chance of winning strong bipartisan support.

Looking at the American party system from the perspective of Hamiltonian nationalism versus Jeffersonian localism, Hamilton's triumph is even more complete. During the heyday of party politics, stretching from the Jacksonian Democracy of the 1830s to the Industrial Revolution of the early 1900s, Jeffersonian localism dominated. Party politics was local politics. Partisan affiliation was infused in the workplace and social circles, and influenced how people viewed the issues and candidates of the day. Parties were key mechanisms for integrating whole groups of immigrants into the culture and mores of civic life—and were celebrated by political scientists for the job they did. In the first line of his 1942 book *Party Government*, E. E. Schattschneider solemnly declared, "Modern democracy is unthinkable save in terms of parties."[16]

As this text has documented, party machines of the late nineteenth and early twentieth centuries were not models for democracy. Progressives wanted to clean up the machines, but their reforms transformed political parties into regulated public utilities controlled by federal, state, and local laws. In effect, the Progressives legalized the two-party system of Democrats versus Republicans, thereby making it difficult (but not impossible) for grassroots minor parties to become viable players. By attacking the party machines and focusing on how politics could be better managed, Progressive reformers further isolated people from politics—even as they threw open the formerly closed doors to smoke-filled party back rooms.

The nationalization of party politics during the New Deal era solidified Hamilton's triumph. As government shifted to the national sphere, so did the party system. National party organizations began providing both more cutting-edge services and lots of money to needy candidates, and political parties became professional, centralized organizations. Against this backdrop of strong, centralized parties, a number of important normative questions developed about the role parties should play, including:

♦ Are parties a desirable feature in a democratic system, or do they detract from allowing the will of the people to prevail?
♦ Should parties be more concerned with winning elections or implementing policies, and can both objectives be realized?

♦ Is American-style democracy best served by having nationally centered party organizations where elites can dominate, or by a diverse Jeffersonian-like system of community-level organizations dominated by amateurs? Or is it possible to have some combination of both in today's networked age, with the rise of virtual communities?

♦ Should elected officials use party affiliation as a guide to voting, or should they be independent operators hired to represent their local constituencies?

♦ Is intra-party democracy necessary, or is it a hindrance to electoral efficiency?

♦ Why is the United States one of the few democracies that relies on a two-party model, and is this something we might wish—or be able—to change?

♦ What role should parties play in the presidential nominating process, and can they help presidents to govern?

♦ Should parties be afforded a special place in the campaign finance system, or should they be treated in a way similar to any other group or individual?

♦ Have court decisions and state and national regulations reshaped parties to the benefit or detriment of the party system?

♦ How might we conceptualize the complex, changing relationship between party organizations and voters?

Answers to these and other questions are needed. But as we devise new solutions to old problems, there is an old maxim that still holds true: how our democracy is doing is directly related to how our political parties are faring. Collectively, our polity's answers to the democratic questions we raise will have a direct impact on our political parties.

# PARTY POLITICS IN THE
# TWENTY-FIRST CENTURY

Notwithstanding the dangers of predicting trends in politics, especially in an era of rapid technological change, we close this book with a few informed judgments about what may lie ahead. We have collapsed our projections into three areas: organizational developments, voter trends and legislative politics, and the role of minor parties.

*Organizational Developments.* It is likely that party organizations will continue to grow in power and influence. Party operatives realize that the only way to remain players in electoral politics is to raise money aggressively, provide cutting-edge services to candidates, and stay abreast of technological changes made possible by today's networked age. This accentuates the importance of centralized, Hamiltonian-style professional party organizations. In light of the *Citizens United* and *McCutcheon* decisions by the U.S. Supreme Court, party organizations are likely to grow as they accumulate and dispense ever-larger sums of campaign dollars. The national parties will also have an expanding role to play in state and local politics. This growth from the top will make national party officeholders—including the chairs of the Democratic and Republican National Committees and their congressional counterparts—vital political players at all levels.

At the same time, however, party organizations will be challenged by Super PACs, whose purposes can be at odds with the national parties and even cause wealthy donors to abandon the parties altogether. George Soros on the left and the Koch brothers on the right have become major national players, along with many others. So far, many of these wealthy donors have largely aligned themselves with the purposes and candidates of their preferred political parties, but there is nothing preventing them from creating organizations whose goals are at odds with their partisan preferences.

The one significant exception to this trend toward the nationalization of politics is the community-centered, volunteer-oriented activity one finds in many corners of the political blogosphere. The so-called netroots have become important in gauging the national mood (especially among activists), and they have played an outsized role in partisan politics. But even these online activists seek not to weaken party organizations as much as to democratize them, both in form and function. The activity of so many Bernie Sanders supporters online and in social media in 2016 is an example of such activity. Despite Sanders' loss, there is no sign that these highly motivated individuals are slackening in their political activity. Indeed, they have remained active players in Democratic politics—especially in making their preference for Minnesota representative Keith Ellison as the next chair of the Democratic National Committee known to its voting members. Ellison narrowly lost to Tom Perez, but assumed the position of vice chair of the Democratic National Committee.

***Voting Trends and Legislative Politics.*** Throughout U.S. history, there have been times when voters have moved away from parties, only to be reconnected to them through an economic crisis or war. In each instance, realigning elections reestablished the party connection. Some have suggested that party brand loyalty may again swell under similar conditions. And there are signs that the bases of the Democratic and Republican parties have solidified during the past decade. The result is that the major-party candidates have depended upon overwhelming support from their partisans. Republican nominees John McCain, Mitt Romney, and Donald Trump, respectively, won the backing of 90 percent of their fellow Republicans in 2008, 93 percent in 2012, and 88 percent in 2016. Democratic candidates Barack Obama and Hillary Clinton won equally sizable support from their partisans: 89 percent of Democrats voted for Obama in 2008 and 92 percent did the same in 2012; 89 percent of Democrats backed Hillary Clinton in 2016.[17]

Increased partisanship has resulted in a heightening of incivility, both in the public dialogue and within the halls of Congress. When President Obama went before Congress to argue for his healthcare reform plan, his address was interrupted by South Carolina Republican Representative Joe Wilson, who shouted the words, "You lie!" Wilson's breach of protocol made him something of a folk hero among Republicans, and he has been reelected ever since. In 2016, Donald Trump affixed the appellation "#Crooked Hillary" to his active Twitter account, and his supporters repeated the chant "Lock Her Up" at his rallies, even repeating their calls after the election. Hillary Clinton labeled Trump's backers "a basket of deplorables," decrying their tendency to tolerate (or accept) some of Trump's most blatant racial and ethnic slurs. Following the election, 86 percent of Republicans said they were excited or relieved that Trump won, while 90 percent of Democrats described themselves as disappointed or angry at the result.[18] In the days following the balloting, many Democrats took to the streets and social media to proclaim, "#NotMyPresident."

As Americans continue to grow apart, their divisions are accentuated by their policy and lifestyle choices. In 2016, an astonishing 45 percent of Republicans described policies advocated by the Democratic opposition as threatening the nation's well-being; 41 percent of Democrats had the same viewpoint of Republican programs.[19] Today there is no middle, no center, and virtually no swing constituencies. Nationwide landslides for either party are almost impossible to attain, even though Republicans narrowly won control of the federal government.

All of this is in stark contrast to a time not so long ago when Democrats and Republicans were willing to work together. One small example: it was Republican Bob Dole who sponsored legislation to name the Health and Human Services building in Washington, DC, after the late Hubert H. Humphrey, who was the Democratic presidential nominee in 1968. Such acts of comity, fairly common in the post–World War II era, now appear quaint. In a 2010 commencement address, President Obama bemoaned the prevailing media culture and the tendency of Americans, both inside and outside of government, to listen only to those voices with whom they agree:

Today's 24/7 echo chamber amplifies the most inflammatory sound bites louder and faster than ever before. And it's also, however, given us unprecedented choice. Whereas most Americans used to get their news from the same three networks over dinner, or a few influential papers on Sunday morning, we now have the option to get our information from any number of blogs or websites or cable news shows. And this can have both a good and bad development for democracy. For if we choose only to expose ourselves to opinions and viewpoints that are in line with our own, studies suggest that we become more polarized, more set in our ways. That will only reinforce and even deepen the political divides in this country.

[I]f you're somebody who only reads the editorial page of the *New York Times*, try glancing at the page of the *Wall Street Journal* once in a while. If you're a fan of Glenn Beck or Rush Limbaugh, try reading a few columns on the Huffington Post website. It may make your blood boil; your mind may not be changed. But the practice of listening to opposing views is essential for effective citizenship. It is essential for democracy.[20]

Following the 2016 election, there remains every indication that U.S. politics will continue to be characterized by a vast partisan divide—an electoral chasm that manifests itself in public opinion polls, presidential and congressional elections, and an impenetrable partisanship in the hallowed halls of Congress.

*Minor Parties.* In the current hyper-partisan atmosphere, voters may be poised for new choices, and this could provide an opening for minor-party candidates. Information technology has afforded minor parties a greater opportunity than ever before to communicate with a large pool of voters at minimal cost; thus, the contemporary third parties mentioned in Chapter 9 will have a ready way to reach potential supporters through cyberspace. Although we do not foresee an end to the two–party model, stress points in the political system caused by growing polarization may increase the appeal of alternative voices. Looking to our closest allies, we have already seen the dismemberment of established two–party democracies in Canada and Great Britain.

The 2016 Libertarian Party ticket of Gary Johnson and William Weld, both former Republican governors who were liberal on social issues and conservative spenders, may signal a revival of third parties in the years ahead. Johnson proved himself to be a flawed candidate, and the Johnson-Weld ticket scored a disappointing 3 percent in the final vote tallies. But Americans continue to say that they want more choices, and a survey taken immediately after the 2016 election found 55 percent expressing dissatisfaction with the presidential choices offered by the two major parties.[21] *If* Donald Trump turns out to be a disappointment, and *if* the two major parties grow even further apart in both policies and lifestyle choices, third parties have an opportunity—*if* they can seize it with the right formulation and candidates.

# A PARTY OF GRIEVANCE VERSUS A PARTY OF GOVERNMENT

Almost two decades into the new millennium, Americans are beset with a public life that is marked by the failure of parties to effectively run the government. On the eve of the 2016 election, 42 percent of Americans held an *unfavorable* view of the Democratic party, while 49 percent said the same about the Republicans. (Only 39 percent and 26 percent, respectively, held a favorable opinion of the Democratic and Republican parties.[22]) The same poll found 62 percent holding a negative opinion of Donald Trump, while 50 percent viewed Hillary Clinton unfavorably.[23] Simply put, in 2016 Americans found themselves voting for parties and presidential candidates they did not like. None of this bodes well for the health of our two–party system. And even while the parties grow in organizational strength and institutional importance, Americans find themselves reacting negatively to the political polarization that is reflective of their newfound strength.

Although Americans may hold the parties in low regard, they still expect them to get things done. Perhaps more than in the distant past when Jeffersonian localism was ascendant, Americans continue to look to the party in government to keep them both financially secure and physically safe—in short, to carry out the desires of the Framers expressed in the Preamble to the Constitution: "to form a more perfect Union, establish Justice, insure domestic Tranquility, provide for the common defense, promote the general Welfare, and secure the Blessings of Liberty." Undoubtedly, public opinion of the two major parties is diminished when both are perceived as failing to deliver. But that does not mean we stop seeking results within the confines of a two-party system that has been the hallmark of U.S. politics for generations.

Thus, we are presented with a paradox: an era when the two parties are stronger than ever is also an age when the party system deeply disappoints. If the past is a good predictor, we are likely to see the parties struggle to respond to public pressure and manage to adapt, albeit imperfectly, to demands for more effective performance. This is what they have always done. And while it is possible that our networked age will eventually herald a return to the amateur politics of a redefined localism, for the time being the major parties hold the upper hand as large, mass-based institutions, for we live in a time of nationalized politics. Hamilton might be unnerved by how poorly these institutions are currently received, but even Jefferson would have to concede that, for the time being, Hamilton is winning the debate.

# NOTES

1.   See Alexis de Tocqueville, *Democracy in America*, Richard D. Heffner, ed. (New York: New American Library, 1956), p. 194. See NBC News/*Wall Street Journal*, poll, December 12–15, 2016. Text of question: "Compared with the past—say a generation ago—do you think the American Dream is easier to attain today, harder to attain, or is it about the same?" Easier to attain, 10 percent; harder to attain, 69 percent; about the same, 20 percent; not sure, 1 percent.

2.   NBC News/*Wall Street Journal*, poll, December 12–15, 2016. Text of question: "Next, I am going to read a list of institutions in American society, and I'd like you to tell me how much confidence you have in each one—a great deal, quite a bit, some, very little, or none at all? . . . The federal government." A great deal, 9 percent; quite a bit, 13 percent; some, 42 percent; very little, 26 percent; none at all, 8 percent; not sure, 2 percent.

3.   Gallup poll, September 7–11, 2016. Text of question: "Some people think the government is trying to do too many things that should be left to individuals and busi nesses. Others think that government should do more to solve our country's problems. Which comes closer to your own view? Government is doing too much, 54 percent; government should do more, 41 percent; no opinion, 5 percent.

4.   See PPRI, poll, November 9–20, 2016. Text of question: "Now as I read some statements on a few different topics, please tell me if you completely agree, mostly agree, mostly disagree, or completely disagree with each one. . . . The federal government has far too much influence in our daily lives." Completely agree, 37 percent; mostly agree, 30 percent; mostly disagree, 23 percent; completely disagree, 9 percent; don't know/refused, 1 percent. See also Greenberg Quinlan Rosner Research, January 7–11, 2015. Text of question: "Now I am going to read you some things being proposed by Republicans as part of their plan to deal with the economy. After each item, please tell me whether that policy makes you feel much more positive about their plan, somewhat more positive about their plan, a little more positive, or not at all positive. Cut government spending immediately and pass a constitutional amendment requiring a balanced budget every year, so that we aren't spending more than we can afford." Much more positive, 46 percent; somewhat more positive, 21 percent; little more positive, 13 percent; not at all positive, 18 percent; don't know/refused, 1 percent.

5.   Social Science Research Solutions, poll, January 13–24, 2016. Text of question: "Do you think the federal government should or should not fund scientific research on developing new gene therapy treatments?" Yes, they should, 64 percent; no, they should not, 30 percent; don't know/refused, 6 percent.

6.   Associated Press/GfK Knowledge Networks, poll, April 23–27, 2015. Text of question: "Do you think the government should increase or decrease spending on each of

the following, or is the current level of spending about right? . . . Building and improving roads, highways, and interstates." Increase spending, 53 percent; decrease spending, 11 percent; current level of spending is about right, 34 percent; refused/not answered, 2 percent.

7.   Quinnipiac University, poll, November 17–20, 2016. Text of question: "Do you think there should be more government regulation of financial institutions, or do you think increased regulation hurts the economy?" More regulation, 46 percent; hurts economy, 43 percent; don't know/no answer, 11 percent.

8.   Gallup poll, February 3–7, 2016. Text of question: "There is much discussion as to the amount of money the government in Washington should spend for national defense and military purposes. How do you feel about this? Do you think we are spending too little, about the right amount, or too much?" Too little, 37 percent; about right, 27 percent; too much, 32 percent; no opinion, 5 percent.

9.   McClatchy/Marist Poll, December 3–5, 2013. Text of question: "Which of the following comes closest to your view about how to reduce the federal budget deficit? Mostly cut government spending including entitlement programs like Medicare and Medicaid, mostly increase revenues such as limiting tax deductions on higher income, do both, cut spending including entitlement programs and increase revenues by limiting tax deductions on higher income." Mostly cut government spending including entitlement programs like Medicare and Medicaid, 16 percent; mostly increase revenues such as limiting tax deductions on higher income, 37 percent; do both, cut spending including entitlement programs and increase revenues by limiting tax deductions on higher income, 38 percent; unsure, 9 percent.

10.   Quoted in Sarah Kliff, "Why Obamacare Enrollees Voted for Trump," *Vox*, December 13, 2016.

11.   Salena Zito, "Taking Trump Seriously, Not Literally," *The Atlantic*, September 23, 2016.

12.   George F. Will, "No More Jury Duty," *Washington Post*, January 19, 1989, p. A-27.

13.   George Gallup, survey, 1936. Text of question: "Which theory of government do you favor: concentration of power in the federal government or concentration of power in the state government?" Federal government, 56 percent; state government, 44 percent.

14.   Gallup poll, June 14–23, 2016. Text of question: "Which theory of government do you favor: concentration of power in the state government or concentration of power in the federal government?" State government, 55 percent; federal government, 37 percent; no opinion, 8 percent.

15.   Chris Edwards, "George W. Bush: Biggest Spender Since LBJ," *Cato at Liberty*, December 19, 2009.

16.   E. E. Schattschneider, *Party Government* (New York: Rinehart, 1942), p. 1.

17.   See Edison Media Research and Mitofsky International, exit poll, November 4, 2008; Edison Research, exit poll, November 6, 2012; and Edison Research, exit poll, November 8, 2016.

18.   Carroll Doherty, Jocelyn Kiley, and Bridget Johnson, "In Election's Wake, Partisans Assess the State of Their Parties," Pew Research Center, report, December 20, 2016, p. 3. Thirty-eight percent of Republicans said they were "excited," while another 48 percent said they were "relieved" Trump won. Sixty-four percent of Democrats said they were "disappointed" and 26 percent said they were "angry" at Trump's victory.

19.   Carroll Doherty, Jocelyn Kiley, and Bridget Jameson, "In Partisanship and Political Animosity in 2016," Pew Research Center report, June 22, 2016.

20.   Barack Obama, Commencement Address, University of Michigan, Ann Arbor, Michigan, May 1, 2010.

21.   Princeton Survey Research Associates, poll, November 10–14, 2016. Text of question: "Now that the campaign is over, how satisfied were you with the choice of (2016) presidential candidates? Would you say that you were very satisfied, fairly satisfied, not very satisfied, or not at all satisfied?" Very satisfied, 19 percent; fairly satisfied, 25 percent; not very satisfied, 26 percent; not at all satisfied, 29 percent; don't know/refused, 1 percent.

22.   NBC News/*Wall Street Journal*, poll, October 10–13, 2016. Text of question one: "Now I'm going to read you the names of several public figures, groups and organizations, and I'd like you to rate your feelings toward each one as very positive, somewhat positive, neutral, somewhat negative, or very negative. . . . The Democratic party." Very positive, 15 percent; somewhat positive, 24 percent; neutral, 18 percent; somewhat negative, 16 percent; very negative, 26 percent; don't know, 1 percent. Text of question two: "Now I'm going to read you the names of several public figures, groups and organizations, and I'd like you to rate your feelings toward each one as very positive, somewhat positive, neutral, somewhat negative, or very negative. . . . The Republican party." Very positive, 8 percent; somewhat positive, 18 percent; neutral, 24 percent; somewhat negative, 24 percent; very negative, 25 percent; don't know, 1 percent.

23.   NBC News/*Wall Street Journal*, poll, October 10–13, 2016. Text of question one: "Now I'm going to read you the names of several public figures, groups and organizations, and I'd like you to rate your feelings toward each one as very positive, somewhat positive, neutral, somewhat negative, or very negative. . . . Donald Trump." Very positive, 15 percent; somewhat positive, 14 percent; neutral, 8 percent; somewhat negative, 10 percent; very negative, 52 percent. Text of question two: ""Now I'm going to read you the names of several public figures, groups and organizations, and I'd like you to rate your feelings toward each one as very positive, somewhat positive, neutral, somewhat negative, or very negative. . . . Hillary Clinton." Very positive, 20 percent; somewhat positive, 20 percent; neutral, 9 percent; somewhat negative, 10 percent; very negative, 40 percent.

# Index

164, 180; netroots activists and 125; in primaries 65, 67–8, 79–87, 116, 120; Progressive Caucus 194; *see also* Congressional Caucus; Iowa caucus
CBS network 99, 172
Census Bureau (US) 12
Chafee, Lincoln 67, 182
*Changing American Voter, The* (Nie, Verba, Petrocik) 97
Chesterton, G. K. 187
Christianity 33, 189; *see also Catholicism; Protestantism*
Citizens for Eisenhower 55
Citizens United 147–9; *see also Citizens United v. Federal Election Commission; Hillary: The Movie*
*Citizens United v. Federal Election Commission* 70, 133, 148–9, 151–3, 185, 209
Civilian Conservation Corps (CCC) 53
civil rights: debates 97; Democratic Party and 75, 78, 102, 106, 181, 194, 207; legislation 165–6, 198
civil service 50, 140; *see also* merit system
Civil Service Commission 50
Civil Service Reform Act 140
Civil War 23, 39, 41, 96, 101, 136, 190–1, 194–5, 207
Clark, Champ 74
Clay, Henry 37–8, 189
Clean Politics Act 140
Cleveland, Grover 41, 47, 192
Clinton, Bill: and campaign finance 182, 185–6, 196–7; as a Democratic speaker 1; as president 60, 114, 121, 123, 144, 161–2, 168, 173
Clinton, George 33
Clinton, Hillary: and 2008 election 60–1, 68, 80, 88, 118; and 2016 election x, 1, 3–8, 60–1, 65–8, 70, 83–7, 93–5, 97, 104, 113–14, 130, 182, 184–6, 197, 212; basket of deplorables 210; and Democratic Party 14, 108, 210; First Lady 168; and fundraising 137–8, 147; and *Hillary: The Movie* 148–9; and private email server 179
Club for Growth 127
CNN 99
Coburn, Tom 108
Coelho, Tony 59

cognitive voter model 97; *see also* party identification
Colbert, Stephen 174
cold war 54, 62, 96, 165, 193, 207
colonial America 30; *see also* political parties
Colorado (US) 81, 128, 196
Comedy Central 174
Comey, James 179
Commission on Presidential Debates 186
Commission on the Role and Future of Presidential Primaries 85
Committee for Party Renewal xi, 15
Committee on Party Structure and Delegate Selection 77; *see also* McGovern-Fraser Commission
Committee on Political Parties 166
Committee to Re-elect the President (CREEP) 141
Common Cause 141
*Commonsense* (journal) 58
*Common Sense* (Paine) 30
communism 6, 54, 105, 188, 193
Communist Party (US) 193
Concord Conferences 57
Congress: campaigning 15, 38, 55, 58–60, 69–70, 137–8, 163–4; and Civil Service Commission 50; Democrats in ix, 5, 40, 53, 56, 97, 120, 122, 124–7, 161; and districting 2, 68; House ratifies president 35, 37; and "little arts of popularity" 174–5; partisanship within 19, 34–5, 46–7, 108, 130, 162, 165–71, 206, 208, 210–11; party leadership 18, 32, 37, 88, 108, 127, 159, 162–5, 168–73, 180; president pro tempore 164–5; Republicans in 6, 37, 48, 74, 103–4, 107, 115, 159–62; role in government 11, 24, 32–3, 36; and Senate voting x–xi, 34, 67, 71, 118; Supreme Court 133–4, 139–46, 150, 152–4; and third parties 41, 128–9, 144, 180, 184, 189–92, 194–6, 198; *see also* Civil Service Commission; congressional committees; whips
Congressional Caucus 37, 71–2, 87; *see also* caucuses
congressional committees: Appropriations (House) 169–70; Commerce (House) 169; District of Columbia (House) 169;

*Human Events* publication 143
Humphrey, Hubert 76–7, 94, 102, 211
Hunt, James 86
Hunt Commission 86

Idaho (US) 51, 81–2
Illinois (US) ix, 11, 41, 67, 78, 81, 94, 104,
106, 118, 135, 144, 194; Chicago 41–2,
47, 77–8, 94; Cook County 78; *see also*
Daley, Richard J.
immigration: anti-immigration sentiment
40; and electoral changes 41, 136;
European immigration 41, 74, 102;
policy ix, 25, 162; and political parties
40–1, 74, 102, 190–1, 208; rise of
Hispanic and Asian immigrants 104
Impeachment xi, 121
independents: in elections 14, 39, 83, 96,
127–8, 180–2, 197; and political parties
4, 8, 19, 58, 98–9, 105–6, 180–1; and
realignment 9; and reform 47, 52
Indiana (US) 80, 82, 171–2
Industrial Age 12, 19, 23
Industrial Revolution 41, 46, 136–8,
207–8
Information Age 19
Instagram 20, 173; *see also* social media
intelligence community (US) 6
interest groups 12, 15–17, 59, 138, 145;
*see also* political action committees;
political parties
Internal Revenue Service 148
Internet: as a democratizing tool 16, 20,
60–2, 99, 109, 136–7; fundraising 9; and
netroots 121–2, 124–6, 130, 207; and
party leaders 84; and politics 114–15,
118–20, 129, 173, 175; and third parties
115–18, 127; *see also* political parties;
social media
Iowa (US) 65, 67–8, 80–1, 83–5, 104,
116–17, 191
Iowa caucus 65, 67–8, 80–1, 83–5,
116–17; *see also* caucuses
Iraq War 3, 14–15, 115, 121–2, 170, 207
Ireland 35, 40–1, 74, 190

Jackson, Andrew: and caucus system 71–2;
as a Mason 189; and his party 37–9,
189; and realignment 102

Jackson, Jesse 78
Jacksonian Democracy 39, 189, 208
Jay, John 34
Jay Treaty 34, 163
Jefferson, Thomas: Democratic-
Republicans 32–6, 38, 163;
disagreements with Hamilton 8–9,
22–3, 33, 38, 43, 71, 205, 213; election
and presidency 34–5, 69, 174, 187; and
*Federalist Papers* 68–9, 160, 174–5; and
Federalists 31, 34–7, 163; and political
parties 12–13; print media support 135
Jeffersonian localism: and congressional
party leaders 175; and money in politics
134, 137; and New Deal 24, 52–4;
and political parties 26, 46, 61–2, 76,
109, 207–9, 212; and presidency 73–5;
public attitudes toward 25, 206; struggle
with Hamiltonian nationalism 23, 33,
36, 43, 46, 62, 72, 74, 130, 182, 188,
199; and Supreme Court 78; and third
parties 129, 200
job approval rating xi, 1, 127
Johnson, Andrew 58
Johnson, Gary 180–2, 184–6, 188, 212
Johnson, Hiram 50
Johnson, Lyndon B. 4, 54, 76, 165, 169,
181, 195, 207–8
judicial review 36
Judiciary Act of 1789 36
Judis, John B. 104

Kaine, Tim 93
Kansas (US) 81
Kansas-Nebraska Act 40, 191
Kennedy, Anthony 149, 149–50
Kennedy, Jacqueline 94
Kennedy, John F. 4, 12, 41, 66, 69, 80,
87–8, 94, 159, 165, 207
Kennedy, Robert F. 76–7
Kentucky (US) 18, 41, 49, 81–2, 93, 104,
127–8, 144–5
Kerry, John F. 108, 117, 147
Key, V.O. Jr. 101–2, 104–6, 108
Kimmel, Jimmy 174
King, Angus 180–1
King-Making Caucus *see* Congressional
Caucus
Klein, Joe 122

Michigan (US) xi, 1, 24, 41, 81, 85, 95, 169, 182, 194, 197
MiGente.com (website) 119
Mikulski, Barbara 85
Mikulski Commission 85
Millennials x, 7, 61, 97, 180
Miller, Warren 96
Minnesota (US) 76, 81, 104, 142, 181–2, 196, 210
minor parties *see* third parties
Mississippi (US) 75–6, 81
Mississippi Freedom Democratic Party 75
Missouri (US) 82
Missouri Compromise 40
Mondale, Walter F. 58
Monroe, James 14, 34, 36–7, 71
Montesquieu 11
Monticello 205
Morgan, J.P. 46, 136
Morgan, William 189
Mormonism 188
Moulitsas, Markos 122–3
MoveOn.org (website) 7, 121, 147
MSNBC 99, 172, 174; *see also* cable television; Maddow, Rachel; Matthews, Chris
muckrakers 49
mugwumps 47, 50
municipal ownership of utilities 49–50
Murkowski, Lisa 180
MyBO (website) 119
MySpace (website) 120

Nader, Ralph 143–4, 182, 185–6, 196–7
National Association of Manufacturers 17
National Association of Realtors 138–9
National Beer Wholesalers Association 138
National Council of the United States of America 190
*National Gazette* (newspaper) 33, 135
National Recovery Administration (NRA) 53
National Republican Congressional Committee (NRCC) 58
National Republican Senatorial Committee (NRSC) 152
National Rifle Association (NRA) 17
National Union banner 14

Natural Law Party 196
NBC network 99, 172
"netroots" phenomenon 25, 121–7, 130, 129–30, 207, 210
networked age: elections in 118–21, 25, 213; and news 99–100; opportunities of 19–20, 26, 42–3, 207, 209; third parties in 200; *see also* Internet; political parties; social media; television
Nevada (US) 80–1, 127–8
New Deal 23–4, 53–4, 96, 100–1, 103, 105–7, 160, 165, 196, 208
New England 22, 32, 36–7, 101–2, 174
New Hampshire (US) 33, 76, 80–1, 85, 144, 173, 191, 197
New Jersey (US) 40, 74–5, 82
New Mexico (US) 82, 180
New Politics Democrats 78; *see also* Democratic Party; McGovern-Fraser Commission
New York (US) 3, 7, 18, 22, 30, 35, 37–8, 41, 47–8, 51, 53, 67, 74, 76, 82, 88, 94, 96, 101, 128, 142, 189–91, 194; New York City 33, 35, 40–1, 136, 190, 207
New York Civil Liberties Union 143
New York State's Independence Party 2
*New York Times, The* (newspaper) 3, 86, 99, 211
Ney, Matt 198
Nie, Norman 97
Nielson television ratings 88
Nineteenth Amendment 51
Nixon, Richard: election of 14, 54, 78, 94, 102–3, 107, 159, 161, 195; and policy 162; and realignment 105; use of television 55–6, 59; and Watergate xi, 141
No Child Left Behind 116, 170
nonpartisan municipal elections 49, 51
nontraditional families 104
North Carolina (US) 82, 86, 93, 174
Northern Mariana Islands 81–3

Obama, Barack: 2008 election 66–8, 80, 86, 95–7, 120, 161; Hamiltonian tendencies 24–5, 207–8; money raised 147; Obama administration x, 65, 123, 125, 127, 208; online presence 20, 60–2, 118–20, 125–6, 130; as party leader ix,